THE INTERNATIONALISATION OF CONSTITUTIONAL LAW

In this book, one of the longest-standing members of The Venice Commission reflects on the work of the institution to show how constitutional law in Europe (and beyond) has become increasingly borderless.

The book tracks the work of the Commission, illustrating the law both in action and in its broader political and historical context. It looks at its treatment of the judiciary and judicial conflicts, including the present crisis of the rule of law among Member States in the region of central eastern Europe. Finally it suggests how all this can only be sensibly understood as a feature of the broader trend towards the internationalisation of constitutional law.

Volume 5 in the series Parliamentary Democracy in Europe

Parliamentary Democracy in Europe

The European Union is founded on the idea of 'representative democracy'. Its citizens are directly represented in the European Parliament, but Union democracy is equally based on indirect forms of representation especially through the European Council and the Council – two Union institutions whose members will be democratically accountable to their national parliaments. The good functioning of the Union democracy assumes, therefore, the good functioning of the democratic institutions of each Member State.

What is the role and relationship between the European and the national parliaments in the democratic functioning of the Union? Do they exercise distinct or complementary functions? Has the European Parliament adopted a structure similar to national parliaments; and how do national parliaments assume their 'European' functions? These questions have gained particular relevance in recent years. Not only has the Lisbon Treaty conferred new functions upon national parliaments, especially concerning the scrutiny on the compliance with the subsidiarity principle (the so called 'Early Warning System'), the coordination of fiscal and economic policies at the European level has led to significant restrictions of national parliamentary powers.

The new Hart Series on 'Parliamentary Democracy in Europe', encompassing both monographs and edited collections, aims to answer some of these questions. The series offers new insights into rules and conventions shaping parliaments and parliamentary democracy in Europe. Its aim is to provide a better understanding of the role parliaments are playing in European constitutional law and its idea of 'representative democracy'.

Series Editors

Nicola Lupo
Robert Schütze

Interparliamentary Cooperation in the Composite European Constitution
Edited by Nicola Lupo and Cristina Fasone

The Italian Parliament in the European Union
Edited by Nicola Lupo and Giovanni Piccirilli

The Principle of Subsidiarity and its Enforcement in the EU Legal Order: The Role of National Parliaments in the Early Warning System
Katarzyna Granat

Parliamentary Oversight of the Executives: Tools and Procedure in Europe
Elena Griglio

The Internationalisation of Constitutional Law

A View from the Venice Commission

Sergio Bartole

• HART •
OXFORD • LONDON • NEW YORK • NEW DELHI • SYDNEY

HART PUBLISHING

Bloomsbury Publishing Plc

Kemp House, Chawley Park, Cumnor Hill, Oxford, OX2 9PH, UK

1385 Broadway, New York, NY 10018, USA

HART PUBLISHING, the Hart/Stag logo, BLOOMSBURY and the Diana logo are trademarks of Bloomsbury Publishing Plc

First published in Great Britain 2020

A catalogue record for this book is available from the British Library.

Library of Congress Cataloging-in-Publication data

Names: Bartole, Sergio, author.

Title: The internationalisation of constitutional law : a view from the Venice Commission / Sergio Bartole. Other titles: Internationalization of constitutional law

Description: Oxford, UK ; New York, NY : Hart Publishing, an imprint of Bloomsbury Publishing, 2020. | Series: Parliamentary democracy in Europe; volume 5 | Includes bibliographical references and index.

Identifiers: LCCN 2020031740 (print) | LCCN 2020031741 (ebook) | ISBN 9781509941476 (hardback) | ISBN 9781509941490 (ePDF) | ISBN 9781509941483 (Epub)

Subjects: LCSH: Constitutional law—International unification. | Constitutional law—European Union countries. | European Commission for Democracy through Law. | Law and globalization.

Classification: LCC K3165 .B37475 2020 (print) | LCC K3165 (ebook) | DDC 342—dc23

LC record available at https://lccn.loc.gov/2020031740

LC ebook record available at https://lccn.loc.gov/2020031741

ISBN: HB: 978-1-50994-147-6
ePDF: 978-1-50994-149-0
ePub: 978-1-50994-148-3

Typeset by Compuscript Ltd, Shannon

To find out more about our authors and books visit www.hartpublishing.co.uk. Here you will find extracts, author information, details of forthcoming events and the option to sign up for our newsletters.

FOREWORD

The Venice Commission is now 30 years old and it is time to write the first volume of its memoirs – or, in other words, to assess the success of the principles it has developed, in order for more successes to take place in the future.

The Venice Commission started as a tool of emergency constitutional assistance in the time when constitutional developments took place overnight in Eastern Europe. Now changes are not so quick, and the Venice Commission has contributed to the dissemination of the values of the European constitutional heritage in hundreds of reports and opinions on national law, not to mention multilateral and bilateral seminars.

What are these values, or principles? How are they put into practice through international standards? Stemming from the constitutional traditions of Western Europe, how were they received in the rest of the continent and beyond? On paper, most of them are universal; and in real life? From a purely legal point of view, are they international law, and, if so, are they hard or soft law? Or, to be somewhat provocative, are they comparative law – if this is law?

All these questions are in the background of the book. It is not intended to answer them all, but, rather, to provide guidelines for reflection. The author, Professor Bartole, is particularly well placed for such an exercise. He has been one of most long-serving and active members of the Venice Commission, which he joined after its creation. He is therefore particularly well qualified to evaluate the progress made, but also the difficulties and the steps backwards which have occurred during its three decades. He has dealt with nearly all aspects of the work of the Commission, in particular in the fields of the organisation of the state, federalism, protection of minorities, ordinary and constitutional justice, referendums, fundamental rights and the rule of law.

Professor Bartole is therefore the right person to evaluate the contribution of the Venice Commission to constitutionalism in the world, with realism, not with complacency.

This book's contribution is particularly precious because it is not intended to give good or bad marks, but to see where the problems arise and their cause. This is, of course, essential to finding a solution. A solution which should not be uniform. The main principles are to be complied with, but the situation of each state in the field has to be taken into account. The European Court of Human Rights, and even national courts, especially in federal states, recognise a margin of appreciation to domestic, respectively federate, regional or local authorities. As a specialist of, inter alia, the federal and regional states, as well as of the protection of minorities, Professor Bartole will not deny this.

Despite its adolescence being long over, the Venice Commission is still young. For a long time, it has been, and still is, called upon to assess the progress – and, unfortunately, from time to time, the regression – of democracy through law in Europe and beyond. This is a perennial task, since our world is not expected to become perfect. All of its citizens, and not just members of international bodies or high-ranking public officials, are called upon to contribute to the implementation of democracy, human rights and the rule of law. This should be the main message to be retained from this contribution to the science of constitutional law.

Dr Gianni Buquicchio
President of the Venice Commission

ACKNOWLEDGEMENTS

This book draws inspiration from my experience as a member of the Venice Commission. The book is a result of a substantial rewriting and new drafting of many papers I wrote during that experience. I am deeply indebted to Antonio La Pergola, founder and first President of the Commission, and to Gianni Buquicchio, the incumbent President, for his foreword. During my more than fifteen years at the Venice Commission, I greatly profited from the exchanges of view with my colleagues Kaarlo Tuori, Hanna Suchocka, Jeffrey Jowell, Jean Claude Scholsem, James Hamilton and Giorgio Malinverni, as well as with the members of the Secretariat of the Commission Simona Granata-Menghini, Schnutz Dürr, Pierre Garrone.

I am very grateful to Nicola Lupo and Robert Schütze who accepted to propose this book to Hart Publishing, where I met an excellent team: especially Sinead Moloney, Sasha Jawed, Chris Myers, and Tom Adams who have been very helpful in the editorial work. Eventually, I cannot forget the generous and intelligent support that my young colleague Pietro Faraguna gave me in dealing with the digital difficulties of the process of publication, and the supportive contribution of Alessia-Ottilia Cozzi in cooperating in the editorial work. Roberto Bin stimulated the planning of this book when he invited me to introduce a seminar at the University of Ferrara on the internationalisation of the constitutional law.

I thank the board of the *European Constitutional Law Review* for authorising the publication in Appendix 2 of this book of my article 'Comparative Constitutional Law – an Indispensable Tool for the Creation of Transnational Law', originally published in volume 13 (2017) of the Review.

TABLE OF CONTENTS

Introduction

The primary purpose of this book is to provide an analytical summary of the Venice Commission's activity in the field of constitutional law. The European Commission for Democracy through Law, established by a partial agreement within the framework of the Council of Europe in 1990, is nicknamed the 'Venice Commission' since it holds its quarterly meetings in Venice, Italy. The Commission's primary function is to provide constitutional assistance to the bodies of the Council of Europe and to the Member States of the European Union. The Venice Commission is a technical body whose members are appointed one from each Member State and work in their personal capacity without a mandate. The activity of the Commission was recently criticised for having 'often displayed an unsettling degree of militancy'.[1] This book tries to contest this position and to show that the Commission's Opinions are the result of a process of legal reasoning. The steps of this process are illustrated by the chapters of the book, connected by a common *fil rouge*.

The first chapter provides an analysis of the first 10 years of the Venice Commission's activity. Accordingly, this chapter presents an insight into the making of the role of the Commission that is the first step of the process of legal reasoning we are dealing with. An illustration of cases dealt with by the Commission is preferred to an abstract and formal analysis of the functions of the body. The history and activity of the Commission were largely conditioned by the fall of the Berlin Wall and by the dissolutions of the Warsaw Pact, the Soviet Union and the Yugoslavian Federation. Practical experiences profoundly shaped the actual identity and mandate of the body. Therefore, the first chapter commences by examining the central role played by the Venice Commission in the monitoring of constitutional reforms in the new Central and Eastern European democracies. The exercise of the advising and monitoring functions required the identification of the yardsticks to be applied in dealing with the cases submitted to the attention of the Commission. For instance, the elaboration of guidelines and standards was necessary to suggest the possible alternative models of the systems of government of the concerned states, of the mutual relations between their governing bodies and of the relevant functions of these bodies. The Commission saw the convenience of such an approach when it organised, in cooperation with the University of Lund, a seminar about the initial 10 years of its activity. The reports submitted by many scholars on that occasion focused on the developments of the Commission's Opinions. All of those reports paid special attention to the identification by the Commission of necessary specific yardsticks to be applied in the exercise of the advising and monitoring functions.

[1] B Iancu, 'Quod licet Jovi non licet bovi? The Venice Commission's Norm Entrepreneur' (2019) 11 *Hague Journal on the Rule of Law* 189, 219. See also M Bobek and D Kosar, 'Global Solutions, Local Damages: A Critical Study in Judicial Councils in Central and Eastern Europe' (2014) 15 *German Law Journal* 7, 171; M De Visser, 'A Critical Assessment of the Role of the Venice Commission in Process of Domestic Constitutional Reform' (2015) 63 *American Journal of Comparative Law* 4, 963.

The basis for this construction is in the concept of a European constitutional heritage. D Rousseau provided an important contribution on the topic in a report submitted at another seminar of the Commission.[2] Two main sources of the heritage were identified by the Lund rapporteurs: (i) the case law of the European judges and related legal literature; and (ii) the constitutional traditions and principles of the European constitutions. On this basis, the European constitutional heritage was a consolidated point of reference that could be generally accepted in the practice of the Commission. At the very beginning of the activity of this body, transnational actors were only in the position of perceiving the necessity of organising materials emerging from the European constitutional tradition, in view of their practical utilisation. A lot of work had to be done to identify the principles and standards to be applied to the cases that were continuously submitted to the attention of the Venice Commission.

The next step of the process (chapters two and three) I am describing regards the legal relevance of the adopted yardsticks. The effects of their practical utilisation depended in the nineties on the functioning of the strategy of conditionality within the framework of the Council of Europe. The compliance with the principles and values of the European tradition of constitutionalism conditions and governs accession and continuous membership to the Council. Therefore, the observance of those yardsticks is the main purpose of conditionality. Consequently, conditionality has a legal relevance as far as it is the basis of operational doctrines of European principles and of the relative activities of the advising and monitoring bodies. Day-to-day principles and standards were derived from the European constitutional heritage, whose content acquired a true normative nature. This is the road towards the formation of a transnational constitutional law binding both the states and the supranational monitoring and advisory bodies. Two different approaches to the monitoring activity have to be considered. In the first years of the transition of the ex-communist countries to liberal democratic values, the adhesion of those countries to the Council of Europe was at stake. Attention was paid to the political engagements of those states to implement the European constitutional values in practice and through future reforms. It was an evaluation that pertained to the political governing bodies of the Council of Europe. Technical profiles of the monitoring activity regarded the modalities of the compliance of the concerned states with the identified yardsticks. The understanding of these yardsticks could be facilitated by the utilisation of the concept of the living constitution.[3] There was cause to involve the Venice Commission, since the beginning of the constitutional transition occurred alongside the prevailing political evaluation of the Parliamentary Assembly and the Council of Ministers of the Council of Europe. The involvement of the Commission acquired new importance at the moment of the accession of new Member States to the European Union, because of the increasing technical dimension to ascertaining the actual compliance with the European parameters by the new Members in drafting the required constitutional and ordinary legislations. The piecemeal scrutiny of constitutional legislations and drafts took centre stage in this part of the process. In the new century, the activity of the Commission has progressively enlarged the scope of its monitoring, resulting in partially covering the relations

[2] D Rousseau, *The Constitutional Heritage of Europe* (Strasbourg, Council of Europe, 1997) 16.
[3] D Strauss, *The Living Constitution* (Oxford, Oxford University Press, 2010) 1–5.

between the European Union and its Member States. Within this frame, the recent phenomenon of constitutional backsliding opens the debate on the strategy of conditionality again.

The analysis of the legal reasoning that supports the Venice Commission requires the identification of the materials used in the monitoring process. Herein, the question arises: is the concept of the European constitutional heritage the expression of common European experiences? The research takes into consideration the different experiences of the Western European countries and their Central European counterparts. The distinction between them, far from being the mere result of academic speculation on the cases considered in the monitoring activity, has historical roots. The Venice Commission was confronted with the inclusion of the Central European countries in supranational institutions that were created and controlled by Western countries following the Second World War. The European constitutional heritage appears to be the result of Western European experience. The tradition and history of Central and Eastern Europe are missing a continuous conformity to the constitutional values. They reveal a different attitude to the state's problems, not only in the twentieth century and during the Soviet hegemony, but also before that. Therefore, it was difficult to consider the Central and Eastern European experiences as a part of the liberal democratic European patrimony. An example is the Hungarian Bulla Aurea, whose history is very different from that of the Magna Carta in the UK. Similarly, the 1791 Polish Constitution was not directly implemented and cannot be seen as a constructive stone for the formation of the European constitutional traditions. The presence of some old constitutional provisions on paper that looked interesting is not sufficient to establish the continuity of a tradition if those provisions were not applied in practice. Analogous conclusions can be drawn, for example, with regard to the old Lithuanian customs. Jarasiunas correctly summarised these developments, underlining the peripheral character of these experiences with respect to other parts of the European constitutional civilisation.[4]

The central chapters of this book focus on the analysis of the described system in action. Chapter four analyses some recent developments in European constitutionalism from the point of view of the Venice Commission's activity. Thus, the chapter provides an overview of the transition from the generic, overall concept of European constitutional heritage to the more specific and detailed principles of international constitutional law. It offers elements useful to the knowledge of the experience of the concretisation of the European constitutional heritage, which has only recently acquired large resonance. The description of that transition has to be supported by a further elaboration of the concept of international/transnational constitutional law and by examples of cases settled through the contribution of the Opinions of the Commission. This analysis will be integrated by the concluding chapters, where attention will be paid to recent constitutional backslidings. The reactions of the monitoring institutions to the violation of the relevant obligations accepted by the Member States at the moment of their accession to the European Union will be examined.[5]

The identification of the constitutive elements of the transnational constitutional law requires a review of the relevant sources and materials. The Western European ascendancy

[4] E Jarasiunas, 'The Prehistory of Constitutionalism: The Sources or the Archetype?' (2009) 118 *Jurisprudencija: Mokslo darbu Zurnalas* 4, 21.

[5] See J Scholsem, 'Risks of Backsliding', report submitted to the seminar organised by the Venice Commission in cooperation with the Lund University at Lund on 6–7 May 2019.

of those elements is testified by the number of constitutional documents quoted in the Opinions of the Venice Commission and in the acts of the other supranational advisory and monitoring bodies. These documents and acts are the basis of the interpretative legal reasoning that opens the way to the new epiphany of the constitutionalism. In addition, an important influence from the 'we the people' American experience is present in the developments we are studying. The European sources, and the American ones, are not only contemporary; some date back to the eighteenth and nineteenth centuries. This implies that the operational construction of the relevant yardstick draws inspiration from: (i) the living constitutions of the relevant Western states during more than two centuries; and (ii) the identification of the political and cultural backgrounds of the law in force throughout those years. Attention has also been paid to the safeguarding of human rights and fundamental freedoms in the international documents. Notwithstanding that the evolution of transnational law has departed from the background of international treaties,[6] the judicial and monitoring practices have considered those documents as constitutive parts of the European constitutional heritage. They are the legitimising bases of the activities of the monitoring and advising bodies – and, therefore, of the formation of international constitutional law. The geographical spectrum of the analysis is completed by the presentation of some examples of the diversity of Central and Eastern European constitutional experiences. Finally, special attention is given to the judicial aspects of the rule of law, which was recently put at the centre of an EU initiative adopted with the help of the Venice Commission.

The new European policy in the field of the rule of law justifies the attention given in the following two chapters (chapters six and seven) to the Opinions of the Venice Commission regarding judiciary and constitutional justice in Europe. The intention of these chapters is to ascertain the consequences of this new policy for the advent of a common transnational constitutional order in Europe, taking into consideration the behaviour of the states that have not complied with the yardsticks elaborated by the European Union with the help of the Commission. Chapter seven explores possible models of an institutional guarantee of the independence of the judiciary. The preference of the Commission was accorded to the so-called Mediterranean model, which provides for the establishment of a superior judicial council the majority of whose members have to be elected by the judicial personnel. The commission drew specific principles and rules that are corollaries of this model and concern the separation of the state's powers, the independence of the judges from the Executive and the appointment of judges. Notwithstanding its preference for the Mediterranean model, the Venice Commission does not radically exclude the possibility of adopting an alternative model in which the Executive is entrusted with functions concerning the career of the judges. However, this solution is only possible in countries with an old constitutional tradition. In these cases, a strict observance of the principle of the rule of law and the safeguard of the personal right to judicial protection are guaranteed. In recent times, Poland and Hungary have contested the Venice Commission's 'case law' and have adopted legislative measures that conflict with it. These initiatives affect the relationship between those countries and the governing bodies of the EU. Chapter eight is specifically devoted to the analysis

[6] As demonstrated by K Tuori, 'Transnational Law. On Legal Hybrids and Legal Perspectivism' in M Maduro, K Tuori and S Sankari (eds), *Transnational Law* (Cambridge, Cambridge University Press, 2014) 11, 21.

of the political and legal consequences of conflicts between national and supranational institutions. It is convenient to compare the delaying reactions of the political authorities with the innovative position of the European judges in this matter.

The Venice Commission has been loyal to the Kelsenian model of judicial review of legislation.[7] On this basis, the Commission has construed principles and rules to guarantee the independence and autonomous functioning of constitutional courts. Some recent cases have offered the Commission an opportunity to confirm its guidelines with the adoption of constitutional reforms by some states. Again, Hungary and Poland have adopted constitutional and legislative amendments that violate the common European constitutional traditions. It is evident that these interventions are aimed at settling possible tensions between elected assemblies and constitutional courts by modifying the normative status of courts. The interferences in the composition of these bodies were of great relevance, as they showed many novelties. We can count among them political behaviours that affected the actual duration of the mandate of the judges and their choice; the new regulations of the judiciary; and the organisation of the judicial review of legislation. Important Opinions have signalled that these interventions were unconstitutional intrusions into the functioning of the constitutional courts. These dangerous effects would only have been avoided in a fair way if the relevant constitutions had provided for one of the arrangements Mark Tushnet includes among the concept of 'weak judicial review' in contraposition to the 'strong' one.[8]

On one occasion, the Commission admitted the possibility of guaranteeing the superiority of the Constitution in a legal system without the establishment of a constitutional court. It was conceded that in Finland the respect of the Constitution was guaranteed by the uniform conformity of the ordinary judges with the declaration of unconstitutionality of a statute adopted by the highest judicial authority – that is, the Court of Cassation.

The purpose chapter eight is to summarise the process of legal reasoning that is at the base of a peculiar phenomenon of international law-making from the point of view of the Venice Commission. Since the inauguration of the monitoring and advising activities of the Commission, attention has been paid to the development of that role in the frame of the principle of conditionality. Conditionality requires the identification of a yardstick of the monitoring of the compliance with the commitments made by the concerned states. This yardstick was identified in the European constitutional heritage. It was a choice that had to be implemented through a constructive process, to be drawn from the statement of very general constitutional principles, leading to the construction of the more detailed principles and rules to settle the cases at stake. Relevant sources and materials have been identified by looking at the history of Western constitutionalism in particular. The conclusions of the process of legal reasoning were shared by the governing bodies of the Council of Europe and of the EU, and were also accepted by the European judges. Gradually, these successive steps induced the formation of international constitutional law through the cooperation of the authorities concerned. It is possible to envisage some similarities with the formation of law in a customary modality (or of the judicial case law).

[7] H Steinberger, *Models of Constitutional Jurisdiction* (Strasbourg, Council of Europe, 1994).

[8] M Tushnet, 'Forms of Judicial Review as Expressions of Constitutional Patriotism' (2003) 22 *Law and Philosophy* 353.

In recent times, reasoning has been concentrated on the implementation of the rule of law. This development is due to a new policy of the EU. The European political initiatives were strictly connected with the recent backsliding of European constitutionalism. The epiphany of the so-called illiberal democracies has put in danger the geographical extension of the described results. Some Central and Eastern European states have recently distanced themselves from Western Europe. These developments were supported by the concerned states relying on the protection of their constitutional identity. Thus, the questions arise: (i) how far can the divergence from the principles of European constitutionalism extend in the name of national identity; and (ii) are we in presence of interpretative transformations of traditional constitutionalism or are we facing new alternative tendencies? A useful approach may be offered by the combination of the hermeneutic concepts of transformation and interpretation of the constitutional orders. The safeguarding of the constitutional identity of those states cannot be seen as a justified return to previous constitutional traditions if these traditions are clearly in conflict with the contemporary European constitutionalism. This is especially true if we examine the histories of Poland, Hungary and Romania. In these countries, the previous continuity of a true constitutional heritage is missing because the communist regime had substituted for the authoritarian or corporative state's constitutional orders. The histories do not offer a point of reference for going back to a coherent admissible constitutional identity.

At the beginning of the activity of the Venice Commission, a proposal was made to qualify its activity as soft law and to separate it from hard law. Taking into consideration recent developments, it does make sense to consider the possible coexistence of hard and soft law. A choice between the two approaches depends on the exigencies and characteristics of the cases at stake. It is useful to distinguish the principles from the standards of transnational law. While principles can require strict compliance,[9] standards allow some elasticity in the practical implementation of those values. Nevertheless, it is possible to prefer soft law only as far as there is no danger to the unity and cohesion of the European institutions. Useful suggestions can be drawn from the recent 'revolutionary' case law of the European Court of Justice,[10] which has reacted effectively to the Hungarian and Polish backslidings. Thus, the judges compensated for the political difficulties encountered by the Article 7 TEU. In the meantime, they confirmed the legal status of the new international constitutional law. The place of this result in the process of globalisation can be debated, but the activity of the Venice Commission shall be considered in the European frame to avoid misunderstandings and misconceptions.

The book is completed by two appendixes. The first appendix presents a paper prepared by Sergio Bartole for a seminar organised by the Council of Europe entitled 'The International Legal Order in a Changing World: Challenges for the Monitoring Procedure of the Parliamentary Assembly', Helsinki, 16 May. The paper offers an overview of the developments of the relations between the Venice Commission and the Parliamentary Assembly of the Council of Europe. The bodies of the Assembly frequently request the intervention

[9] The problem is complicated by the fact that the principles themselves imply a certain flexibility of application: R Dworkin, *Taking Rights Seriously* (London, Duckworth, 1978) 24.

[10] D Kochenov and P Bard, 'The Last Soldier Standing? Courts vs Politicians and the Rule of Law Crisis in the New Member States of EU' (2019) *European Yearbook of Constitutional Law* 243.

of the Commission by submitting questions about relevant pieces of legislation adopted or under discussion in the Member States. This move is an alternative to the monitoring process requested by the Member States looking for advice. It is justified by the peculiar position of the Commission in the order of the Council of Europe and by the strategy of conditionality. Conformity with the European constitutional values is required both at the moment of accession to the European Institutions and during the continuity of membership. The strategy of conditionality has to be interpreted not as a downgrading of the sovereignty of the states concerned, but as a peculiar and valuable improvement of their identity due to accession.

The second appendix deals with a general problem whose interest is not limited to the Venice Commission, and tries to emphasise the persisting utility of the studies in the field of comparative constitutional law studies following the epiphany of international constitutional law. It is a reprint of an article[11] written as a follow-up to an intervention of Mark Tushnet[12] that argued a hypothetic diminishing relevance of the traditional boundaries of comparative law as a scholarly field. The appendix reacts to these conclusions, suggesting that the global and European points of view may be different. An explanation of the difficulties envisaged by Tushnet can be found in the different geographic extension of European transnational law with regard to the universal developments of the globalisation of law that Tushnet has in mind. The pluralism of the European system (see the contributions of MacCormick, Walker, Maduro etc) requires us to focus on the common constitutional elements of the European states. Therefore, the comparative constitutional law appears to be an indispensable tool for the creation of transnational law at the European level.

[11] S Bartole, 'Comparative Constitutional Law – an Indispensable Tool for the Creation of Transnational Law' (2017) 13 *European Constitutional Law Review* 601.

[12] M Tushnet, 'The Boundaries of Comparative Law' (2017) 13 *European Constitutional Law Review* 13, 13.

1

The Development of the Role of the Venice Commission

The European Commission for Democracy through Law was established by the Representatives on the Committee of Ministers of the Council of Europe, which adopted the relative partial agreement with Resolution (90)6, confirmed by the decision taken at the 484bis meeting of the Ministers' Deputies in December 1992. The Commission was entrusted with the function of providing legal advice to its Member States[1] in view of helping to ensure the dissemination and consolidation of a common constitutional heritage. Today, the areas of its main concern are: (i) the constitutional, legislative and administrative principles and techniques that serve the efficiency of the democracy and strengthen the rule of law; (ii) fundamental rights and freedoms; and (iii) local and regional self-government. It is better known as the Venice Commission, as it meets in Venice, while the permanent secretariat is located in Strasbourg at the headquarters of the Council of Europe.

I. The Transition to Democracy and Rule of Law in Central and Eastern Europe

From the very beginning, the role of the Venice Commission has been deeply shaped by the experience, and especially by the attention paid by the European institutions to the advent of the new democracies in the countries of Central and Eastern Europe after the fall of the Berlin Wall. The importance of these developments was recognised by the Commission, which held a seminar with them specifically in mind, on democracy in a society in transition, in May 2000 in Lund.[2] In his opening speech, the President of the Parliamentary Assembly of the Council of Europe underlined that democracy is not just an element of the transition, but is often the transition itself. 'If there is not democracy, there is nowhere to transit.' This is true, but it is also true that there is no democracy without law. Law is not a precondition for democracy or a facilitating factor in carrying out democracy; law is democracy. It is impossible to have democracy without a suitable legal framework providing rules for its fair exercise and for the correct functioning of democratic institutions. Democracy is true only if the will of the people is properly expressed in the form of law, whose adoption provides a guarantee against the arbitrariness of the exercise of power.

[1] At the moment, members of the Venice Commission number 62.

[2] The papers presented at the seminar were published in (2000) 26 *Review of Central and East European Law* 3. In the following pages of this chapter, reference will be frequently made to those papers.

The connection between the concepts of transition, democracy and law characterises the experiences of the advent of the new democracies in Central and Eastern Europe. Therefore, it has had special relevance in forming the role played by the Venice Commission during the first 10 years of its activity. This chapter is devoted to commenting on the help given by the Commission to states in the process of transition, which did not end with the Lund Seminar, even if some commentators thought the contrary. Recent events have demonstrated that the Commission had not yet terminated its task after 10 years of activity.

It is common opinion that the transition of former communist regimes to liberal and constitutional democracies can be described as a peculiar process. The contextual presence of pieces of the old institutions and of elements of reform creates a framework which can be compared with previous experiences, but has – at same time – its own distinguishing features. It requires special attention, but its evolution also needs the support of the people concerned; it is therefore a true exercise of democratic political rights. An important contribution by Luis Lopez Guerra reminds us that the Spanish transition to a constitutional democracy was also characterised by the effort of achieving 'a maximum degree of consensus' through negotiations and agreements between the main actors of the transition – the political parties, trade unions and business associations.[3] The evolution of the Central European transition took place at an international level. Therefore, national and supranational actors were involved. The Venice Commission did not substitute itself for the interested electors, but gave its advice on the steps to be taken in view of implementing the transition to liberal democracy. Its mandate was helping the governing authorities of the European institutions in the evaluation of the constitutional reforms adopted by the states in the light of agreed values and principles.[4] The Commission participated in the monitoring processes with auxiliary but decisive functions.

Implementation of the negotiations and agreements required that the main political actors in the process of transition were in control of the bodies of the states entrusted with the task of adopting the necessary constitutional reforms. This aspect of the democratic transition was present in the Central and Eastern Europe countries even where democratic institutions were gradually introduced without breaking the formal continuity of the legislative decision-making process of the previous regimes. The completion of the reforms was obviously not very easy notwithstanding arrangements and round tables. The former 'nomenklatura' remained in control of important state structures, many former communist practices were still complied with and the civil society was weak. Internal efforts aimed at the renewal of the constitutional system needed major assistance from abroad. The Venice Commission participated in these efforts of cooperation, which took place under the control of various international organisations. The fall of the Berlin Wall suggested the moving of the concerned states from the framework of the Warsaw Pact, of the Soviet Union and of the Yugoslavian Federation to the framework established by the Western democracies after the end of the Second World War. This choice implied the accession to supranational organisations. If admitted, the interested countries could get a new international status

[3] L Lopez Guerra, 'The Application of the Spanish Model in the Constitutional Transition in Central and Eastern Europe' (1998) 19 *Cardozo Law Journal* 1937.

[4] Therefore, its activity is not affected by the doubts about 'what an outsider can offer' expressed by M Tushnet, 'Some Skepticism about Normative Constitutional Advice' (2008) 49 *William and Mary Law Review* 1473.

as members of the complex Western network of liberal democracies and market economies. However, to achieve such results, the ex-communist states were required to comply with values and principles shared by the members of these institutions. The acceptance of these principles and values was the condition to which the accession of new members was subject and the necessary cooperation was subordinated. Therefore, many international negotiations were undertaken with the view to insuring the observance of this condition. Even the Organisation for Security and Cooperation in Europe, which former communist states had joined in the past, had an important role in the process of transition. The main roles were played by the Council of Europe, the European Union and the International Monetary Fund.

When they cut their links with the Warsaw Pact, the Central and Eastern Europe countries were instructed that all the Western states shared many values and principles with which they had to comply. The notion of a common European constitutional heritage was at stake. It limited in some way the scope of their self-determination. Did it imply dealing with those states within a framework similar to that of the Warsaw Pact, when their sovereignty was limited by the subordination to the ideologies, policies and interests of the USSR? There was a difference. The new democracies were bound to comply with the Western constitutionalism because they had freely accepted to enter into the network of the Western institutions the membership of which was conditional on the acceptance of European traditional constitutional values and principles. The Central and Eastern Europe countries, as new members of the Council of Europe, accepted the statute of this organisation and ratified the relevant Conventions, especially the European Convention for the Protection of Human Rights and Fundamental Freedoms. Afterwards, some of them subscribed to preliminary agreements in view of the accession to the European Union, and – at a later stage – to treaties of accession. As far as all these developments were freely accepted without external subjection, their sovereignty was not endangered. The subordination to the international monitoring could not be construed as an interference of the supranational organisations, but it was the result of a process which had put the new democracies in a position of equal standing with the old Western democracies. Therefore, all of them participated, and participate today, in the collective decisions of the concerned institutions on an equal footing and with similar powers.

II. The Take-Off of the Activity of the Venice Commission

Having in mind these peculiar aspects of the relations between the ex-communist countries and the European institutions, the Venice Commission has always been very careful in developing the guidelines for its activity. The identification of the necessary yardstick to be adopted in the exercise of its functions implied a proper balancing between the principles of European constitutionalism and the constitutional identity that the states wanted to be preserved. However, the necessity for clear limitations to national sovereignty was to be accepted as far as the continuity of the concerned supranational institutions and their common guidelines was concerned. Special attention needed to be given to the debate on the relation between the constitutional principles and the distinguishing requirements of the market economy, whose concepts were (as presently are) under continuous revision and updating. The subsequent experience of the Commission shows minor attention to the problems of the economic and social reforms of the new democracies. However, during the first decade, differences of opinions between European states, European or international organisations and financial or economic international institutions were intense. They became more marked when some decisions required the adoption of decisions in cooperation with the International Monetary Fund, the World Bank and the USA.

The Venice Commission has been always concerned to preserve its identity as a technical body which works under the umbrella of political bodies, such as the Parliamentary Assembly and the Committee of Ministers of the Council of Europe. These bodies are authorised to avail themselves of its advice and cooperation.[5] This peculiar position has allowed the Commission to avoid adopting political choices,[6] while it defends the values and principles of constitutionalism even against the pretense of national sovereignty. The involvement of the concerned states in the preparation of the Commission's Opinions has been suggested as being 'in line with one of the classic rules of natural justice, viz the principle of *audi alteram partem*'.[7] The proposal cannot be shared, because the Commission is not part of a contentious relationship with those states, but is a neutral body bound by an auxiliary link to the Council of Europe and other European institutions.

A case concerning Ukraine serves as a suitable illustration of the apolitical attitude of the Commission. The case concerned a conflict between the head of state and the parliament, which had been explained according to different interpretations by different international actors. A former US ambassador in Moscow had emphasised the need to strengthen the executive in Ukraine in view of the implementation of economic reforms.[8] Instead, the Council of Europe was seriously concerned by the unconstitutional presidential tactic of enhancing the political authority of the President by submitting to the people a constitutional revision specifically concerning his own powers. Through this referendum, he tried to bypass the parliament, which obviously was fearful of the enlargement of the presidential powers. The Parliamentary Assembly of the Council of Europe asked the advice of the Commission. The Commission had not previously had a chance to express a preference for the adoption of a parliamentary or a presidential system in Ukraine. It refused to draw practical inspiration from the referendum called by President De Gaulle in 1962 to revise the French Constitution outside the constitutional provisions concerning the procedure for constitutional amendments.[9] In the past, the Commission had only been able to underline the different effects of the alternative systems of government at stake. In its Opinion on the Ukrainian case,[10] the Commission severely criticised the presidential solution because it would have disrupted the balance between the powers.

[5] See Appendix 1.

[6] For a different opinion, see B Iancu, 'Quod licet Jovi non licet bovi? The Venice Commission as Norm Entrepreneur' (2019) 11 *Hague Journal on the Rule of Law* 189. Iancu's analysis will be dealt with in the following chapters.

[7] M De Visser, 'A Critical Assessment of the Role of the Venice Commission in Processes of Domestic Constitutional Reform' (2015) 4 *The American Journal of Comparative Law* 963, 995.

[8] JF Matlock, 'The Nowhere Nation' (2000) XLVII(3) *The New York Review of Books* 41.

[9] G Burdeau, *Droit Constitutionnel* (Paris, LGDJ, 1988) 447–50.

[10] Venice Commission, CDL-INF(2000)011-e.

The example of Ukraine is in fact a good one. It reminds us of the comments made by Carl Schmitt, when he envisaged a revision of the Weimar Constitution.[11] Schmitt said that at the end of the First World War, Germany had been obliged to choose the Western model of constitutional democracy. The model was not at all suited – according the author – to the needs of the integration of German society. That opinion could certainly be ascribed to the authoritarian tendencies of Schmitt, but it gives us an opportunity to reassess the crisis of the Weimar Germany. Perhaps a revision of that Constitution which had taken into consideration the problems of 1920 German society would have avoided the later developments which favoured the advent of Nazism. A constitutional decision could have been substituted for the seizing of power by an authoritarian political party. Should similar reasoning have been applied to Ukraine, even with the absence of authoritarian tendencies in the head of state's project? It is difficult to answer this question, but it is in any case fair, considering that the Venice Commission correctly insisted on favouring the compliance with the constitutional rules concerning the revision of the Constitution of Ukraine.

In the Lund Seminar, special attention was paid to the problem of the duration of the transition time. Harutunian and Suchocka[12] both claimed that it was not yet over in 2000. Some constitutional choices made immediately after the fall of the Berlin Wall probably required revision. In fact, the Commission had to deal with two different alternatives. On the one side, it had to elaborate the yardstick of the monitoring according to the exigencies of the transition time. On the other side, it was necessary to comply with the requirements of the later stages of the transition, bearing in mind the results of the experience and the perspectives of the institutionalised establishment of the principles of the constitutionalism. The choice was not always easy.

Leaving aside the problems of the relations between the Commission and its 'political clients' (the Parliamentary Assembly and Committee of Ministers of the Council of Europe, for instance), whose discretion had to be respected, the choice of yardstick had to take into consideration the assumed freedom of choice of the concerned states. The states' choice could not be excluded in an all-or-nothing fashion, at least as far as there were no problems in safeguarding the basic European constitutional values. These exigencies explain the preference accorded by some authors to the configuration of the guidelines of action of the Commission as standards.[13] In any case, the flexibility of the standards had to be partially restricted when the states were bound by specific international conventions affecting their choices, for instance with regard to the safeguarding of human rights and fundamental freedoms. This was the case with the European Convention on Human Rights (ECHR), which concerns the protection of fundamental rights of citizens. However, its provisions frequently concern the organisation of the state, and especially the structure and independence of the judiciary, as Suchocka correctly underlined in her contribution.[14] Therefore,

[11] C Schmitt, 'Reichprasident and Weimarer Verfassung' [1925] *Die Schildgenossen*, republished in C Schmitt, *Staat, Grossraum, Nomos*, G Mashke ed (Berlin, Duncker & Humblot GmbH, 1995) 24.

[12] G Harutunian, 'Democratic Processes and Present-Day tasks of the Constitutional Court of the Republic of Armenia' (2000) 26 *Review of Central and East European Law* 259; H Suchocka, 'The Separation of Powers in the Polish Constitution' (2000) 26 *Review of Central and East European Law* 329.

[13] W Hoffmann-Riem, 'The Venice Commission of the Council of Europe – Standards and Impact' (2014) 25 *The European Journal of International Law* 579.

[14] Above n 12.

special international rules converged with the general principles governing the constitutional state's institutions.

Sometimes, international agreements were recognised as having pervasive effects. In Bosnia and Herzegovina, the duration of the transition was the subject of heated discussion. The Republic aimed to recover its own sovereignty by establishing a new constitutional order on its own initiative. However, it had to deal with the obligations flowing from the Washington and Dayton Agreements, whose provisions affect the adoption of a constitutional reform. The implementation of the Agreements was under the control of the international authorities, whose support, as well the support of the major members of the international community, would have been required to amend the actual constitutional order. On the other side, this order was only partially effective at the time. Every innovative intervention could endanger the efforts of the international community aimed at the establishment of peace and order in Bosnia and Herzegovina. Notwithstanding these difficulties, the Venice Commission made a great contribution to the growth and integration of the institutions of the Republic through interpretative technical elaboration of the frequent lacunae of the Agreements. Many novelties have been introduced, even in the absence of a full exercising of sovereignty through constitutional legislation by Bosnia and Herzegovina. Special attention should be paid to the Opinions concerning the creation of the Ombudsman, the internal judicial cooperation and the necessity of a judicial institution not provided for by the Agreements, as well as numerous questions in the matter of the protection of human rights and of ethno-linguistic groups.[15] The importance of all of these innovative interventions to the establishment of the Republic is evident, bearing in mind the great deal of creativity they display.

III. Rule of Law and Separation of Powers

Two other items were especially addressed in the initial decade of activity of the Commission: the rule of law and the separation of powers. The Opinions of subsequent years show the progressively central position taken in developing the yardstick for monitoring the rule of law. At the same time, the Commission's connection with the principle of the separation of powers has become increasingly evident.

The rule of law has always been a complex concept. Its content differs when we look at the German *Rechtsstaat*, the French *état de droit* and the English rule of law.[16] However, step by step, it has acquired a substantially common meaning in the practice of the European institutions. The contribution of the Venice Commission to these developments has been very relevant. In the contemporary legal experience, a common understanding has taken place within the framework of the European constitutional heritage. The concept implies some structural elements, such as the separation of powers between the legislative and judicial authorities of the state and the independence of the judiciary from the executive. It also

[15] For the Ombudsman, see Venice Commission, CDL-INF(1998)012; for judicial cooperation, see Venice Commission, CDL-INF(1998)011 and CDL-INF(1998)017; for the protection of human rights, see Venice Commission, CDL-INF(1996)009, CDL-INF(1998)018, CDL-INF(1999)012 and CDL-INF(1999)016.

[16] See A Magen, 'Cracks in the Foundations: Understanding the Great Rule of Law Debate in the EU' (2016) 54 *Journal of Common Market Studies* 1050.

includes the democratic formation of the legislative bodies, procedural guarantees in the decision-making processes, the protection of some human rights and fundamental freedoms. Moreover, the states have to comply with a number of standards of conformity with constitutional values in the exercise of the judicial functions and in the equal implementation of legal principles.

Obviously, the actual functioning of this model depends on the attitudes of the civil society, on the discontinuity (or continuity) of the legacy of the former communist regimes, and on the developments and achievements of the civic education of the social actors. A clear reference has been made to the moral, political and economic theories which are the basis of the fundamental aims pursued in the transition.[17] The presence of all these peculiar requirements of the rule of law depends on the passage of time: it would be unthinkable to expect a coherent and complete implementation of the rule of law in just a few years. This circumstance implied that the monitoring institution should extend its attention to the legislation for the implementation of the constitutional reforms adopted in the period of the immediate transition and years following the first constitutional reforms. In fact, even where some structural requirements had been introduced, there were not only new judicial procedural rules that were lacking. According to the Venice Commission, the independence of the judiciary had to be refined through the creation of a High Judicial Council system as was, and still is, present in many European countries.[18]

The absence of procedural guarantees is of greater concern than the absence of a High Judicial Council. Moreover, the immediate establishment of so-called judicial self-government raised some doubts. Entrusting the majority of the judges of the communist regime still in office with administrative functions concerning the careers of judges did not seem convenient. Not only were the electoral rights for the election of the High Council at stake; attention had to be paid to the appointment of new judges, compliance with the standards of judicial fairness and implementation of the judicial reforms, all matters that fall within the competence of the elected members of the Council and directly affect the identity of the judiciary. According to a largely shared opinion, it would have been possible to create a body elected by the judges and mainly composed of judges only if a change in mentality was taking place among the judges.

Therefore, the implementation of the constitutional reforms in the judicial field required a progressive approach and flexibility. At the beginning of the transition period, the appointment of judges could be entrusted to the political bodies which were supposed to be able to understand the needs of the new political and constitutional order. However, this guideline was not always adopted because of the risk of unjustified political interference. In any case, the professional requirements of the judges had to be satisfied. The legislators should have in mind the purpose of restricting the time of the transition as much as possible. It would have been advisable to award self-government powers to the judges only after a number of years. In the meantime, basic human rights had to be guaranteed. As Suchocka highlighted,[19]

[17] See F Feldbrugge, 'The Rule of Law in the European CIS States' (2000) 26 *Review of Central and East European Law* 213.

[18] R Maruste, 'Democracy and the Rule of law in Estonia: Progress Achieved and Problems Remaining (2000) 26 *Review of Central and East European Law* 311.

[19] Above n 12.

in the ECHR the interpreters can find useful principles that concern not only the procedural aspects of the exercise of the judicial functions, but also the organisation of the judiciary. Even if the judges were appointed by a political body, their independence had to be ensured.

The efficiency of the judiciary is also an essential factor in view of the implementation of the safeguard of human rights and fundamental freedoms. This could be uncertain in a period of transition. Evidently many promises could not be immediately satisfied. It was a difficult task to find a satisfactory arrangement. Even a monitoring body has to take into consideration these difficulties. There are many signs of partial dissatisfaction with newly adopted initial reforms. They may seem preferable to the heirs of the past communist order, but they do not always comply with the hopes and desires of the citizens. A maximalist approach has to be avoided. Time is required for the establishment of the new institutions in conformity with the principle of constitutionalism and for the evolution of a new mentality among the public actors.

Moreover, the idea that a High Judicial Council system is the preferable model for implementing the independence of the judiciary has to be married with the reality of the adoption of different systems of judicial organisation in some European states, such as Germany, Austria and Switzerland. If these different systems are traditionally able to guarantee the independence of the judiciary, for instance through a strict application of the rule of law, the monitoring body has to be very careful in advising the new democracies to establish a Judicial Council. It should have been possible to leave the choice between these different solutions to the states, so long as the principle of the separation of the powers was not endangered. A supranational organisation should be more concerned with this principle than with the modalities of its implementation. As we will see in the next chapters, some states claimed their intention to be faithful to their legal traditions. On this point, the Venice Commission has taken the position that this choice deserves respect so long as the European constitutional heritage is safeguarded. For instance, in the Czech Republic, the preference was expressed for a system of independence of the judiciary without a High Council, but the intervention of the Commission was not required in view of an analysis of this choice.

IV. Forms of Government

A similar attitude has been adopted with regard to the reforms in the matter of the form of government. It has been extremely difficult to suggest a preference between the different alternatives of parliamentary, presidential and semi-presidential governments. The main purpose of such a choice should be the elaboration of a solution that could guarantee a democratic decision-making process and the parliamentary control of the executive in conformity with the European tendencies. A fair separation of powers and a balance between the executive and the legislative assemblies should be required. If the Venice Commission had shared the opinion that the direct election of the head of state is the solution best fitted in a period of constitutional transition to democracy in a modern pluralist society, it would have had to have confronted two different alternatives. On the one side, there was the intent occasionally claimed by the Central and Eastern countries that their legislators had to take into account the desire of the people to have a role in choosing the head of state. The discontinuity with the communist regime had to be achieved through an enlargement of the electoral powers of the citizens. The system would have emphasised the unity of the state and reduced the fractional impact of the political parties on the selection of the political actors. On the other side, there were opinions that a presidential system would have increased the authoritarian tendencies of government which were historically present in some ex-communist states, for instance members of the Commonwealth of Independent States. These guidelines contrasted with the European model of representative democracy. The purpose of the new democratic reforms had to be to substitute an institutional pluralism for the previous communist concentration of power. The direct election of the head of state could have favoured the return of old practices of government under the cover of the need to strengthen the powers of the executive. Therefore, even if there was no justification to contest in principle the legitimacy of the choice of the direct election of the head of state, practical reasons suggested alternative solutions.[20] It looked advisable to emphasise the importance of the parliamentary control of the executive and of a fair balance of powers. For instance, frequently a preference for semi-presidential government did not meet the hostility of the Commission. This choice ensured that control of the executive was exercised by the legislative assemblies, which is more difficult in a presidential system.[21]

It is true that, according to political analysts, a semi-presidential government favours forms of possible, difficult 'cohabitation'. Also, parliamentary systems can be the source of potential danger in a period of transition. It is well known, for instance, that in the Czech Republic President Havel strongly supported the adoption of a proportional electoral legislation for the parliament in view of the adoption of the new post-communist constitution. That choice was correct. The deliberation of a new constitution has to encompass all the political positions that are present in the society. This has always been the position of the Venice Commission. The correction of proportional electoral systems is frequently suggested in the name of efficiency of governance. However, even in a parliamentary system of government it would be unfair to concentrate all powers of decision-making in a parliamentary majority elected according to a non-proportional electoral system. Therefore, parliamentary government can also present problematic aspects and risks.

The Commission held that it is also true that the direct election of the head of state by the people can increase the rifts present in a society. The concentration of the supreme representation of a nation in one person elected outside a parliamentary agreement (which normally implies a qualified majority) can endanger the credibility of governmental institutions. In a period of transition, attention had to be paid to perilous developments for the unity of a country. Legal considerations had to be balanced with political and social concerns. Legal doctrine should research the cooperation between the sociology and political science.

After 10 years of the transition process in Central and Eastern Europe, the political conflicts in the ex-communist states signalled further, new problems. As Holovaty clearly

[20] In its Opinion on the draft of the new Constitution of Iceland, CDL-AD(2013)010-e, the Commission appreciated the choice of keeping the national tradition of the direct election of the head of state as a safeguard of the people's power. The decision to maintain the parliamentary form of government was appreciated, but concern was expressed about possible risks of political blockage and instability due to the marked complexity and 'lack of consistency' of the draft. The Commission evidently had in mind the traditional European model of parliamentary government.

[21] For a different opinion, see B Ackerman, *Revolutionary Constitutions* (Cambridge, MA, Belknap Press, 2019) 227 and 257, discussing the influence of the French semi-presidential model on the Polish constitutional system.

remarked in his intervention at the Lund Seminar,[22] the case of Ukraine[23] implied that there were questions regarding more than just the powers of the head of state. The country had adopted its new Constitution in June 1996, but it had still not been implemented. The President, being dissatisfied with the present Constitution, tried to overcome the difficulties of the transition through authoritarian measures and blamed the parliament for the delay. He proposed a referendum concerning not only the revision of relevant aspects of the form of government, but also the actual tensions of the political situation of the country. However, the Commission stated in an Opinion that the initiative did not deserve international support.[24] The President aimed to bypass the procedure for the revision provided for by the Constitution. Moreover, the proposed amendments were not acceptable according to the generally shared constitutional yardstick, even if a lot of the incumbent deputies were connected with the old communist nomenklatura and a change of the political personnel was needed. Inter alia, there were provisions concerning the reduction of the number of members of the incumbent legislative assembly and the limitation of parliamentary immunity. Both novelties were regrettable. Obviously, the change in the number of deputies could be adopted only with regard to a future parliament and could not be used as a weapon in the conflict with the incumbent chamber. And the curtailment of the immunity contrasted with a historical achievement of parliamentary independence. Eventually there was an evident risk of destroying the present balance of the powers. The all-Ukrainian referendum was substantially conceived as a vote on the question whether the present assembly enjoyed the confidence of the electors. The vote had to be expressed at the same time of the vote on the constitutional reform of the parliament. The combination of the two questions contradicted the principle requiring the unity of the subject matter of the question submitted to the electors in a referendum. Moreover, it was proposed that in the event of the withdrawal of the confidence in the incumbent assembly, the President was authorised to dissolve the parliament. Therefore, the proposal was aimed at substituting a direct relation between the head of state and the electors for the link between the people and the deputies. The President wanted to become the centre of the constitutional system with the disruption of the present equilibrium of the powers. There was a danger of the personalisation of the state's power and of an increase in authoritarian tendencies. The assembly risked no longer being the representative institution of all the political groups present in Ukrainian society. There were sufficient reasons to justify a negative Opinion of the Commission. All these purposes contrasted with the intention of the supranational institutions to favour the establishment of a fair and mature democracy and to encourage a free political choice between the different political alternatives of the people.

At the centre of the political conflict in Ukraine was the problem of the economic policy required by the transition to a market economy. According to Holovaty,[25] the President had adopted many decrees, which created parallel regulations alongside numerous statutes that were already in force. He had thus enlarged the scope of his functions. He was able to do so

[22] S Holovaty, 'Ukraine in Transition: From Newly Emerged Democracy towards Autocracy' (2000) 26 *Review of Central and East European Law* 267.

[23] Venice Commission, CDL-INF(2000)011.

[24] ibid.

[25] Above n 22.

because the Constitution allows him to adopt decrees dealing with economic matters not yet regulated by parliamentary legislation. In fact, the definition of economic matters or issues is not an easy task. An arbitrary elaboration is always possible. A great deal of private or commercial law is connected with the establishment of a market economy. The exercise of the presidential powers should have been balanced by an effective parliamentary control. If the best solution of the adoption of presidential decrees in the framework of a previous, insufficiently updated legislation was not possible, the best alternative would be the adoption of decrees to be submitted for parliamentary approval by a fixed deadline. The decrees should lose their legal effect in the case that the parliament failed to give its approval. These proposals were only discussed in an academic frame, as happened for the solution of entrusting the parliament with the power to provide general guidelines for the adoption of presidential decrees. There was a possibility of substituting formal and procedural guarantees for the substantive bonds provided by a previous legislation, but the inherent difficulties could not be overcome.

V. Judicial Review

Since the very beginning, the Venice Commission had been interested in questions concerning the establishment and functioning of constitutional courts in the new democracies of Central and Eastern Europe. Constitutional courts play an essential role in guaranteeing respect for the procedural and substantial constitutional provisions. Their creation had immediately been perceived as a fundamental step towards the establishment of the rule of law. Constitutional review had to be provided for from the period of the transition to safeguard the needs of the reform in the face of the obstinacy of the previous authoritarian practices.

Hans Kelsen[26] had underlined in his contribution to a European theory of the judicial review of legislation that the appointment of constitutional judges implied the intervention of the state's political bodies. According to Kelsen, this move should not present the institutional and practical difficulties which usually complicate the advent of a new ordinary judiciary. Notwithstanding that recent developments have raised doubts about the credibility of this idea, it helped explain the political agreement reached in Poland in the 1980s for the creation of a Constitutional Tribunal which paved the way to that country's transition. However, we cannot forget that such a result is not satisfactory if the independence of the constitutional judge is not guaranteed. A problem arises which concerns not only the personal status of the judges, but also the distribution of the powers of nomination and appointment of the members of a constitutional court or tribunal. The Venice Commission underlined the delicacy of this problem when it expressed its preference for a balanced and pluralistic composition of the constitutional courts.[27] This result cannot be achieved if the mentioned powers are concentrated in one body of the state (for instance, the head of state,

[26] H Kelsen, *La garantie jurisdictionnelle de la Constitution (La justice constitutionnelle)* (Paris, Laval, 1928) ch 4, para 1.

[27] Venice Commission, CDL-STD(1997)020.

without the advice or the control of the parliament). A court with such a membership would be the expression of the will of the President, and therefore would not be completely independent. Even when the power of appointing the constitutional judges is entrusted to more than one body of the state, the independence would not be guaranteed if all the concerned state's institutions were under the control of one body (for instance, the parliament) and specific rules concerning professional skills and independent personal status are missing.

The position of the Commission with regard to the constitutional courts has taken into consideration two caveats. On the one side, it has always avoided substituting constitutional courts for ordinary judges, when constitutional cases are not at stake. According to the Commission, for instance, a constitutional court could not replace other judges when the judiciary does not function well and does not comply completely with its tasks. During a mission of the Commission in Armenia, authorities of that country suggested increasing direct access to its constitutional court through a creative interpretation of the personal right to access judges. The idea was to open the access to the court for cases which were not satisfactorily dealt with by the ordinary judges, even in the absence of constitutional rules providing for some kind of constitutional complaint. This proposal of increasing direct access to the Court was not welcomed. It was objected that a constitutional court is a special judge that does not have a general competence. It has enumerated functions, which are precisely listed in the relevant legislation. A court cannot risk its credibility by extending its intervention outside the scope of its attributions which define its role in a legal system.

The Armenian position had probably been influenced by suggestions that can be found in the American constitutional literature, which was at that time extensively read in Europe by the drafters of the new constitutions. This literature could offer useful suggestions for the interpretation of a written constitution. But it was not advisable to forget that the Supreme Court of the USA is a common law judge and can easily substitute itself for a constitutional legislator. Certainly, the American scholars wrote fascinating tracts about transformations of the American Constitution introduced through judgments of the Supreme Court. However, the new European constitutional courts should avoid following that example. In principle, they should leave space for the legislative political decision-making processes and refrain from giving the impression that they share the responsibilities of the politically elected bodies of the state. Sometimes the creative intervention of a court may be necessary where there is a lack of parliamentary legislative initiatives. If a court wanted to learn from the American experience, it would preferably stick to the minimalist suggestions of Sunstein's interpretation of the case law of the Supreme Court.[28] Instead of taking on the functions of parliaments, constitutional courts should restrict their judgments to cases submitted to their attention and work to open the way for political decisions. In the presence of controversial and hard constitutional cases, their task should be to favour the democratic deliberative decision-making processes.

The years 1990–2000 were years of transition for the countries of Central and Eastern Europe, but also for the Venice Commission. At that time, it started to elaborate on its philosophy and its guidelines of activity. Perhaps it might have given the impression that its Opinions were too doctrinal and abstract, and not really rooted in a complete knowledge

[28] C Sunstein, *One Case at a Time* (Cambridge, MA, Harvard University Press, 1999) passim.

of the actual situation of the country being dealt with. The work of the Commission was certainly based on written drafts of constitutional and legislative reforms, even if it was supported by missions of its members in the interested states. Sometimes the transition was accelerated, as in the cases of Hungary and Poland, which were admitted to the Council of Europe without having formally adopted a new and complete constitution. In contrast, Bulgaria and Romania had to wait longer to join, notwithstanding that their new constitutions were already in place. The transition was always controlled by the governing bodies of the Council of Europe (and later on by the European Union) according to a realistic examination of the real situation of the interested states. This way of reasoning did not bypass the necessity of a strictly textual legal monitoring, but it did take into account the living constitution[29] – that is, the practical and concrete adhesion by the authorities of a state to the principles of the European constitutionalism, or their still defective behaviour. In any case, the European constitutional heritage was at the centre of attention. *Rebus sic stantibus*, the examination of the reforms to be adopted acquired special relevance and involved, with increasing frequency, the Venice Commission, which was becoming aware, step by step, that 'at the level of the implementation of the constitutional texts important problems remain'.[30] The future was open to new and major perspectives.

[29] 'A "living constitution" is one that evolves, changes over time, and adapts to new circumstances, without being formally amended': D Strauss, *The Living Constitution* (Oxford, Oxford University Press, 2010) 1. Strauss lists examples of changes of the constitution through the lawmaking of the Supreme Court. He adds that 'the important distinction is between nations that have well established liberal tradition and those that do not. The distinction does not track the one between written and unwritten constitutions' (D Strauss, 'Common Law Constitutional Interpretation' (1996) 63 *The University of Chicago Law Review*, 924).

[30] A La Pergola, 'Introduction' (2000) 26 *Review of Central and Eastern European Law* 209.

2

European Conditionality, Living Constitution and Constitutional Drafting

I. The Many Faces of Conditionality

Conditionality is a peculiar strategy introduced by specific provisions (frequently referred to as 'HR clauses'[1]) in international treaties or agreements. The purpose of these provisions is the adoption of 'a basic strategy through which international institutions promote compliance by national governments' with the main guidelines of the relevant treaties and agreements.[2] The focus herein is on conditionality in Europe as far as the principles of European constitutionalism and the European market are concerned. The experience of the Venice Commission started from the strategy of conditionality adopted by the Council of Europe. The collaboration with the European Union pertains to a later stage of that experience due to the attention paid by the Union to the constitutional choices of its Member States. European policies aimed at the establishment of a common free market are not in the competence of the Commission.

If we want to have a full understanding of the functioning of the policies of conditionality, we have to keep in mind that the EU is concerned not only with the compliance of its Member States with the common values and principles, but also with the establishment of preferential trade schemes with third countries. Negotiations with third countries are seen by the governing European authorities as occasions for the promotion of human rights and democracy. This holds true even if the matters dealt with in the trade treaties and agreements are outside the scope of the promotion of the principles of constitutionalism.[3] When third countries are ready to accept the insertion of the HR clause in the international schemes that regulate their relations with the EU, they accept the opening of a process of negotiations whose final objective is their compliance with the relevant engagements. Nonetheless, conflicts frequently arise because third countries at times view the implementation of democratic and human rights principles as a violation of their sovereignty. Therefore, machinery entrusted with the task of settling these divergences is necessary. However, the Venice Commission has not been involved in this exercise.

As chapter one discussed, the birth of the Venice Commission coincides with the transition of the Central and Eastern European countries from communism to liberal-democratic

[1] F Zwagemakers, 'The EU Conditionality Policy: A New Strategy to Achieve Compliance' (2012) IAI Working Papers No 3.

[2] JT Checkel, 'Compliance and Conditionality' (2018) ARENA Working Papers WP 00/18, 1.

[3] See B Brandtner and A Rosas, 'Human Rights and the External Relations of the European Community: An Analysis of Doctrine and Practice' (1998) 9 *European Journal of International Law* 468.

constitutionalism. The actuality of the passage has in certain ways been certified by the accession of those states to the Council of Europe. The membership to this institution has been always conditioned to the will to collaborate sincerely and effectively in the realisation of its aims as specified in chapter 1 of its Statute. The concerned states had to give evidence of this commitment by fulfilment of the provisions of Article 3, which stipulates that 'every member of the Council of Europe must accept the principles of the rule of law and of the enjoyment by all persons within its jurisdiction of human rights and fundamental freedoms'. The compliance with these provisions required first, a general overview of the constitutional systems of the candidate states, and secondly, the monitoring of their legislation adopted in the fulfilment of the commitments taken at the moment of accession. This chapter is devoted to the analysis of these two steps.

The accession of Central and Eastern European countries to the Council of Europe was only the first step to membership of the EU. Their next request to access to the EU opened a new phase of transition, where the principle of conditionality once again played a crucial role. Conditionality is an essential strategy for the cohesion of the Union in central matters such as the rule of law, the principle of democracy and the safeguarding of human rights. Therefore, compliance with those European values is required from the moment of accession. In the documents of the EU, the internal stability and observance of the principles of the constitutionalism are considered as important factors for the protection of relations between Member States. Internal and supranational stability was one of the principal commitments that the EU required of the new European democracies. In particular, the common guarantee and observance of the European constitutional heritage by all participants in the process of European unification is a main mission of the EU.

It has been frequently remarked in the literature that the modalities and purposes of the strategy of conditionality concerning the accession of new Member States are different from the policies adopted by the EU in the case of trade agreements with third states. In this last case, special attention is paid to the protection of human rights and the principles of democracy. The objective is the establishment of a constitutional order that is considered 'a facilitating condition for accomplishing development through trade'.[4] In contrast, the accession of new Member States to the EU is seen as an occasion for starting an overall process of constitutional transformation. The innovations are strictly connected with the implementation of the commitments previously undertaken by the states at the moment of accession to the Council of Europe. There is a continuity between the two events. The whole process should make the post-communist democracies 'more receptive to the EU institutional paradigms … because EU models are being presented at the same time as CEE policymakers are seeking institutional models to replace or to create new structures'.[5] *Rebus sic stantibus*, the internal constitutional homogeneity of the EU is at stake.

Therefore, the documents concerning accession to the Council of Europe and to the EU (for instance, the document adopted at the Copenhagen European Council 1993) go further than the HR clauses of the EU's trade agreements. Accession to the Council of Europe may be seen as a preparatory step to the process of European unification. The EU's purpose is the

[4] Zwagenmakers (n 1) passim.

[5] H Grabbe, 'How Does Europeanization Affect CEE Governance? Conditionality, Diffusion and Diversity' (2001) 8 *Journal of European Public Policy* 1014.

stability of institutions guaranteeing democracy, the rule of law, human rights and respect for protection of minorities. The commitment to this purpose is the *sine qua non* political condition of accession.[6] The choice is evidently aimed at establishing a political organisation of Europe that requires Member States to share the same constitutional principles and values. These criteria of accession affect the whole structure of the concerned states and its functionality. The national political actors have to balance the internal costs of implementation of the Statute of the Council of Europe and of the Copenhagen document with the national domestic interests connected with the accession. Member States cannot complain about a loss of their sovereignty, as they consciously accepted to embark on the road to accession.[7]

Conditionality implies that the country bound by a given yardstick for its constitutional legislation and the international institution requiring compliance with the given yardstick enter into a relationship. On the one hand, states that are partners in trade relations see the apparent slimness of the direct link between the economic engagements and the HR clauses as an easily acceptable violation of their sovereignty. On the other hand, at the moment of accession to the Council of Europe, the conditionality placed upon the ex-communist countries was suffered as a coercion which endangered their sovereignty and was perceived almost as a return to Breznev's doctrine. The same reaction was evident when faced with the strategy of conditionality for accession to the EU of new Member States. However, the scholarly debate correctly underlines in both cases that compliance with conditionality is a matter of voluntary choice. For instance, in the case of the accession to the EU, it was remarked that 'all applicant countries have the option of not entering the EU and thus of not complying with the enlargement conditionality'.[8] A country that envisages the possibility of the accession should be ready to accept the limitation of their sovereignty. The purpose of the strategy of conditionality is to shape the internal order of the Member States according to commonly shared constitutional principles. The introduction of a monitoring system is a necessary consequence of this choice.

The absence of any explicit mention of conditionality in the texts of the European Treaties in view of the accession of new Member States to the EU is remarked on by Kochenov in an important contribution about overestimating conditionality.[9] The lack of an explicit provision of conditionality in the Treaties does not imperil the credibility of the strategy. Conditionality is an implicit principle in the complex regulations that subordinate the accession to, and continued membership of, the EU to compliance with the European constitutional values. On the other hand, how rigid or flexible the conditionality is in practice depends on how rigid or flexible the required engagements to the Member States are, and on their interpretation by the monitoring authorities. Evidence of these alternatives is given by the processes followed in the adhesion of the ex-communist countries to the Council of Europe.

[6] F Schimmelfenning, S Engert and H Knobel, 'Costs, Commitment and Compliance: The Impact of EU Democratic Conditionality on Latvia, Slovakia and Turkey' (2003) 41 *Journal of Common Market Studies* 495, 497.

[7] ibid passim.

[8] H Agné, 'European Union Conditionality: Coercion or Voluntary Adaptation? Alternatives' (2009) 8 *Turkish Journal of International Relations* 1.

[9] D Kochenov, 'Overestimating Conditionality' (2014) University of Groningen Faculty of Law Research Paper Series No 3, 2–3, 6.

II. From the Council of Europe to the EU – The Living Constitution

When dealing with the functioning of the strategy of conditionality in the Council of Europe and in the EU, authors frequently use the expression 'political conditionality'.[10] The open texture of the relevant terms of reference – basically the European yardstick – leaves a lot of discretion to the monitoring authorities. Therefore, political choices are required, but they have to be based on a technical legal analysis. The entire process requires the contribution of different skills and abilities. On the one hand, the flexibility of the yardstick to be adopted is apparent. This flexibility implies reference to the European constitutional heritage, the content of which has gradually acquired a consolidated meaning. Reference to the European constitutional heritage is made under the control of both the legal scholarship and public opinion. The process of relative implementation has to guarantee the cohabitation of different states and people within the frame of a homogeneous constitutional order. On the other hand, the attention of the monitoring authorities must be focused on the effective constitutional developments in the concerned states. Attention must be paid not only to the establishment of new institutions, but also to the effective constitutional practices of the authorities of those states. From this perspective, the Copenhagen criteria defined in 1993 play an essential role. Accordingly, the stability and continuity of a state's institutions have to be guaranteed. The democratic formation of the governing bodies, the rule of law, the safeguarding of human rights and the protection of minorities are all at stake.[11] However, authors add to these elements 'the strengthening of the state capacity', which implies a reference to the administrative reforms in view of a complete implementation of the obligation to the conditionality.[12]

The strategy of conditionality has implied, especially in recent times, a piecemeal approach, insofar as single constitutional provisions or single legislative acts have been at the centre of the monitoring authorities' attention. However, the process of accession of the ex-communist countries to the Council of Europe in the years after the fall of the Berlin Wall was characterised by a different, more flexible and general approach of the governing bodies of that institution. Attention was paid to the overall attitude of the concerned states with regard to the transition from the past authoritarian or dictatorial regime to the liberal democratic constitutional order. From this perspective, the commitments of the states to future constitutional reforms acquired a special relevance. Moreover, the adoption of liberal and democratic practices by the national authorities was considered by the monitoring authorities to be an important forerunner to the legislative implementation of those commitments. Liberal and democratic practices were seen as symptoms of the credibility of the application submitted by the states for membership of the Council of Europe. This

[10] W Sadurski, 'Accession Democracy Dividend: The Impact of the EU Enlargement upon Democracy in the New Member States of Central and Eastern Europe' (2004) 10 *European Law Journal* 371, 374.

[11] G Pridham, 'Status Quo Bias or Institutionalization for Reversibility: The EU's Political Conditionality, Post-accession Tendencies and Democratic Consolidation in Slovakia' (2008) 60 *Europe-Asia Studies* 423, 433; G Pridham, 'Securing the Only Game in Town: The EU's Political Conditionality and Democratic Consolidation in Post-Soviet Latvia' (2009) 61 *Europe-Asia Studies* 51, 60.

[12] Pridham, 'Status Quo Bias' (n 11) passim; Pridham, 'Securing the Only Game' (n 11) passim.

behaviour, therefore, was welcomed by the Parliamentary Assembly and by the Committee of Ministers of the Council. If we wanted to use a theoretical concept for these choices, we could argue that the mentioned authorities decided on the basis of the 'living constitution' of the applicant states.

The concept of a living constitution[13] is frequently used by scholars who are not satisfied with a formalistic approach to the study of constitutional law. They think that knowledge of the law in force requires something more than the reading and construction of constitutional and legislative texts. A scholarly approach to the constitutional systems implies the construction of an effective legal practice. Not only the formally adopted legislative provisions, but also the concrete acts and behaviours of the constitutional actors deserve to be taken into account. Therefore, only a living constitution can allow lawyers to capture effective guidelines for a constitutional order. This methodological choice is useful if we want to understand the prevailing interpretation of the words used in these texts. However, the concept of a living constitution can also help the observer in the absence of specific legislative texts, as it is a useful tool in dealing with the effective practices of a constitutional order.

The living constitution is a concept that has emerged from the analysis and understanding of the acts and behaviours of constitutional authorities, of the conventions of the constitution agreed between them, and of the case law of the constitutional courts and judges.[14] In the presence of a constitution that is actually in force, the concept is also a yardstick for the credibility of our construction of the constitution's text and symptomatic evidence of the compliance (or non-compliance) with the constitution itself. The usefulness of the concept is especially evident when we are dealing with developments in the interpretation of the constitutional legislation. These developments normally imply various and serious transformations of the meaning given by the interpreters to the relevant acts and behaviours. These developments may determine the transformation of a state's order.[15] The written constitution is concerned with such a phenomenon insofar as its practical implementation changes according to the changing interpretations by the constitutional actors. Moreover, even if the text of a written constitution is missing, we can perceive the constitutional tendencies through the use of the concept of a living constitution. This analytical attitude was evident in the reactions of the governing bodies of the Council of Europe when dealing with the problem of the accession of the ex-communist countries.

Moreover, the concept of a living constitution may be useful in the ordinary exercise of monitoring functions. Interpretations of a single provision currently in force that conflict with the constitutional principles of a given constitutional order can always be judicially reviewed. This is the typical piecemeal result due to the existence of the internal judicial review of legislation. However, the interpreters may need a more general approach to, and an overall vision of, a constitutional order. This can be the case of the international or supranational institutions that can take advantage of the concept of a living constitution.

[13] For two different approaches, see D Strauss, *The Living Constitution* (Oxford, Oxford University Press, 2010); B Ackerman, '"The Living Constitution" 2006 Oliver Wendell Holmes Lectures' (2007) 120 *Harvard Law Review* 1738. While Ackerman is especially attentive to the modalities of the transformation of the constitution, Strauss underlines the importance of the practice for the knowledge of the actual constitutional orders.

[14] According to the definition of Strauss (n 13) 1, 'a "living constitution" is one that evolves, changes over time, and adapts to new circumstances, without being formally amended'.

[15] B Ackerman, *We the People – Transformations* (Cambridge, MA, Belknap Press, 1998).

An overall scrutiny of the general constitutional practice of a state, in light of the principles enshrined in its constitution, can require the adoption of a wider perspective illuminated by the concept of the living constitution. The usefulness of the concept may appear evident, for instance, in the presence of recent developments concerning the application of Article 7 TEU.

The Opinions of the Parliamentary Assembly of the Council of Europe adopted at the end of the twentieth century[16] on the applications for membership submitted by the Central and Eastern European states are examples of the use of the concept of a living constitution. These documents confirm that the concerned states were 'able and willing' to fulfil the provisions of Article 3 of the Statute of the Council of Europe[17] and were ready to collaborate 'sincerely and effectively' in the realisation of the purposes of the Council of Europe. However, the presence of a liberal and democratic written constitution was not always considered strictly necessary. For instance, Hungary's admission was justified with reference not only to new constitutional provisions, but also to the effective establishment of a parliamentary democracy and the commitment to sign the European Convention on Human Rights.[18] In the case of Poland, special importance was given to the Polish 'pioneering role in the democratisation process in Central and Eastern Europe'. Evidence was offered by the organisation of 'partially free' parliamentary elections.[19] The organisation of democratic parliamentary elections held by a universal, free and secret ballot had an important impact on the admissions of Bulgaria and Lithuania some years later.[20] Estonia was evidently required to settle questions concerning citizenship before accession to the Council, which was justified by the holding of parliamentary elections and other commitments.[21]

The existence of written constitutions was underlined by the Parliamentary Assembly when it welcomed the applications of the Czech and Slovak Republics. The relevance of commitments and obligations of both states was not forgotten.[22] In the case of the admission of Romania, the state's authorities were asked to pay attention 'to the necessity of instituting separation of powers, guaranteeing the real independence of the media, and insuring the conditions for the free functioning of local administrative bodies':[23] something was evidently missing at the moment of the accession. The procedure of welcoming Latvia was engaged especially in the problems of the citizenship: the adoption of both new legislation and relative commitments were needed to avoid arbitrary and discriminatory practices in the field.[24] Finally, much attention should be paid to the admission of Russia, whose application was welcomed notwithstanding the fact that the Assembly expressed deep concern for the violation of human rights by the Russian authorities and the consequent shortcomings in many fields of constitutional interest.[25]

[16] These Opinions are specifically referred to in the following pages.

[17] It stipulates that 'every member of the Council of Europe must accept the principles of the rule of law and of the enjoyment by all persons within its jurisdiction of human rights and fundamental freedoms'.

[18] Opinion 153/1990.

[19] Opinion 154/1990.

[20] Opinions 161/1992 and 168/1993.

[21] Opinion 170/1993.

[22] Opinions 174/1993 and 175/1993, respectively.

[23] Opinion 176/1993.

[24] Opinion 183/1995.

[25] Opinion 193/1996. For some useful comments, see PA Jordan, 'Russia's Accession to the Council of Europe and Compliance with European Human Rights Norms' (2003) 11 *Demokratizatsiya* 281.

The documents mentioned above reveal that the new Central and Eastern Europe democracies were admitted to the Council of Europe on the basis of complex evaluations. The compliance of their existing constitutional practices with the European principles and values was taken into special consideration by the authorities of the Council. A positive welcome of the applications of membership was approved by the Parliamentary Assembly even in the absence of a formally adopted written constitution. Moreover, the commitments of the interested states to the new extensive constitutional reforms played a relevant role. Inter alia, these commitments were at the base of the transition that implied the functioning of the strategy of conditionality. Conditionality evidently played a different role according to the different evaluations and interpretations of the governing bodies of the Council. In the following years, special authorities were set up to monitor the compliance to the obligations and commitments made in the engagements at the time of accession. A new phase of the relations between the Council and the new Members States started. The examination of the individual constitutional and legislative drafts prepared by the competent national authorities took the place of the monitoring and appreciation of the overall constitutional situations of the concerned states. The piecemeal implementation of the obligations of the membership was at stake in view of the adoption of the necessary constitutional and legislative reforms. In this phase, the Venice Commission had a relevant role, as described in chapter one. At this stage, an understanding of the machinery of the conditionality may be facilitated if we focus on the admission of new Member States to the EU.

III. Accession of New Member States to the EU

The legal literature has correctly underlined the importance of the Copenhagen criteria in strengthening the 'tight monitoring procedures detailing the satisfaction of the political conditions by candidate countries' applying for accession to the EU.[26] The stability of democratic institutions was impacted by the growing importance of the Copenhagen criteria. 'The EU's political conditionality did not embrace all tasks of democratic consolidation.'[27] The working of democratic government and the competitive role of political parties on the basis of genuine and unrestricted pluralism were at the centre of the monitors' attention.[28] The monitoring activity did not require a piecemeal examination of the details of the legislative reforms; rather, a general consideration of the relations between the state's authorities, between those authorities and the citizens, and finally between the citizens themselves was needed. The concept of a living constitution revealed its utility again in this context. And conditionality was interpreted with some flexibility and understanding.

Two cases of postponement of the accession of candidate states are exemplary. A Report of the European Commission, dated July 1977, declared that Slovakia 'does not fulfill in a satisfying manner the political conditions set out by the European Council in Copenhagen'.

[26] See Pridham's contributions quoted at n 11 above. For an analysis of the EU enlargement requirements for the accession of new Member States, see A Albi, *EU Enlargement and the Constitutions of Central and Eastern Europe* (Cambridge, Cambridge University Press, 2005) esp chs 4 and 5.

[27] Pridham, 'Securing the Only Game' (n 11) 81.

[28] ibid.

The document underlined 'the instability of the Slovakia's institutions, the lack of rootedness in political life and the shortcomings of its democracy'.[29] The refusal to consider the compliance of Latvia with the Copenhagen criteria as satisfying was considered an example of how broadly focused the EU's conditionality was, if compared with the piecemeal approach of other international organisations.[30]

Considering the overall process of the enlargement of the Union, European authorities feared that many candidate countries of Central and Eastern Europe would have found difficulties in implementing the Copenhagen criteria. The troubled developments experienced by Romania and Bulgaria are well known. In these cases, the process was complicated by the activation of special procedures for monitoring. A generous attitude in welcoming the applications of some states would have increased the risks in the admission process. The Union's authorities would have been deprived of the leverage of conditionality after the accession of the new members. The consideration of effective constitutional practices was considered no longer sufficient. The examination of specific legislative acts was acquiring primary importance. The way to piecemeal detailed negotiations was opened. It is true that in the case of Slovakia, the EU still preferred a flexible approach. The Councils of the European Union, the European Parliament and the European Commission all modified their mindsets in the face of political and personal change in the composition of the Government of Slovakia. The substitution of the Dzurinda Cabinet for the Meciar Cabinet changed the relations between Slovakia and the EU notwithstanding that 'the outcome of the political conditionality by the actual accession in May 2004 was one of imperfect implementation'.[31] The same conclusion was adopted with regard to the application of Latvia. This 'new democracy could not be seen as a consolidated one by the time the Country joined the EU in 2004'.[32] However, the governing bodies of the EU made a positive decision. In the cases of both Slovakia and Latvia, the will of the political parties and the explicit acceptance of the European constitutional principles as leading guidelines of the national policies were considered decisive. The actual constitutional practices were seen as credible evidence of the satisfaction of the requirements for accession to the EU. The political and cultural attitudes of the concerned states guaranteed a future transformative modification of the existing legislation in conformity with the principles of the European constitutional heritage.

A severe approach was taken by the EU in the cases of Bulgaria and Romania. To make the conditionality work, the behaviour of the concerned states was monitored both in the pre- and post-accession years.[33] A possible delay of the accession was not considered sufficient. The recognition of a gap between the desire for accession and the actual compliance with the necessary requirements suggested the adoption of 'new mechanisms like sanctions and infringements procedures'.[34] These new mechanisms applied especially to Bulgaria and Romania, whose performances were subject to a monitoring process.

[29] The document was the basis of the conform decision adopted in December 1997.

[30] Pridham, 'Securing the Only Game' (n 11) 69.

[31] G Pridham, 'The European Union's Democratic Conditionality and Domestic Politics in Slovakia: The Meciar and Dzurinda Governments Compared' (2002) 54 *Europe-Asia Studies* 203.

[32] ibid passim.

[33] U Sedelmaier, 'Pre-accession Conditionality and Post-accession Compliance in the New Member States: A Research' in W Sadurski, J Ziller and K Zurek (eds), *Aprés Enlargement: Legal and Political Responses in Central and Eastern Europe* (Florence, European Institute, 2006) 806.

[34] Pridham, 'Securing the Only Game' (n 11) 57.

IV. Post-Accession Conditionality and Compliance

With the adoption of the Treaty of Amsterdam, Article 7 TEU was introduced. According to this provision, the EU has competence to impose sanctions on Member States who do not respect the fundamental principles of democracy and the rule of law. The EU is a political community of states that share the common principle of constitutionalism. The purpose of the Union is to guarantee the stability of the reciprocal relations and the general acceptance of common institutions shaped according to those principles. In January 2000, the EU had not adopted sanctions under Article 7 TEU against any Member State. The inclusion in the Austrian Cabinet of representatives of the Freedom Party of Austria (Freiheitliche Partei Österreichs; FPÖ) induced the Member States of the EU to adopt measures that resembled the sanctions provided for by Article 7 TEU.[35] FPÖ was considered to be 'a right wing populist political party with extremist expressions'.[36] FPÖ officials were reported to have made 'statements that can be interpreted as xenophobic and which indicate praise for Austrian Waffen SS veterans'.[37] Apparently, an interpretation of constitutional practices and interpretations of the existing legislation in violation of the principles of constitutionalism were considered a plausible and undesirable scenario. This risk did not emerge from the mere observation of the letter of the constitutional law, but mostly from the possible epiphany of an illiberal living constitution.[38] However, in June 2000, a mission of three 'wise men' from the Council of Europe suggested that the international obligations and the constitutional and legislative provisions of Austria allowed the lifting of measures adopted by the Council of Europe. The governing bodies of the institution followed this advice and accepted the recognition that the existing guarantees in Austria did not justify the initial fears.

In November 2002, the Bureau of the Parliamentary Assembly of the Council of Europe asked the Venice Commission to provide an Opinion on the conformity of the proposed revision of the Constitution of Liechtenstein with the fundamental principles of the Council of Europe. The Commission went further and examined the impact of the proposed draft amendments on democracy in the Principality. The identification of the actual compliance with the principles of democracy, which 'in Europe … [is] the only accepted form of government', was at stake.[39] This reasoning referred to the principle of conditionality, which requires conformity with the democratic principle. Democracy is a condition for the continuity of membership of the Council of Europe and the EU. According to the Commission, the existence of democracy requires: (i) free parliamentary elections of a representative body; (ii) the effective enjoyment of individual rights; (iii) the admissibility of the restrictions of rights only to uphold the democratic system; (iv) the accountability of the executive

[35] A Duxbury, 'Austria and the European Union. The Report of the "Three Wise Men"' (2001) 1(10) *Melbourne Journal of International Law* 169; E Regan, 'Are EU Sanctions against Austria Legal?' (2000) 55 *Zeitschrift für Offentliches Recht* 299.

[36] I Bantekas, 'Austria, the European Union and Article 2(7) of the UN Charter' [2000] *ASIL Insights* February, 1.

[37] ibid.

[38] As Sadurski correctly says, a statement was adopted by 14 Member States, without consulting any supranational bodies of the Union, to freeze any bilateral contact with Austrian Government officials: W Sadurski, 'Adding Bite to Bark: The Story of Article 7, EU Enlargement and Jorg Haider' (2010) 16 *Columbia Journal of European Law* 385, 398.

[39] Venice Commission, CDL-AD(2002)032.

to the people; (v) the primacy of the power of the elected assembly; (vii) compliance with the rule of law; and (viii) objective guarantees for the independence of the judges. According to the Commission, the proposed amendments to the Constitution of Liechtenstein enlarged the powers exercised by the Prince Regnant in the legislative and executive field without any democratic control or judicial review. A serious step backwards was considered a possible development, while a further transition towards a fully fledged constitutional monarchy could be endangered. All these developments could lead to the isolation of Liechtenstein within the European community of states.

Notwithstanding the critical opinion of the Venice Commission, the proposal to amend the Constitution of Liechtenstein was adopted and published in the Official Journal on 15 September 2003. The new text stated that the Prince Regnant 'is not subject to the jurisdiction of the Courts and does not have legal responsibility'. The powers of the Prince Regnant in respect of the government were enlarged and he was entrusted with the power to veto bills voted for by the Diet. A compromise solution was adopted for the appointment of the judges. The move by the Principality induced the Parliamentary Assembly to initiate a political dialogue with the Liechtenstein Diet. The Venice Commission has not been called upon to issue any other Opinion in this case. The focus of the monitoring activity was on the overall system of government of the Principality, while the piecemeal technical approach of the adopted measures was set aside.

A general approach to the internal constitutional order of Romania was again at the centre of an intervention of the European authorities. Romania was admitted to the EU in 2007; however, its shortcomings in implementing the European principles and values suggested the establishment of a Cooperation and Verification Mechanism to monitor the progress in implementation of the obligations of membership. According to a Report of the European Commission dated 18 July 2012, the behaviour of the Romanian authorities 'raised serious doubts about the commitment to the respect of rule of law or the understanding of the meaning of the rule of law in a pluralist democratic system'. Romania's compliance with the European engagements was at risk due to 'political challenges to judicial decisions, the undermining of the constitutional court, the overturning of established procedures and the removal of key checks and balances'.[40] The EU focused not only on specific acts of the Romanian authorities, but also on concrete political events and the interpretative attitudes of the Romanian authorities in constitutional matters. The European initiative required something more than a monitoring of legislative and administrative measures.

This approach was adopted by the Secretary General of the Council of Europe when he asked the opinion of the Venice Commission on the compatibility with constitutional principles and the rule of law of actions taken by Romania. The request was evidently submitted in the interest of the Council of Europe, but was also on behalf of the European Union. It implied an evaluation of the overall behaviour of Romanian authorities. An ascertainment of factual elements appeared essential in view of the compliance with the Commission's mandate. The Commission was not convinced of the constitutionality of ordinances, decisions and procedures. According to the Opinion,[41] restricting the powers of the parliament

[40] European Commission, 'On Progress in Romania under the Cooperation and Verification Mechanism', COM (2012) 410 final.

[41] Venice Commission, CDL-AD(2012)026.

and bypassing judgments of the constitutional court by governments' emergency ordinances raised doubts and perplexities. Many events and even several statements of the concerned authorities demonstrated 'a worrying lack of respect among representatives of State institutions for the status of other State institutions, including the Constitutional Court as the guarantor of the supremacy of the Constitution'.[42] As stated by the Commission, the respect for a constitution cannot be limited to the literal execution of its operational provisions.

> The very nature of a Constitution is that, in addition to guaranteeing human rights, it provides a framework for the State institutions, and sets out their powers and their obligations. The purpose of these provisions is to enable a smooth functioning of the institutions based on their loyal cooperation.[43]

The institutions shall have 'the interest of the State as a whole in mind, including, as a consequence, the interests of the other institutions and those of the parliamentary minority'.[44]

V. Constitutional and Legislative Drafting

The introduction of the principle of loyal cooperation in the Opinion concerning Romania was a novelty that enriched the contribution of the Commission to the identification of the European constitutional principles. Such a development is frequent in the Commission's monitoring of constitutional and legislative drafts. While the overall consideration of the situation of the constitutional order of a state requires general considerations, the examination of individual acts implies the identification of the specific principles and rules to be implemented. The functioning of the conditionality favours the punctual contribution to the elaboration of international constitutional law by the Commission.

In the opinion of the legal literature, Central and Eastern European countries 'have undergone a major process of external governance'.[45] The adoption of new rules and their implementation in national political systems have been at the centre of important developments controlled by the strategy of conditionality.[46] The process required time to come into effect. The internal compliance with the European constitutional principles and values had to be coordinated with the national policies of the concerned governments. At times, the adopted reforms were induced by internal factors. In many cases, the relations of those governments with the European authorities were conditioned by internal 'veto players'.[47] Therefore, it has been correctly emphasised that the entire processes implied a great deal of negotiation and bargaining that has in some way compensated for the loss in autonomy and power of the candidate states.[48] These relations had a political dimension that fell in the competence of the governing bodies of the Council of Europe, the European Union and the

[42] Ibid.
[43] ibid.
[44] ibid.
[45] F Schimmelfenning and U Sedelmeier, 'Governance by Conditionality: EU Rule Transfer to the Candidate Countries of Central and Eastern Europe' (2004) 11 *Journal of European Public Policy* 661, 669.
[46] ibid.
[47] ibid 672–75.
[48] F Schimmelfenning and H Scholtz, 'EU Democracy Promotion in the European Neighborhood: Conditionality, Economic Development, and Linkage', Paper presented at the EUSA Biennial Conference, Montreal, May 2007.

states. Nevertheless, political decisions frequently (if not always) depended on the technical opinions of the monitoring and advising bodies. In this space, the Venice Commission played an important role in the identification and implementation of the principles and rules of law to be applied in dealing with the cases at stake.

The technical contribution of the Venice Commission was especially relevant in the follow-up of the accession of the above-mentioned states to the Council of Europe and the EU. In the 1990s, the Commission produced Opinions that dealt with the new constitutions of some states, in particular Albania, Moldova, Armenia, Poland, Ukraine and Russia. In the following years, the trend changed and the interventions of the Commission interested a large number of countries because Opinions have been required in view of the legislative implementation of the engagements taken by the states at the moment of their accession to the Council of Europe and the EU. Therefore, monitoring and advising activities were undertaken in the face of particular individual acts of the new members. The specificity of these cases has been the cause of the Commission's detailed elaboration of international constitutional law. Gradually, the Opinions have cumulatively enriched the normative meaning of the European constitutional heritage – that is, the whole complex of traditions, historical doctrines and materials that have conditioned the accession to, and continued membership of, the concerned supranational entities by the Central and Eastern Europe countries. The final results of the monitoring and advising activity of the Venice Commission depended on the decisions of the governing European authorities responsible for relations with Member States. Sharing the conclusions of the Commission's Opinions, those authorities gave them formal relevance and legally engaged the responsibility of the Members. However, these decisions would not have been effective or credible without the technical contribution of the Commission. The role and importance of this contribution is the focus of attention in the next chapters.

3

The European Constitutional Heritage as a Yardstick for the New Democracies

I. The Research of a Parameter

The activity of the Venice Commission takes places between the Scilla of the European constitutional heritage and the Cariddi of the national constitutional identities of the European states. From its inception, the Commission had frequent difficulties in identifying the meaning of the references to the old traditional legal institutions that were and are present in the new European constitutions. For instance, what are the legal institutions evoked by Article 131 of the Russian Constitution? What are the historical and other local traditions of that country[1] according to which the functions of local self-government shall be exercised? What are the legal consequences of Article 13 of the Bulgarian Constitution, which considers Eastern Orthodox Christianity to be 'the traditional religion in the Republic'? What are the implications of mentioning the spiritual bequest of Cyril and Methodius in view of the interpretation of the Constitution of the Slovak Republic? And why is the mentioning of historical Moravia in the same constitution relevant?

According to its preamble, the Lithuanian Constitution is historically based on two sources: the sixteenth-century Statutes of Lithuanian and the Constitutions of the Republic of Lithuania. However, the legal value of these two sources is not always clear. Is the interpreter of the Lithuanian legal order allowed to draw inspiration from the old historical Statutes? Does the reference to the Constitution of the Republic regard it as having been established after the First World War? Does this reference acquire a special meaning from the preamble's reference to the 'reborn State' of Lithuania? Does the Lithuanian history authorise an approach that is incompatible with the experience of other European states, where authoritarian regimes were established?

Many similar questions have also interested the Venice Commission, whose advising and monitoring activity has focused on the discontinuity/continuity of the new democracies with the old historical traditions and the regimes previously present in the concerned states. The accession of those states to the liberal and democratic European Community often implied not only the refutation of the communist principles of government that were at the base of the supranational frame established by the Warsaw Pact, but also the

[1] M Ignatieff, '"The Discovery of Chance," by Aileen M Kelly' *New York Times*, 20 May 2016 and GS Morson, 'Herzen: The Hero of Skeptical Idealism' (2016) 63 *New York Review of Books* 18 underline the importance given to these traditions by Alexander Herzen, whose hopes for their realisation were betrayed by the Soviet Regime. The new Russian Constitution would have implied a reaction to the Soviet practice.

abandonment of the authoritarian principles of the governments established in the years between the First and Second World Wars.[2] The Commission had to understand the meaning of the references to the past, because the identification of that meaning was essential to the exercise of the Commission's advising and monitoring functions.[3] Due to the principle of conditionality, all states were interested in continuing their newly acquired membership of the supranational institutions. Therefore, the states were bound to comply with the engagements mainly subscribed at the moment of the accession to the Council of Europe and the European Union. Were those historical references compatible with the European yardstick, which transnational practice has identified with the European constitutional heritage? Moreover, the novelty of the introduction of this safeguard of the constitutional identity of the Member States of the European Union brought new issues to the attention of interpreters: was there the possibility of tensions and conflicts between the supranational authorities and the states due to Article 4(2) TEU, which obliges the EU to respect the equality of the Member States before the Treaties as well as their national identities?[4] What are the limits of the protection of the national identities with regard to the common principles and exigencies of the European Union?

II. Paradoxes and History of the Concept of the European Constitutional Heritage

The Venice Commission's focus on the concept of European constitutional heritage[5] is required by the need to rely on certain, commonly accepted and clear yardsticks when exercising its functions. Many difficulties derived from the variety of constitutions of the concerned states. The yardsticks had to be based on the values enshrined in the constitutive documents of the European institutions. Among these values, the Commission included: respect of human rights and fundamental freedoms; a system of checks and balances; the independence of the judiciary; and constitutional justice.[6] However, the identification of these yardsticks implied a participation of the European states in the elaboration of the concept of a European constitutional heritage. Moreover, it was possible to derive this concept from a survey of the national legal orders and their contribution to the development and elaboration of the principles of the constitutionalism. Comparative constitutional law is an indispensable tool for this enterprise.[7] It follows that the European constitutional

[2] For instance, the regimes of Horty and Gombos in Hungary, King Charles in Romania and Pilsudski in Poland: see the many references in B Mirkine-Guetzévitch, *Les nouvelles tendances du droit constitutionne* (Paris, M Giard, 1931); B Mirkine-Guetzévitch, 'L'echec du parlamentarisme "rationalize"' [1954] *Revue international d'histoire politique et constitutionnelle* 1.

[3] 'The presence of the past is a fact in the construction of Europe': C Joerges, 'Introduction to the Special Issue: Confronting Memories: European "Bitter Experiences" and the Constitutionalization Process: Constructing Europe in the Shadow of its Pasts' (2005) 6 *German Law Journal* 245, 253.

[4] L Besselink, 'National and Constitutional Identity before and after Lisbon' (2010) 6 *Utrecht Law Review* 36.

[5] D Rousseau, 'The Concept of European Constitutional Heritage' in *The Constitutional Heritage of Europe* (Strasbourg, Council of Europe, 1997) 16.

[6] A La Pergola, 'Introduction' (2000) 26 *Review of Central and East European Law* 209.

[7] See Appendix 2.

heritage is made up not only by the European Treaties and conventions in the field of human rights and the rule of law, but also by the concrete, common constitutional experiences of the European states.[8] The European constitutional heritage covers not only the legal provisions in force in the European states, but also the scientific elaboration that favoured the historical process of growth of those legal orders. Its developments have also drawn inspiration from European transnational law and from the case law of the two main supranational courts, the European Court of Justice (ECJ) and the European Court of Human Rights, which have a significant but different role in Europe. Even the language of the ECJ was taken into account insofar as it evoked the common constitutional traditions of the Member States in the fundamental rights that were considered constitutive parts of the European general principles of law.[9]

At the base of all this reasoning there was a paradox. The yardstick adopted for advising and monitoring the constitutional reforms of the new democracies was supposed to be derived from the common heritage of the constitutional experiences of all the European states. It could include the principles and values of the legal orders of the states that aimed to become members of the European supranational institutions and required the advice and monitoring of the Venice Commission. The paradox could be bypassed only through a historical analysis of the European developments of constitutionalism. It is true that many states had been in the position of offering an effective contribution to the formation of the relevant values and concepts of the constitutionalism. The history of these states provides evidence of the past and present contributions to the implementation of those concepts and values. Moreover, their participation in the scholarly elaboration in that field is important. However, it was only a group of the European states that participated in this process. Some European states, included in the Warsaw Pact in the second part of the twentieth century, had not been involved in these developments, as a connection with the traditions of constitutionalism was missing. These states had to leave behind their previous constitutional experiences, in particular where these experiences were connected with the bonds of the Warsaw Pact. In fact, the former members of the Warsaw Pact had to gain a new credibility via cooperation with the supranational institutions.[10]

Therefore, the identification of a European constitutional heritage implied that the constitutional experience of all other European states that were involved in the elaboration of values and concepts of European constitutionalism was taken into due consideration. The principles of constitutionalism were deeply rooted in these states since the creation of their modern legal orders and/or after special historical events. The French Revolution, the spread of national states after the First World War and the fall of authoritarian regimes in Europe in the 1940s and 1970s had all been peculiar transitions. The heritage of the French

[8] 'The development of a common European Constitutional Tradition ....embraces constitutional diversity': M Kumm, 'The Jurisprudence of Constitutional Conflict: Constitutional Supremacy in Europe before and after the Constitutional Treaty' (2005) 11 *European Law Journal* 262, 269.

[9] European Court of Justice Case 11/70 *Internationale Handelsgesellachaft GmbH v Einfurh und Voratstelle fuer Getreide und Futermittel* (1970) ECLI:EU:C:1970:114; Case 4/73 *J Nold, Kohlen und Baustoffgrosshandlung v European Commission* (1974) ECLI:EU:C:1974:51.

[10] The 1791 Polish Constitution requires an approach different from that adopted with regard to Western Europe documents, according to MM Banach, *La Costituzione polacca del 3 maggio 1791 – Un'ipotesi interpretative sulla debolezza del primo testo costituzionale europeo* (Roma, Aracne, 2018).

Revolution in particular had been of primary importance in the progressive epiphany of contemporary states. Therefore, legal and political actors have to pay attention to the events that occurred in Europe after the French Revolution.

At this point, it is necessary to look at documents and events which preceded the advent of the Enlightenment. The origins of the modern state are certainly European, and are strictly connected with the developments of the European systems of law. According to Harold Berman, who studied the great 'revolution', which initiated the Western legal tradition, the birth of the modern state in Europe coincides with the pontifical revolution of Pope Gregorius VII in the eleventh century.[11] At that time, the emphasis on the separation of the Roman Church from the civil authorities opened the way to the advent of new legal doctrines. Developments of the practice of the living law and of the scientific legal researches were strictly connected. Inspiration has been especially drawn from the history of the English law of the twelfth century, the so-called 'legal century'. According to Pollock and Maitland,[12] the age of Glanvill, the age of the first compilation of the English law and customs, coincides with the advent of the European legal schools in the frame of the newly established universities. The complexity of the new society required a new approach to legal studies. There was a similar occurrence in Italy when the lawyers started reading the *Corpus iuris* through the eyes of the late Middle Ages.[13]

The rebirth of Roman law and the growth of Church law were decisive influences. Legal doctrines and theories offered the necessary support to the elaboration of the concept of the state, of its institutions and of their authority. The twelfth century saw the advent of the initial elaboration of the principle *rex in regno suo est imperator*:[14] the sovereignty of the monarchy was construed as the basis of the sovereignty of the kingdom. However, as Antonio Marongiu remarks,[15] during the autumn of the Middle Ages, the idea of limiting the powers of kings and princes through agreements stipulated with the nobles or the gentry took root. In France, the authority of the king was restrained by the traditional and customary *lois fondamentales*. The example of the Magna Carta (1215) was not isolated, but was followed in Central Europe by the Bulla Aurea in Hungary in 1222. Both of them deserve special consideration as starting points for the advent of constitutionalism in Europe. However, the histories of these documents show great differences. Significant peculiarities emerge when we look at the institutional implementation of these charters and the connected elaboration of their provisions in the legal literature. Notwithstanding the fact that they were contemporaneous, general attention is paid only to the Magna Carta. It is very frequently quoted in all the European legal scholarship and is considered as a basic source of European constitutionalism. In contrast, the Bulla Aurea is rarely quoted. Certainly, it is not considered by the main scholars as a constitutive part of the European constitutional heritage.

[11] See HJ Berman, *Law and Revolution. The Formation of the Western Legal Tradition* (Cambridge, MA, Harvard University Press, 1983) ch I.

[12] F Pollock and FW Maitland, *The History of the English Law before the Time of Edward* (Indianapolis, Liberty Fund, 2010).

[13] P Grossi, *L'Europa del diritto* (Rome, Laterza, 2007) 37.

[14] F Calasso, 'Origini italiane della formula rex in regno suo est imperator' [1930] *Rivista di storia del diritto italiano* 213. Weiler also finds the roots of the sovereign equality of the states in the pre-state chivalrous world of feudalism: see JHH Weiler, 'The Geology of International Law – Governance, Democracy and Legitimacy' (2004) 64, *ZaöRV*, 547.

[15] A Marongiu, *Il Parlamento in Italia nel Medio Evo e nell'Età moderna. Contributo alla storia delle istituzioni parlamentari dell'Europa occidentale* (Milan, Giuffrè, 1962) 506–09.

The difference certainly depends on the message of the two documents. It is true that the Magna Carta stayed in force for a short period of time, while the Bulla Aurea is considered to have been a stable element of the continuity of Hungarian legal history. The Bulla Aurea played a crucial role in shaping the Hungarian state. However, it is also true that the legal force of the Magna Carta was updated more than 30 times in the following years and was frequently amended over the centuries. Moreover, the English document was certainly aimed at ensuring the privileges and special rights of certain persons and classes. However, it simultaneously displayed great attention to the protection of all the persons of the kingdom, and anticipated modern theories and practices of the universal safeguarding of human rights. The clauses of the Magna Carta guarantee a general extension of the protections insured by the customs and freedoms it mentions. It requires their compliance by 'tam clerici quam laici … quantum ad se pertinet erga suos'. Therefore, the guarantee has been progressively extended to all people who were subjected to the mentioned *clerici* and *laici*. Eventually, in the seventeenth and eighteenth centuries, both Edward Coke and William Blackstone contributed greatly to these developments, but they found the basis for their constructions in the earlier legal literature.[16] The Bulla Aurea was instead inspired by a restrictive idea of freedom. It introduced a guarantee that was partially connected with the exploitation of the land and was strictly concerned with the privileges of the ruling class. Under Matthias Corvinus, some judges tried to interpret the Bulla with the aim of extending its protection to other persons. With the advent of the Jagellonian Dynasty, this case law was overruled and rejected. Many scholars share the opinion of Balogh that the Bulla Aurea exerted 'a vitally important influence upon the development of the Hungarian constitution'.[17] However, it is also accepted that the Bulla was the basis of the Hungarian corporative constitutional choice. Hungarian history had shown across the centuries the emergence of principles different from those which have been at the core of the modern and contemporary European constitutional heritage.[18] The Magna Carta reveals a different effective orientation. It favoured progress towards the establishment of the principles of modern constitutionalism, as is often confirmed by the developments of legal doctrines. The UK could correctly claim to have a priority in this field.

If we compare these different developments, we can understand Jarasiunas's opinion that research should avoid the Procrustean bed of the present categories of constitutionalism, at least with regard to the prehistory of constitutionalism.[19] However, it is difficult to adopt such an approach when we are dealing with modern and contemporary European history, which highlights the distance of the Central and Eastern European countries from Western civilisation. It should be recognised that in the historical European literature those countries are described as having a peripheral character with respect to other parts of Europe.

[16] M Caravale, *Magna Carta Libertatum* (Bologna, Il mulino, 2020) 78–84.

[17] E Balogh, 'The Place of the Golden Bull in Hungarian Constitutional History' in L Besenyei, G Erszegi and M Pedrazza Gorlero (eds), *De Bulla Aurea – Andreae II Regis Hungariae MCCXXII* (Verona, Valdanega, 1999) 203.

[18] The point was underlined by KF Geiser, *Democracy versus Autocracy. A Comparative Study of Governments in the World War* (Boston, MA, DC Heath & Company, 1918), a book that was devoted to the knowledge of the constitutional traditions of the countries of the dissolved Austro-Hungarian Empire, in which he remarked that the idea of European liberties 'was almost completely annihilated' in the centuries after the adoption of the Bulla and appeared completely abandoned at the time of the French Revolution (42–44).

[19] E Jarasiunas, 'The Prehistory of Constitutionalism: The Sources or the Archetype?' (2009) 118 *Jurisprudencija: Mokslo darbu Zurnalas* 21.

They always appear to be trying to reach Western yardsticks. However, they have not always got the results they hoped for. According to common opinion, the history of Central and Eastern Europe has been characterised by gaps in statehood, national calamities, and social and economic difficulties. This past especially deserves to be explored today, when the ideals of Western constitutionalism 'seem to have lost their mobilizing strength'.[20]

III. Comparing Western and Eastern Europe Traditions

The peculiar institutions and the unpredicted achievements of the ancient constitutional systems of the Central and Eastern European countries have impressive characters for scholars exploring their development.[21] They are not studied as a part of the European common constitutional heritage. Their experience is not considered by the majority of scholars to be a constituent element of the European constitutional tradition. This is surprising, as the Hungarian Bulla Aurea is a very ancient constitutional document. However, only those documents and institutions that are at the base of the constitutional developments, for instance, of the UK and France, or, in more recent times, of Belgium, Italy and Germany, are studied and elaborated in assessments of the progressive formation of the European constitutionalism. The impression is that only liberal democratic states that have been successfully established for a long time are considered as adequate terms of reference for modern constitutionalism in the elaboration of the European constitutional heritage. Even the Polish Constitution of 3 May 1791, notwithstanding its European priority after the adoption of the American Constitution, has not been the object of special attention in that context. Although it had been in force for only a short time, it was a sign of the spreading of the ideas of the Enlightenment. The Polish Constitution was aimed not only at guaranteeing the privileges of the gentry and the rights of the burgers, but also at insuring a protection by law of the peasants. Some elements of its content would have probably deserved to be taken into account by the historians even before the dissolution of the Warsaw Pact, which is the starting point of new studies about the Polish legal traditions. The unfortunate developments of Poland prevented its consideration by the doctrines and theories that are the basis for the scientific and judicial construction of European common constitutionalism. Does this fact oblige us to deny the existence of a Polish constitutional tradition? Certainly, this opinion is not shared by those scholars and intellectuals who are interested in keeping alive the historical tradition of the efforts made by the Polish people to safeguard the Polish identity in the

[20] Joerges (n 3) 250.

[21] Recent interesting studies have been devoted to peculiar Polish institutions and their connection with the developments of the European constitutionalism; for articles on the justiciability of power, see T Kucharski, '"Treasury Settlements" Accepted by the General Diet in the Polish–Lithuanian Commonwealth (1569–1791). A Purely Feudal Institution or a Great Step towards Modern Parliamentary Control on the Implementation of the Budget by the Government?' (2019) 37 *Giornale di storia costituzionale* 75; A Tarnowska, '"Willing that the Guard of Law should be responsible to the Nation for their action …". Justiciability of Power in the Era of Polish May Constitution of 1791' (2019) 37 *Giornale di storia costituzionale* 105; M Galedek, 'The Monarchical Sovereignty and the Ministerial Responsibility in the Course of Works on the Constitution for the Kingdom of Poland, 1814–1815' (2019) 37 *Giornale di storia costituzionale* 153; M Byczyk, 'The Fiction of Ministerial Accountability in the Kingdom of Poland (1815–1830). Consideration of the Inefficacy of Extrajudicial Bodies in the Field of Criminal Responsibility' (2019) 37 *Giornale di storia costituzionale* 171.

frame of the European experience. Recently, Hanna Suchocka claimed the existence of a strong Polish constitutional tradition. According to her, the 1791 Polish Constitution 'was built on such principles like sovereignty of the nation, separation of power with independent courts, guarantee of the religious tolerance'.[22]

This position deserves attention. It cannot be denied that documents with the historical characteristics of the Bulla Aurea or of the Polish 1791 Constitution played a specific role in the development of the legal cultures of Hungary and Poland. They can be a positive factor in the recognition of the identity of their country. However, a long continuity of compliance with principles and legal institutions is an essential factor for the identification of a significant constitutional tradition. The existence in the past of interesting and admirable documents is not sufficient to justify the presence of a historical and relevant tradition in the absence of an efficacious implementation of those documents. On the contrary, discontinuities, frequent and long ruptures, continuous inobservance of the past principles and legal institutions make difficult the recovery of old historical constitutional doctrines. After the ancient epiphanies of primitive constitutionalism, the Central and Eastern European countries have been impacted by many negative factors, such as: the deprivation of their state's sovereignty in the nineteenth century; the advent of authoritarian regimes after the First World War; and the long presence of the communist dictatorships. These tragic historical events have profoundly affected the characteristics of state institutions in Central and Eastern Europe.[23]

The situation following the fall of the Berlin Wall required the Central and Eastern European States to research new ways and modalities to establish a constitutional system. In recent decades, the exigencies of the time had opened the way to a rethinking of the doctrines of constitutionalism, which had been all-but ignored in those countries. They have had to be compensated for the time lost, and their history has not always been helpful to this purpose. Ideas of constitutionalism have evolved profoundly and the reappraisal of old experiences has not been sufficient. The factor of continuity was missing even in those countries where interesting constitutional experiences had taken place in the first part of the twentieth century. These experiences are rarely mentioned. In Czechoslovakia, for example, the epiphany of the judicial review of legislation in Europe in the 1920 Constitution would have deserved attention. However, the application of the relevant law of 29 February 1920 was interrupted at the end of the first term of the Czech Constitutional Court. New judges were appointed in 1938, but the Court was overwhelmed by the dissolution of the state in 1939.[24] Authoritarian developments affected in a similar way the life of the 1920 Estonian Constitution, which was widely considered the most democratic order anywhere in the world due the important presence of direct democracy provisions. The social rights introduced by the provisions of the 1921 Yugoslav Constitution also had an ephemeral life.

[22] H Suchocka, 'Constitutional Heritage and the Form of Government', report presented at the conference Global Constitutional Discourse and Transnational Constitutional Activity, Venice, 7 December 2016. For a different opinion, see Banach (n 10).

[23] M Avbelj, 'Central Europe as a Legal Phenomenon' (2015) 7 *European Perspectives* 53 says that the legal tradition of Central Europe 'cherises a strong central authority' and 'has also always been extremely hierarchical'.

[24] See P Cruz Villalon, *La formacion del Sistema europeo de control de constitucionalidad (1919–1939)* (Madrid, Centro de Estudios Constitucionales, 1987) 277.

Instead, in some Central and Eastern European countries, it is possible to find an attempt to legitimise the present choices through the quotation of ancient documents in the preambles of their national constitutions. This is the case in the Czech Republic, whose Constitution makes a generic reference in the preamble to the 'sound traditions of the ancient statehood of the Crown of Bohemia as well as of the Czechoslovak statehood'. The preamble of the Georgian Constitution mentions not only the 'centuries-old traditions of the Georgian Statehood' but also the 'main principles of the 1921 Constitution'. All these statements apparently make greater claims to the national identity of these countries than their constitutional heritage.[25] They are connected with complex and contradictory experiences that are not taken into consideration in the elaboration of the main doctrines of the European constitutional heritage. The preamble of the Constitution of Croatia is equally destined to confirm and support the 'historical, national and natural right of the Croatian nation'. It opens the text and precedes all of its provisions with reference to important events in Croatian history and to relevant deliberations of the Croatian Sabor in the past centuries. The specific purposes of these preambles make their elaboration in view of the identification of a common European constitutional heritage very difficult. They are especially concerned with specific claims to the national identity of the state. This does not mean that those claims are unfounded. However, the recognition of the right to self-determination does not depend on the specific vindication of a single country only. It has to be the result of the common construction of the community of European states, or of the majority of them. The recognition of the states emerging from the dissolution of the Yugoslavian Federation offers clear confirmation of this opinion. Only the common elaboration of the problem could give evidence of the general acceptance of the right to self-determination and of the values and requirements that underpin it.

Easier acceptance can be guaranteed to the individual choices of a state concerning particular aspects of its organisation. Such specific arrangements should still comply with the European constitutional principles. However, this guideline was disregarded in the case, for instance, of the provisions of the Czech Republic Constitution that concern the independence of the judiciary. The Czech Republic was admitted to the Council of Europe notwithstanding that its Constitution does not provide for judicial 'self-government' similar to the Mediterranean model. While Article 81 of that Constitution states the principle of independence of the judges, Article 93 entrusts the function of appointing judges for life to the President of the Republic. Moreover, Article 93 of the Constitution reserves the regulations of the procedures of appointment of the judges by the President of the Republic and of the professional requirements of the new judges to parliamentary legislation. This choice resembles those of other states of Central Europe, such as Germany and Austria.

In fact, the constitutional history of some countries can offer examples of 'paradoxical subjects–unpredicted achievements'[26] of the political-legal system, which are characteristic of Central and Eastern Europe according to Jarasiunas. This author is obviously referring to Lithuania, where the Constitution makes reference in its preamble to Statutes defined by the framers as 'legal foundations of the Lithuanian Nation'. Has this reference the same

[25] For this distinction, see Besselink (n 4) passim.

[26] See Jarasiunas (n 19).

meaning of the above-mentioned quotations that are present in the preamble of the Croatian Constitution? Does it concern something more than the Lithuanian national identity? The reference ambiguously covers also 'the Constitutions of the Republic of Lithuania'. Does this reference allow for a connection of the foundations of the Lithuanian Nation to the European constitutional heritage? The Lithuanian Statutes of 1529,[27] 1566 and 1588 have a larger content than the documents quoted, for instance, in the preamble of the Croatian Constitution. These Statutes not only deal with the claim of the Lithuanian nation to its own identity and sovereignty, but also cover civil, criminal and procedural matters. In these fields, Europe has had innovative developments in the principles of the protection of human rights, which are a constituent part of the European constitutional heritage. The Lithuanian Statutes entered into force in the frame of a country where the presence of the *ius commune* offered evidence of the influences of the Roman legal culture. The establishment of the University of Kraków and the jurisprudence of the judges of Vilnius and Kraków also played important roles in this picture. However, legal historians share the opinion that the content of the Statutes is strictly linked with the social and political situation of the country in the sixteenth century. The Statutes are recognised as having special importance as one of the first examples of a full written codification, which followed the path of the codification of the old Lithuanian customs started by Casimir's Code in 1468. The Statutes aimed to balance factors of centralisation (including support of the king, ensured by the preservation of elements of Roman law) with the guarantee of special powers and privileges for the Lithuanian magnates. Therefore, the Statutes are seen by historians to be the result of very peculiar Lithuanian developments.

The Statutes distanced the country from the evolution of the Western part of Europe. As Lithuania and Poland made up a common kingdom, Lithuania was involved in the European Enlightenment through the adoption of the Polish Constitution of 3 May 1791. Notwithstanding the traditional cultural links of both these countries with European civilisation, the events of the nineteenth and twentieth centuries have been an obstacle for the participation of Lithuania in the elaboration of the European constitutional heritage. Even the reference in the preamble of the present Constitution to the 'Lithuanian Constitutions' does not help. That reference is probably to the Lithuanian Constitution of 1922, and can be likened to the resumption by the newly independent Latvia of its Constitution of 1922 (significantly amended in 1998). Both of these constitutions are considered by the framers of the new Latvian and Lithuanian constitutional orders as factors in the continuity of sovereignty in the concerned states. However, in both cases, the important element of the continuity of adhesion to the principles of constitutionalism is missing. In the 1920s and 1930s, both countries suffered the advent of authoritarian regimes, followed, in 1940, by their inclusion in the Soviet Union. There was a rupture in the continuity of the progress of constitutionalism that was taking place in other parts of Europe after the Second World War. At the moment of their transitions to a liberal democracy, both Lithuania and Latvia had to regain the same level of principles of constitutionalism that had been obtained in the Western European countries.

[27] For the collection of these statutes, see S Lazutka, I Valikonytė and E Gudavicius (eds), *Pirmasis Lietuvos Statutas* (Vilnius, Faculty of History, 1991).

IV. The Impact of the Western Tradition

The discussions and the examples presented in this chapter lead to the conclusion that, in the experience of the Venice Commission, the traditions and principles of Western European constitutionalism have had a primary, if not exclusive, relevance even in the creation of the constitutional orders of the new democracies in Central and Eastern Europe. Two historical factors displayed special influence and oriented the work of scholars.

On the one side, the political and constitutional history of the Central and Eastern countries signalled the presence of long-standing authoritarian and dictatorial regimes that blocked the maturation of a modern constitutionalism in those countries.[28] The experiences of the nineteenth and twentieth centuries prevented even Hungary and Poland – countries that proudly claimed interesting epiphanies of primitive constitutionalism – from being in step with the Western European countries. In addition, in the twentieth century, some of these Western countries had experienced dictatorships, such as Italy and Germany. However, the authoritarian heritages in Italy and Germany were successfully cancelled at the end of the Second World War. New constitutions were adopted, and these have had an important influence on the following European constitutionalism developments. Moreover, legal and political actors had to take into account that the new Western European constitutionalism found promising cradles in the experiences of the UK's rule of law, the French Revolution's Enlightenment and the spreading of constitutional monarchies across Europe in the nineteenth century. In fact, all of these past and new developments are extremely important for our analysis, as they are strictly connected with the second historical factor we are looking for.

In the second half of the twentieth century, the Western liberal democracies advanced the progression towards a modern constitutionalism through the creation of supranational institutions. The Council of Europe and the European Union, whose purposes and values have drawn inspiration from the constitutional experiences of their founding states, deserve special attention. Therefore, when the new democracies looked for international recognition of the abandonment of their dictatorial or authoritarian past, they requested to join the Council of Europe and – subsequently – the European Union. On those occasions, they accepted the sharing of the principles and values of Western constitutionalism. This choice was monitored by competent bodies of the two interested supranational institutions, which elaborated all the materials offered by the national Western traditions and the international efforts aimed at the consolidation of the constitutional values and principles. The results of these activities produced – in a transnational frame – the concretisation of the parameters of the European constitutional heritage, which resulted in the advent of the international constitutional law that is studied in the following pages.

[28] For a useful analysis of the experiences from the first part of the 20th century, see Mirkine-Guetzévitch, *Les nouvelles tendances* (n 2) passim.

4

The Epiphany of the International Constitutional Law

I. Constitutionalism and International Law

Many recent contributions in the field of public law are devoted to the internationalisation of constitutional law. Neil MacCormick correctly concluded an important contribution by underlining that 'the time is … indeed ripe for rethinking jurisprudence and legal philosophy' because sovereignty and constitution are no longer necessarily connected.[1] However, notwithstanding the apparent plainness of the expression 'internationalisation of constitutional law', its meaning is not self-explanatory. The phenomenon partially pertains to the epiphanies of transnational law insofar as it is a law 'beyond the dichotomy of state law and international law'.[2] However, the legal literature refers to a multiplicity of different developments that extend the attention of legal observers beyond the borders of the state.

An example of the internationalisation of constitutional law is the tendency of constitutional courts to look 'for guidance from the decisions in other countries dealing with similar issues'.[3] Even inside the US Supreme Court, this tendency was the object of a controversial debate, with important contributions from its members, especially Justice Antonin Scalia.[4] The legal relevance of this use of foreign precedents is evident, but it pertains more to the cultural background of judicial interpretation than to the legal dimension of lawmaking. Courts are using precedents issued in other jurisdictions as materials for the construction of national law. Moreover, scholars have used the expression 'internationalisation of constitutional law' with regard to the progressive submission of activities and reciprocal relations of subjects of the international legal order to the principles and doctrines of constitutionalism. Sabino Cassese recently dealt with this phenomenon,[5] underlining the fact that the rigid separation between constitutional law and international law is decreasing and we are now confronted with so-called international constitutionalism. The regulation of matters that traditionally fall within the field of international law is shaped in conformity with the basic

[1] N MacCormick, 'Beyond the Sovereign State' (1993) 56 *MLR* 1.

[2] K Tuori, 'Transnational Law. On Legal Hybrids and Perspectivism' in M Maduro, K Tuori and S Sankari (eds), *Transnational Law. Rethinking European Law and Legal Thinking* (Cambridge, Cambridge University Press, 2014) 17.

[3] H Schwartz, 'The Internationalization of Constitutional Law' (2003) 10(2) *Human Rights Brief* 10. See also J Klabbers, A Peters and G Ulfstein, *The Constitutionalization of International Law* (Oxford, Oxford University Press 2009).

[4] An overview of the position of Scalia is provided in MA Waters, 'Justice Scalia on the Use of Foreign Law in Constitutional Interpretation: Unidirectional Monologue or Co-Constitutive Dialogue' (2004) 12 *Tulsa Journal of Comparative & International Law* 149.

[5] S Cassese, *Oltre lo Stato. Verso una nuova costituzione globale?* (Naples, Editoriale Scientifica, 2006).

guidelines of constitutionalism, including the separation of powers and judicial guarantees of personal rights. Furthermore, in these cases, when we are faced with cultural developments, we can observe the translation of models of legal organisation from one field of law to another.[6] Therefore, notwithstanding the difference of subjects, the relevant international law has to be interpreted in the light of the elaboration of the models of internal organisation of the different states. Finally, some authors have adopted another point of view, and looked at different developments in the internationalisation of constitutional law. They have studied the incorporation of international human rights treaties into national legal orders through special constitutional provisions, the convergence of national constitutions due to international bonds and the progressive transformation of treaties in supranational constitutions.[7] According to a recent systematisation, 'international law can be divided into three [...] broad subcategories' (fundamental rules of the international legal system at large, constitutions of international organisations and norms affecting domestic law).[8]

The study of the above new trends has to be connected to the analysis of the establishment of new international institutions aimed at ensuring the uniformity of internal legal regulations through cooperation between states. The phenomenon is progressively interesting the field of constitutional law, as the domestic implementation of international treaties is at stake. These developments started with the adoption of human rights treaties and the creation of the relevant supranational monitoring and judicial organisations, and continued with the protection of minorities. Frequently, these developments are connected with the conclusion of wars and their respective peace accords. Events that followed the end of the Second World War or the agreements of Dayton and Washington concerning Bosnia-Herzegovina offer meaningful examples of the connection of peace accords and the adoption of new constitutions. Moreover, the incorporation of international agreements in national law does not always concern detailed and specific international provisions that can be directly identified and applied. In these cases, an interpretative elaboration is required. The conformity of internal authorities to the accepted international obligations is ensured not only by national judges, but also by the competence of supranational judges, as in the case of the European Court of Human Rights. At times, the follow-up of international agreements requires a more complex lawmaking process. Internal legislation has to be adopted in conformity with the strategy of conditionality. In these cases, the existence of supranational organisations, such as the Council of Europe and the European Union, is again especially important insofar as candidate states intend to first become and then remain their members. Accessions are promoted by the institutions themselves and by their founding members. A basic strategy inspires these developments. The new Members States are accepted and are allowed to keep their membership only if they accept specific principles and values, such as the doctrines of the constitutionalism or the main elements of the economic free market.[9]

[6] See, eg the adoption of the parliamentary democracy models by the European Union: M Avbelj, *The European Union under Transnational Law* (Oxford, Hart Publishing, 2018) 82.

[7] C Wen-Chen and Y Jiunn-Rong, 'Internationalization of Constitutional Law' in M Rosenfeld and A Sajo (eds), *The Oxford Handbook of Comparative Constitutional Law* (Oxford, Oxford University Press, 2012) 1164.

[8] T Kleinlein and A Peters, *International Constitutional Law* (Oxford, Oxford Bibliographies, 2017–2018).

[9] See JT Checkel, 'Compliance and Conditionality' (2000) Arena Working Paper 18, 1.

II. International Law, Transnational Law and National Law

The content of the relevant engagements of stipulating parties are frequently extremely vague and ambiguous. They concisely refer to constitutional and economic theories and doctrines that can be elaborated according to subjective attitudes and orientations. According to Kaarlo Tuori, 'political consensus among States is easy to reach' 'the vaguer the provisions under regulation are'.[10] The peculiar structure of those provisions opens the way to the lawmaking of international judges and monitoring bodies in the field of international constitutional law. For instance, Article 2 TEU states that the European Union is founded 'on the values of respect for human dignity, freedom, democracy, equality, the rule of law and respect for human rights, including the rights of persons belonging to minorities'. The preamble to the European Convention on Human Rights (ECHR) proclaims, inter alia, the respect of human rights and fundamental freedoms, the existence of a democratic political regime and the primacy of law. The specific characteristics of these provisions have a direct effect on the functioning of the conditionality as far as they require the interposition of a monitoring machinery. The machinery must check the compliance of states with those provisions if those states are looking to accede to, and continue their membership of, the relevant institutions. The competent monitoring bodies must elaborate specific yardsticks to evaluate the concrete measures adopted by those states. This elaboration frequently requires the construction and implementation of binding principles and values through apposite guidelines and standards. These standards and guidelines may become generally mandatory, when they are adopted repeatedly to settle specific conflicts concerning different states. Here we have the 'epiphany' of international constitutional law that 'transcends national frontiers' – it is transnational law.[11] The relevant lawmaking is strictly connected with the application of the basic constitutional principles. Therefore, the content of the principles is no longer restricted to a generic reference to the European constitutional heritage or to the cultural circulation of the constitutional models.[12] The practice implies additional elements that may be inspired by the case law of European judges and by the European constitutions.[13] The difficult task of the political and legal actors is to fill the 'open texture' of international documents.

The relations between international law and transnational law are approached on the basis of different constructions. While, for instance, Avbelj qualifies 'international law … [as] an example of public transnational law',[14] Tuori distinguishes between the two fields and concludes that all examples of transnational law have international law as their 'background'.[15] This position is focused on the making of transnational law by supranational judges and monitoring bodies, whose activities affect matters usually reserved to the competence of the internal authorities of the concerned states. According to the traditional opinion, public international law does not interfere in the domestic legal order. However, twentieth-century

[10] Tuori (n 2) 19.

[11] This is the general definition of the transnational law proposed by PC Jessup and accepted as the starting point for a deep analysis of the matter: see Avbelj (n 6) 9.

[12] As happened in previous experiences of the Venice Commission.

[13] See Appendix 2.

[14] Avbelj (n 6) 149.

[15] Tuori (n 2) 21.

developments have shown that international law allows transnational lawmaking to touch on national constitutional organisation and the states' treatment of human rights. Therefore, studying the transnational results of the activity of some supranational bodies in the frame of international law is correct. This is a phenomenon of international law. The distinction between international law and transnational law is not just a terminological one, it reflects their different operational levels. This clarification suggests that we should be very careful when distinguishing between national law, international law and supranational law.[16] According to this differentiation, the existence of an autonomous legal order that is separate from national and international law generates the distinct phenomenon of supranational law. This chapter deals mainly with these kinds of phenomena. Nevertheless, the terminological differentiation may unfortunately cause misunderstanding insofar as it makes it easy to disregard the dependence of transnational law on international law.[17]

This raises questions about the monitoring machinery of transnational law: Who has the authority to fill the open vagueness of the expressions used by the signatories of the treaties? Who is allowed to refer to the traditional theories and doctrines of legal thought and their contemporary construction? The common idea that states are always behind the expansion of international law is controversial today. There is a tendency to look further into the spontaneous horizontal expansion of international law and the increasing public relevance of the international community. The above-described developments can be observed even when the existence of supranational institutions which are supported by the states is at stake.[18] From this perspective, many scholars underline the important role played by international judges. We certainly cannot forget the contributions to international law made by the case law of the ECJ and the ECtHR. A crucial new question arose recently: In whose name do judges of international courts decide? The answer is that their legitimacy derives not from the Member States of supranational institutions, but from the existence of international or supranational fora, which give the citizens a 'cosmopolitan identity'.[19] This answer confirms the usefulness of a horizontal approach.

These conclusions base the claim of authority of international judges on the guarantee of the values of personal rights and freedoms and of democracy. Therefore, this approach is coherent with the purposes of the treaties and conventions that direct the developments of international law towards the implementation of the principles of constitutionalism. However, this approach allows a conception of the legitimacy of international judges, founded on the circulation of the legal culture within the international community. Minor attention is paid by the observers to the relevance of the political decisions of the states. The formal establishment of an institutionalised and distinct body entrusted with legislative power could be paradoxically absent. Even if the epiphany of the mentioned cultural communitarian process is normally linked to the activity of international judicial bodies, we will not always see a unidirectional development. In fact, circularity of relations between

[16] Avbelj (n 6) 10–12.

[17] Instead, the use of the adjective 'supranational' is convenient when we speak about the authorities of the mentioned autonomous order.

[18] A von Bogdandy, 'Il costituzionalismo nel diritto internazionale: commento su una proposta della Germania' in G Gozzi and G Bongiovanni (eds, *Popoli e civiltà* (Bologna, Il mulino, 2006) 183.

[19] A von Bogdandy and I Venzke, 'On the Democratic Legitimation of International Judicial Lawmaking' (2011) 12 *German Law Journal* 1343.

international actors is always possible.[20] As the international operators draw inspiration from international case law, international judges also look at the activity of other international authorities. For instance, the home page of the Venice Commission's website highlights more than 200 judgments and decisions of international judges who have quoted the Opinions of the Venice Commission. There are many ways for constitutionalism to expand in the international field. If the relevant treaties and conventions offer references that require further hermeneutic elaboration, a common effort is needed to identify the possible contents of the bounds provided for by documents on the matter. Choices and interpretative orientations can derive from different sources. However, they are always the fruit of an interpretative construction. The meaning of the treaties and conventions may be clarified beyond any strict textual interpretation. It is this reasoned and justified approach that offers grounds for finding and working out new principles and rules.[21]

Special attention should be paid to conditionality in view of its effects on the expansion of international constitutional law. Conditionality does not necessarily imply the intervention of a judge and the exercise of a judicial function. Frequently, compliance with rules providing for conditionality is connected with the adhesion to an international or supranational institution that requires the observance of specific obligations by its members. The machinery works through the presence of special bodies entrusted with the task of monitoring the conformity of Member States with the purposes of the institution. The shaping of the internal state's organisation or the establishment of the main elements of an economic free market are at stake. One of the competent bodies is usually a political body whose deliberations are frequently supported by the reports and opinions of technical (ie non-political) advisory bodies. Statements that have apparently only political relevance produce important legal normative effects, thanks to the reiterated adoption of similar decisions. Through the elaboration of the values and principles stated in the documents establishing the concerned institution, advisory and technical bodies fill the vagueness of the relevant provisions. The content of these provisions is integrated and completed through an exercise of what eventually appears as a true exercise of lawmaking. And this result is eventually transferred into the deliberations of the competent political authorities.

III. The Making of International Constitutional Law: The Role of the Venice Commission

It is evident that the final purpose of legal and political actors is the adoption of internal legislation by the state in conformity with the recommendations of the monitoring technical bodies insofar as these recommendations are supported by their reception by political bodies of supranational institutions. Both political and technical bodies participate in the exercise of the lawmaking. The statements of the technical bodies only rarely acquire the status of

[20] These developments apparently confirm the idea that relations between legal orders and their coexistence depend on a case-by-case approach: N Krisch, *Beyond Constitutionalism* (Oxford, Oxford University Press, 2010) 298; for comments, see Avbelj (n 6) 28–29.

[21] G Della Cananea, 'Thesis and Dike in the International Arena – Comments on Armin von Bogdandy and Ingo Vetzkès "Democratic" Legitimation of International Judicial Lawmaking' (2011) 12 *German Law Journal* 2059.

international constitutional law without ratification by the superior political bodies. These statements cannot be compared with the judgments of the supranational judges even if the members of those bodies are experts (lawyers, economists, political scientists, etc) who have to be neutral and do not have a political mandate.

The legal relevance of the results of these interpretative elaborations is strengthened by their reiterated and frequent adoption in the monitoring processes concerning even different Member States of a supranational institution (the Council of Europe or the European Union, for instance). The Venice Commission pays special attention to its precedents. In this way, it ensures the coherence and continuity of the results of its work, which can erroneously look arbitrary and discordant to some observers.[22] Therefore, the basis of the binding force of Venice Commission precedents could eventually be identified as a product of customary lawmaking. The reiteration of these processes opens the way to the normative expansion of international constitutionalism. The politicians, the diplomats and the experts who take part in these exercises interpret and elaborate the theories and doctrines that make up the content of the constitutional heritage. The consequent compliance by the concerned states confirms the functioning of the machinery of the conditionality. Simultaneously, however, the content of the legal rules binding the members of the concerned institutions is enriched.

In this way, it is possible to identify the practical consequences of the observance or violation of the adopted yardstick. The actors of these developments are at the same time authors and executors of the international constitutional law whose elaboration is part of their mandate. In this role, they take part in a public forum and make a substantial contribution to a communitarian process that is at the base of the establishment of new relations between European countries. There are exchanges of ideas and opinions that start from the constitutional experiences of the states, the relevant internal legislation and the constitutional case law. These materials are evoked in the light of the traditional theories and doctrines of European constitutionalism and enable the spreading of the relevant legal culture. The mentioned materials acquire international relevance as far as the relations between the states, and between the supranational institutions and the states that are or plan to become their members, are affected. The importance of the results can be compared to that of the international formal documents providing for the protection of human rights and fundamental freedoms, thus contributing to shaping a new dimension of constitutional law.

These developments promote the discussion of a new form of lawmaking; however, the matter requires further thought. The results of the elaboration of the mentioned materials by the technical advisory bodies are rarely directly applied to the concerned facts. They have to be adopted by the political bodies of the interested supranational institutions. In the case of the Venice Commission, the final adoption depends on the will of the Parliamentary Assembly of the Council of Europe and its monitoring committee or of the Committee of Ministers of the Council of Europe. This final step is decisive. In fact, the political bodies may require a more or less strict observance of the conclusions adopted in the technical phase of the monitoring process. In this final step of the process, political considerations may play a crucial role. Moreover, subsequent effects depend on the rational choices of

[22] B Iancu, 'Quod licet Jovi non licet bovi? The Venice Commission as Norm Entrepreneur' (2019) 11 *Hague Journal on Rule of Law* 189; M Bobek and D Kosar, 'Global Solutions, Local Damages: A Critical Study in Judicial Councils in Central and Eastern Europe' (2014) 15 *German Law Journal* 1257.

the states that play a concurrent role as far as the addition of new content to the adopted yardstick by the technicians is concerned. If states comply, the legal binding effect depends on the principle of conditionality. If that conditionality is not observed, the legal normative relevance will depend on the decision of the competent bodies to sanction the behaviour of the states or to recur to a supranational judge, as in the recent cases concerning Hungary and Poland. However, international negotiation implies the concurrence of an internal bargain between governing authorities of the states concerned and opposition, including possible veto, players.[23] Therefore, the reaction of European authorities is not always foreseeable insofar as they may take into consideration internal political conflicts in the implementation of the establishment of democracy in those states.

The legal and political aspects of these developments do not preclude the attention their cultural dimension deserves. Even if the comparative constitutional perspective is not a novelty, the new expansion of the public international discussion is connected with the rise of constitutionalism, as described in a seminal contribution.[24] In recent times, successive waves of adoption of new constitutions have emerged, which have certainly enriched the international constitutional debate. These developments were followed by a large circulation of ideas insofar as the constitutional processes affected not only the internal transformations of the states, but also the relations between the states and the supranational institutions.

The European point of view on constitutionalism is especially important. Western Europe, together with the Eastern Coast of the USA, was the cradle of constitutionalism. However, this area of 'Western constitutionalism' has also been concerned with the modern, contemporary innovative implementation of constitutional principles developed through the different experiences of the old and new democracies. Following the Second World War, the Council of Europe and the European Union contributed to the evolution of international constitutionalism. The support of these supranational institutions had a decisive impact on the adoption of new constitutional legislation in new democracies. The support of technical bodies was offered, as is widely illustrated in this book.

In the context of the frame described in chapter one, the experience of the Venice Commission is a typical example of the illustrated developments. The Venice Commission was designed as a consultative body on issues of constitutional law, the functioning of democratic institutions, fundamental freedoms and rights, electoral legislation and constitutional justice. Its members are in office in a personal capacity, without any representative link with the governing bodies of their states. Therefore, the Commission can provide technical input to the political deliberations of the authorities that seek its opinion on relevant cases. The coincidence of its creation with the fall of the Berlin Wall and the dissolution of the Soviet Union and the Federative Republic of Yugoslavia facilitated the involvement of the Commission in the growth of new democracies in Central and Eastern Europe. The Venice Commission has helped these states with the preparation of the constitutional and legislative reforms needed to move them towards alignment with, and ultimately accession to, the Council of Europe and the European Union.

[23] F Schimmelfenning and U Sedelmeier, 'Governance by Conditionality. EU Rule Transfer to the Candidate Countries of Central and Eastern Europe' (2004) 11 *Journal of European Public Policy* 661, 669.

[24] B Ackerman, 'The Rise of World Constitutionalism' (1997) 83 *Virginia Law Review* 771.

The Commission exercises its main function of constitutional assistance at the request, for instance, of concerned states or of the Secretary General and the Parliamentary Assembly of the Council of Europe.[25] Its Opinions deal with drafts and amendments of constitutions and ordinary legislation on the matter. The purpose is the monitoring of the conformity of these documents with the engagements accepted by the states at the moment of their accession to, or during their continued membership of, the Council. As previously discussed, this exercise of monitoring implies the reference to the principles and values that have to be observed by members of the supranational institution. The elaboration of those principles and values is at the centre of the activity of the Commission. The Commission is required to determine the actual meaning of vague and ambiguous provisions of the treaties and agreements. The final function of the Commission is the creation of a yardstick of evaluation that is commonly accepted and shared. When the Commission began its work, this general yardstick was summarily identified in the European constitutional heritage. The concrete application of this yardstick to specific cases, however, required the identification of specific guidelines and standards. The Commission has slowly developed principles and rules that integrate the generic content of the initial yardstick and concretise the content of the bonds whose observance is mandatory for the Member States.

Obviously, the Commission did not invent *ex nihilo* the rules that have enriched the provisions of the treaties and agreements. It has drawn inspiration from the constitutional experience of the Western European States. Comparing different national experiences requires a complex intellectual and interpretative activity and the identification of their consequences. As discussed above, according to the main legal doctrine, the historical developments of the Central and Eastern European countries are not always taken into consideration in this investigation. Some of those states have significant traditions in the field of constitutionalism. However, they have been substantially marginalised in the progress of the European constitutional traditions. Therefore, these countries did not have the continuity of adhesion to the principles of constitutionalism that was required in the formation of the European constitutional heritage.[26] Simultaneously, the mentioned Western materials needed to be updated in the light of the emergence of new questions and problems connected to the advent of the contemporary post-industrial society. For instance, new problems and questions were not always covered by the ECHR. At times, the most important international documents only provided a starting point of general principles, underpinning suggestions and guidelines. According to Dworkin, principles are not 'applicable in [an] all-or-nothing fashion', as they 'do not set out' the consequences of their application.[27] Therefore, the interpreters are engaged in an effort of concretisation of the law that is needed to arrive at the solution for the cases at stake.[28] The Commission is tasked with providing constitutional answers that become part of the experience of

[25] See Appendix 1.

[26] The experiences of Poland and Lithuania are especially covered by L Garlicki, 'Democracy and International Influence' in G Nolte (ed), *European and US Constitutionalism* (Cambridge, Cambridge University Press, 2005) 263. He tries to overcome the difficulties of the mentioned marginalisation of these countries.

[27] R Dworkin, *Taking Rights Seriously* (London, Duckworth, 1978) 24.

[28] See M De Visser, 'A Critical Assessment of the Role of the Venice Commission in Processes of Domestic Constitutional Reform' (2015) 63 *American Journal of Comparative Law* 963, 972, who, notwithstanding her critical attitude, shares the opinion that for 'the mentioned principles to be meaningful yardsticks, further concretization is necessary'.

European constitutionalism through the machinery of conditionality. The proposed solutions are helpful to other international bodies as well. For instance, quotations of Opinions and Reports of the Venice Commission are found in the case law of European judges and the documents of the bodies of the European Union. This highlights the contribution made by the Commission to the formation of international constitutional law, the basic content of which is integrated and enriched by the Opinions of the Commission. These results not only have cultural relevance; they also have binding effects. Insofar as they are not limited to the cultural dimension, they can eventually be qualified as true expressions of lawmaking activity.

The dialogue between the Commission and states' constitutional courts is an exemplary model of these developments. Since the beginning of its activity, the Commission has devoted particular attention to constitutional justice. In fact, the establishment of constitutional courts was constantly supported by the advice and recommendations of the Commission. Its interventions have affected not only the preparation and adoption of national legislation, but also judgment in some cases. Constitutional judges have frequently asked the cooperation of the Commission, which answers in the form of amicus curiae briefs. The Commission does not pretend to substitute its Opinions for the interpretation of national constitutional law whose guarantee is the mandate of the courts. The construction of a state's internal constitution is a task for the state's judges. The Commission only offers its advice by suggesting the correct interpretation of the principles of the international constitutional law that have to be complied with by national authorities and make up the frame of the deliberations of these authorities.

IV. Precedents and Examples

Many Opinions of the Commission provide important evidence of the contribution of this body to the developments of the European constitutional heritage. For instance, in a case concerning Albania,[29] the Commission suggested that the state's interest in implementing a Lustration Act apparently affecting some judges of the constitutional court must be balanced with the continuity of the judicial review of legislation. Therefore, if the Lustration Act did not provide for their temporary replacement, the judges whose position was suspicious would have to stay in office and refrain from abstention. In this way, the adoption of a decision on the constitutionality of the Lustration Act was possible as the presence of the required number of judges for the adoption of a decision was ensured. The Opinion was evidently based on a doctrine of constitutional justice that has to be effectively present to guarantee the continuity of the compliance of the system with the constitution. Moreover, the suggestion not only provided for the integration of the international yardstick, but also enabled Albanian judges to fill a lacuna of the internal legislation by adopting a new rule. From the Albanian state's point of view, the advice of the Commission implied the exercise of a power of lawmaking by the constitutional court that is a usual feature of constitutional justice.

[29] Venice Commission, CDL-AD(2009)044, concerning Albania and CDL-AD(2010)002 concerning Moldova.

The Commission followed a similar way of thinking when it showed a clear preference for one of the possible solutions of a Moldavan case. The constitutional court of that country was asked to complete the provisions of its constitution by a functional interpretation of the principles concerning the election of the President of the Republic. The mere application of the constitutional text met with some difficulties and required the advice of the Commission. In this case, the approach of the Commission went further than explicit legislative provisions, whose purely textual interpretation was insufficient. Punctual suggestions were given for a broader constitutional approach. A creative interpretation of the role of the constitutional court was envisaged in view of its participation in the process of constitutional lawmaking. This interpretation is a clear and evident result of the elaboration of recent experiences of Western constitutionalism. At least in the field of constitutional law, countries with a long civil law tradition are embracing modalities typical of common law countries.

In an Opinion concerning Romania,[30] the Commission proposed a solution that introduced a principle not always present in the written texts of the constitutions of the European states and was beyond the text of the Romanian Constitution. The Commission suggested to the governing bodies of the state (the President, the government and the parliament) the observance of the principle of constitutional loyal cooperation. The aim was the avoidance of conflicts and intricacies in the mutual relations of those authorities. The idea was that the principle of loyal cooperation has to be complied with in all the models of government. Even in the absence of clear constitutional provisions, loyal cooperation has to be the basis of an efficient functioning of the constitutional systems, notwithstanding the differences and peculiarities that are often present.

The work of the Commission in the field of electoral legislation is especially interesting. It is the product of the activity of its Council for democratic elections established in cooperation with the Congress of Local and Regional Authorities. The results derive from the identification of principles and standards that have been defined as the European electoral heritage.[31] Their identification was derived from Article 3 of the Additional Protocol of the ECHR and the national and supranational case law on the matter. The principle of stability of the electoral legislation benefited from a creative approach. This principle is constructed as a factor of credibility of the electoral process and of the consolidation of democracy.[32] The universality, equality, freedom, secretiveness and directness of the vote have been considered as the basis for the construction of the doctrines of the Commission in the electoral field. Over time, these doctrines have acquired a binding relevance.

According to one authoritative contribution,[33] similar creative processes are apparently missing in the general field of human rights and fundamental freedoms as safeguarded by the ECHR. The interpretation of the ECHR 'takes a predominant place'[34] in the Opinions of the Commission. However, this body 'painstakingly follows' the case law of the European

[30] Venice Commission, CDL-AD(2012)026.

[31] P Garrone, 'Le patrimonie electoral européen' (2001) No 5 *Revue du droit public* 1417.

[32] Venice Commission, CDL(99)41 and CDL(99)67.

[33] P Van Dijk, 'The Venice Commission on Certain Aspects of the Application of the European Convention on Human Rights *Ratione personae*' in S Breitenmoser (ed), *Human Rights, Democracy and the Rule of Law, Liber amicorum Luzius Wildhabh* (Zurich, Nomos, 2007) 183.

[34] ibid.

Court of Human Rights.[35] The Commission has a different perception of its contribution to the innovations in the process of safeguarding human rights. In fact, the Commission has prepared many reports summarising its 'case law' concerning human rights and fundamental freedoms (religion and belief, association, assembly, equality and so on).

At times, the Commission has been confronted with the difficult problem of reconciling the basic conceptions of constitutionalism, on the one hand, with some traditional institutions of the concerned countries, on the other hand. These institutions have not been subject to a process of modernisation. This is the case, for instance, of the Prokuratura in Russia and Ukraine. Draft laws of these countries were aimed at entrusting the office of the Prosecutor with functions that were not always connected with the judicial criminal prosecution of misdemeanours and violations of criminal law. Therefore, the intention of those legislators was to pursue the continuity of the larger role played by the Prokuratura for more than a century. The Commission insisted in recognising in both cases[36] the primacy of modern international principles over those remaining from the past. Therefore, the Commission refused to admit the continuity of the national heritage. This heritage was considered not to be in line with the Council of Europe's values, as it followed the Soviet (and czarist) model, which reflected a non-democratic past.[37] Again, with regard to the legislation of Ukraine, the Commission[38] stated the principle that the protection of national minorities does not always have to be an absolute priority. This protection has to be implemented taking into account the state's identity and national language if the concerned minority group has a disproportionate de facto traditional strong position in society because of historical and political reasons. The Commission concluded that the Russian minority profited, and still profits, in Ukraine from the protection of a powerful kin – the state of Russia. Moreover, the Commission recently contested with Hungary the admissibility of the so-called uniformity procedure, which allowed the highest judicial authority (the Curia) both to adopt obligatory uniformity decisions with binding effect on inferior courts and to check the observance of those decisions. The Hungarian government had defended this system by referring to a tradition from the nineteenth century.[39] Conversely, the Commission considered acceptable the adoption of a model of judicial organisation that entrusted the executive with relevant functions in some Central Europe states. Even in the absence of the Mediterranean model of judicial independence (usually preferred by the Commission), the long tradition of conformity to the principle of rule of law in those states has been judged sufficient to ensure the independence of the judiciary. This position is dealt with in depth in chapter seven.

The Eastern European countries have not been the only ones to benefit from the advice of the Venice Commission. For instance, Belgium was considered to have correctly adopted a temporary derogation of the rules dealing with the revision of the Constitution. The necessity of facing an ongoing constitutional crisis was accepted as a sufficient basis to justify this move from the perspective of international standards.[40] In 2002, the Commission adopted a

[35] ibid.
[36] See Venice Commission, CDL-AD(2005)014 and CDL-AD(2013)025.
[37] See the personal note of H Suchocka in Venice Commission, CDL(2001)134.
[38] Venice Commission, CDL-AD(2011)047.
[39] Venice Commission, CDL-AD(2012)001.
[40] Venice Commission, CDL-AD(2012)010.

severely critical Opinion about the revision of the Constitution of Liechtenstein, which was supposed to distance the country from the other European democracies.[41]

It is evident that the Venice Commission has assigned particular importance to the constitutional yardstick it adopts. This attitude can be explained since the Opinions of the Commission produce binding effects that go beyond the sphere of the Council of Europe. Recently, the spreading of these effects was facilitated by the compilation of documents that collect the main conclusions of the Opinions of the Commission according to a thematic criterion (Reports or Compilations). This initiative confirms that the body assigns a general importance to its Opinions and confirms the coherence and continuity of the 'case law' of the Commission. The initiative of these documents disavows the criticism of those authors who accuse the Commission of arbitrariness.[42] The continuity of the observance of the principles stated in the Opinions excludes the possibility of arbitrariness. The background behind the Commission's documents does not imply the adoption of a codified corpus of detailed provisions. Instead, it is the fruit of interpretative doctrines consisting of principles and guidelines that have become mandatory through their reiterated adoption by the governing bodies of the supranational institutions. The authority of these decisions requires the internal application of those doctrines in the internal constitutional legislation of the states.[43]

The doctrines are developed through a reasoned construction of the models of the constitutional relations and the relative guidelines for their implementation. These materials are compatible with the constitutional legislation of European states. The work of the Commission can imply the introduction of innovative principles and standards. These principles and standards must be considered as the basis for the shaping of the necessary constitutional reforms in the new (but also in the old) democracies. These materials must be taken into account by the interlocutors of the Commission. Actors in charge of applying these doctrines need not to forget the peculiar national situations of the individual countries. The Commission's doctrines are, however, supposed to trump national traditions that have not been updated according the principles of contemporary constitutionalism. Their internal reception is the final step of the process. However, the mandatory effect depends on the adoption of the proposals of the Commission by the governing bodies of the Council of Europe or of the European Union, and also depends on the willingness of those political bodies to enforce the Commission's doctrines according to their special institutional provisions.[44]

[41] Venice Commission, CDL-AD(2002)032.

[42] See the authors quoted in n 22 above.

[43] These developments remind us of the opinion about the intermediate role played by the political, administrative and judicial bodies of the states in the extension of the effects of international constitutional law in domestic legal orders of A von Bogdandy, 'Pluralism, Direct Effect, and the Ultimate Say: On the Relationship between International and Domestic Constitutional Law' (2008) 6 *International journal of Constitutional Law* 401.

[44] The Venice Commission is conscious that the final result of the lawmaking process does not depend solely on its own contribution. In the Reports and Compilations of its Opinions, the Commission always underlines that all these documents are 'frames of reference' that do not preclude the introduction of new points of view or the divergence from earlier ones 'if there is a good reason for doing so'. Opinions relate to specific countries, therefore not all the conclusions adopted by the Commission can be extended to all the concerned states. Moreover, it is sometimes difficult to find the roots of those conclusions in the European constitutional heritage as they regard items and institutions that are not subjects of general interest but are peculiar aspects of the constitutional order of a single state.

The described developments involved many authorities and bodies who do not have lawmaking powers. However, those developments result in the creation of law that we call international constitutional law. We are confronted with the establishment of collective institutions at the supranational level. These institutions engage the responsibility of the concerned states to implement international/transnational law in the domestic legal orders of the concerned states. As discussed in chapter two, this responsibility may be sanctioned at the supranational level on the basis of the internal behaviour of the bodies of the states. Therefore, competent supranational authorities must check this behaviour. The domestic order is no longer impermeable to external interferences. The supranational scrutiny is exercised in the light of the yardsticks identified by the Venice Commission and accepted by political bodies entrusted with the final steps of the monitoring process. The specific single decisions of these bodies do not have general normative effects even if they are mandatory because of the monitoring mandate of their authors. However, insofar as they are repetitively adopted and imposed by the states on a case-by-case basis, they are acquiring a general normative efficacy. This efficacy is not limited to the effects displayed by the decisions in single particular cases. The effect acquires general normative relevance through a process of formation that is comparable to the customary lawmaking.

The innovative content of the decisions goes further than the content of the provisions of the relevant treaties. The formation of new law provides evidence of the normative effects of the 'case law' of the Commission. These aspects are confirmed by two factors. On the one side, an important role is played by the publication of the Commission's Reports or Compilations summarising its 'case law' in its different fields of action. These reports underline the importance of the spreading among the interested states and authorities of the new doctrines adopted by the Commission. On the other side, the frequent quotation of the Commission's Opinions by European supranational and national judges reveals the growing legal importance of the Commission's 'case law'. Opinions are considered useful since they are read as an integration of the frequently ambiguous and vague content of the European constitutional heritage. This is the result of the generally relevant, frequent operational references to the Opinions by the concerned institutions, which help these institutions to identify the actual meaning of the vague normative content of the European principles that are the basis of their judicial or monitoring activities. Therefore, the construction of interpretative and explanatory legal doctrines is a necessary component of the process of legal reasoning aimed at the practical integration of the 'open texture' of the law that has to be applied by the interpreters.[45]

However, the participation of the Commission in international constitutional lawmaking is not free. The body is bound to guarantee the compliance with the basic principles and values of the European constitutional heritage by national authorities. At the same time, the Commission has to respect those principles and values. Utilising a metaphor, the creative effect of the Commission's activities has to proceed according to the model of the rhyming couplet. This model requires the adoption of two lines of poetry of equal length, one after another: the final words of the two lines need to end with the same sound. This model was introduced to justify the creative decision-making of the Italian Constitutional Court,[46]

[45] Important elaborations of this matter are presented in K Tuori, *Ratio and Voluntas. The Tension between Reason and Will in Law* (Farnham, Ashgate, 2011) ch 6.

[46] The metaphor was first used by V Crisafulli, 'La Corte costituzionale ha vent'anni' (1976) 20 *Giurisprudenza costituzionale* 1694.

and may be useful to understand the developments we are dealing with. The Commission's lawmaking has to be the consequence of the principles and values as they are interpreted.

If the will of the Commission is restricted in the elaboration of its own yardstick of evaluation, its activity may be compared to judicial activity. The recognition of this peculiarity is supported by elements pertaining to the legitimisation of the Commission and its monitoring role. Certainly, its activity has a political importance insofar as it contributes to the expansion of the supranational institutions (such as the Council of Europe and the European Union) and to the establishment of the internal constitutional and legal structure of the Member States in conformity with the European doctrines. However, it does not follow that the Commission has a political legitimacy. The founding states entrusted the Commission with a technical mandate that implies the accomplishment of the Commission's task through the elaboration of juridical materials according to the cultural and professional qualifications of its members. Its Opinions derive their authority from the correctness and coherence of the adopted legal methodology. Therefore, they have to be deliberated according to the principles of neutrality and in full respect of the basic requirements of legal reasoning. Compliance with the fundamental rules of professional deontology by its members is at stake. Hence, these members are appointed and work in their own personal capacity. Insofar as the observance of mentioned rules is guaranteed, the legitimacy of the activity of the Commission is beyond dispute. Moreover, this legitimacy justifies the consequent formation of an integrative international constitutional law. The comparison of the activity of the Commission to judicial activity does not preclude this conclusion as the European experience has many examples of judicial lawmaking.

5

International Constitutional Law: Sources and Materials

I. International Law and Transnational Law

The Venice Commission takes part in international constitutional monitoring and participates in the elaboration of international constitutional law through the machinery of conditionality.[1] Conditionality is an essential feature of these developments. Conditionality implies that the effects of the Commission's lawmaking do not depend only on the mere declaration or statement of its Opinions, but are also the result of a complex process. This process leads to the acceptance of those Opinions by the institutions that seek the Commission's advice. These institutions can be political bodies of the concerned state or authorities of the supranational institutions of which the state is a member. At best, the final step of this complex process is the implementation of the Commission's Opinions in the making of the national constitutional or ordinary legislation. Therefore, the lawmaking effects are to be acknowledged only when there is compliance with the Commission's Opinions. Moreover, guidelines and principles recommended by the Opinions of the Commission may assume an institutional relevance when the addressees repeatedly observe them. In these cases, guidelines and principles of the Commission's Opinion may open the way to the establishment of new customary law, consisting of the basic elements of the doctrines elaborated or accepted by the Commission[2] and the other authorities. However, the mentioned legal effects may also depend on the decisions of the governing bodies of the supranational institutions to sanction states that do not comply with the principles stated in the Opinions. These developments may even require the intervention of European judges.

These developments may be especially observed when the Commission draws inspiration from the constitutional experience of Member States. At times, the work of the Commission implies the operational interpretation and elaboration of the content of specific normative texts.[3] In this case, there is a written point of reference and the activity of the Commission favours the formation of the interpretative doctrines of the relevant documents in cooperation with other authorities (for instance, political bodies of the interested country;

[1] S Bartole, 'International Constitutionalism and Conditionality. The Experience of the Venice Commission' (2014) AIC Rivista No 4/2014.

[2] For similar conclusions but with regard to the advisory opinions of the international judges, see K Oellers-Frahm, 'Lawmaking through Advisory Opinions of the International Judges' (2011) 12 *German Law Journal* 1033.

[3] Treaties or conventions on human rights and fundamental freedoms; see, in particular, Document of the Copenhagen Meeting of the Conference on the Human Dimension of the CSCE, 29 June 1990.

the European authorities that asked the advice of the Commission; and international judges frequently quoting the Commission's Opinions).

According to some authors,[4] it is possible to classify these developments as epiphanies of the internationalisation of constitutional law. This is an expression that, on the one side, correctly emphasises the extension of constitutionalism beyond the nation state and, on the other side, underlines the large scope of the phenomenon. The expression covers the incorporation or implementation of different legal sources in domestic constitutions. Among these, the most important are: (i) international treaties aimed at safeguarding human rights and fundamental freedoms; (ii) treaties establishing European institutions that bind Member States to the main principles of constitutionalism; and (iii) the internal rules of global regulatory institutions, such as the World Trade Organization. However, a recent contribution[5] has taken a position on the distinction between transnational law and international law, and has claimed that the evolution of transnational law is strictly linked to phenomena of the disconnection of legal transborder experiences from their international law foundations. Thus, normative and institutional structures of transnational law are based on international law but have distanced themselves from the background of treaty-based international law. They are progressively getting significant autonomy where the existence of supranational institutions is concerned.

An important example of these developments is the system of the European Convention on Human Rights (ECHR) and the case law of the European Court of Human Rights (ECtHR), which is seen as a true instance of international/transnational law making. Insofar as the results of the activity of the Venice Commission concern the safeguarding of human rights and draw inspiration from the elaboration of the precedents of the ECtHR, we could argue in favour of their inclusion in the developments of transnational law. However, where the institutional organisation of states is concerned, the reference to ECtHR case law becomes more tenuous. Within this picture, the international law system could regain new space and relevance through reference to the specific provisions of treaties binding the interested actors to adopt, for example, a peculiar organisation of the judicial institutions (see Article 6 ECHR). Also, in these cases, the final developments of the concerned processes affect the internal order of the states. In short, there is a convergence of the results of the processes of internationalisation and transnationalisation of domestic constitutional law. Both of these processes can be considered as constitutive elements of a progressive tendency to an extension of the area of constitutional law.[6]

In fact, we find at the core of the experience of the Venice Commission its advisory acts (Opinions) on the drafts of adoption or reform of national constitutions submitted to its examination by countries interested in accession to international or supranational institutions, or in maintaining their membership thereof. The Venice Commission is also

[4] Among others, C Wen-Chen and Y Junn-Rong, 'Internationalization of Constitutional Law' in M Rosenfeld and A Sajo (eds), *The Oxford Handbook of Comparative Constitutional Law* (Oxford, Oxford University Press, 2012) 1165.

[5] K Tuori, 'Transnational Law. On Legal Hybrids and Perspectivism' in M Maduro, K Tuori and S Sankari (eds), *Transnational Law. Rethinking European Law and Legal Thinking* (Cambridge, Cambridge University Press, 2014) 11, 20.

[6] Also, the tendency of the national judges to make reference to the case law of judges of other countries is often quoted as a part of the phenomenon we are dealing with: see, eg H Schwartz, 'The Internationalization of Constitutional Law' (2003) 10(2) *Human Rights Brief* 10.

entrusted with the institutional duty to respond to requests initiated by the governing bodies of the Council of Europe and the European Union (the Parliamentary Assembly of the Council of Europe and its Monitoring Committee, for instance).[7] By adopting the acts which are typical of its functions, the Commission concurs in the identification and elaboration of principles, standards and guidelines whose observance is relevant to the goals pursued by interested countries. Increasingly, the documents of the Commission make up principles and standards aimed at the implementation of the doctrine of constitutionalism in different fields. Among these fields, the following are considered crucial: the organisation of the powers of the state, the safeguarding of human rights and fundamental freedoms; judicial review of legislation; and, finally, the relations between states and their participation in international or supranational institutions.

This chapter deepens the understanding of the interpretative process of the participation of the Venice Commission in the formation of international constitutional law by addressing two questions concerning the activity of the Commission. First, it is certainly urgent and necessary to ascertain the geographical extension of the effectiveness of the principles elaborated by the Venice Commission. Nowadays, it is common to connect the growing importance of international constitutional law with developments in so-called globalisation. Therefore, we should investigate whether the activity of the Commission is affected by the expansion of globalisation, and consequently whether the Commission's activity impacts a worldwide legal space, or whether its relevance has to be restricted to the European regional area (as could be suggested by the original institutional connection of that body with the Council of Europe). Even if the Council of Europe claims to pursue universal values.

Secondly, it is important to identify the sources of guidelines and principles, the observance of which the Commission requires from the states that seek its advice and help. The identification of these sources emphasises the historical matrices of the constitutional doctrines taken into consideration by the Commission. The two questions are connected, as the geographic dimension of the Commission's 'case law' is closely related to the historical developments of constitutionalism. The phenomenon depends on the historical formation of European constitutionalism in the frame of the old nation states, even if it implies the extension of constitutionalism beyond nation-state confines.[8]

The rationale of the analysis this chapter develops favours starting with the second question, as the identification of the historical sources of constitutionalism indirectly gives sufficient indication of the geographical extension of the materials taken into consideration in the activity of the Commission. Therefore, a historical approach is necessary. From the very beginning of its existence, the investigations of the Commission have been closely connected with the idea of European constitutional heritage. The Commission looked at the traditional legal experiences of constitutionalism in order to ascertain two important developments. On the one side, the Commission has been sensitive to the origins of those shared values that make up the European constitutional heritage. On the other side, the Commission took into account the spreading of these values from one legal order to another, and the mutual exchange of experiences and suggestions that imply a common

[7] See Appendix 1.
[8] Tuori (n 5) 39.

adhesion to common concepts of constitutionalism. From this historical point of view, the starting point is the experience of those countries that are usually identified as the cradle of constitutionalism, such as the UK, the USA and France. However, we cannot forget the contribution of other countries, such as Belgium, Italy and Germany.

II. The Research of the Historical Roots

If the starting point of our inquiry refers to the general principles of the European constitutional heritage, we have to look first to the Magna Carta. We should consider not only the initial document of 1215, but also the changes and new interpretations aimed at updating it to meet the social and economic developments of the kingdom and its entry into the (then named) Statute Book of the Kingdom.[9] This move is certainly useful if we want to identify the matrices of the doctrine of the rule of law, which – according to A Dicey – is a main characteristic of the constitutional order of England since the Norman Conquest.[10] The English concept of the rule of law was strictly connected with the frame of the common law; therefore, there were differences from its European conception. These differences are partially overcome by recent policies of the European Union. The Venice Commission played an important role in these developments.[11]

If we focus our attention on the models of the organisation of the state and, in particular, on the doctrine of democracy and of the separation of powers, we have to make reference to Article 16 of the 1789 Déclaration des Droits de l'Homme et du Citoyen. Accordingly, all societies where the guarantee of rights is not ensured and the separation of powers is not established do not have a constitution. The correctness of this way of proceeding could be contested as we demand to look at documents that have different origins and pertain to different legal systems. It could be objected that we are not in the position of a jurist who deals with the Bill of Rights of the American Constitution and considers 'the legal texts of other charters of liberty – Magna Carta, Petition of Rights, the English Bill of Rights, state constitutions, and the like' – as materials of his research.[12] In fact, Akhil Reed Amar rightly makes reference to all the quoted English documents as the English system of law is at the origin of the constitutional developments of the American Colonies and of the USA. However, our approach correctly starts from the mentioned English and French documents. In fact, this approach emphasises the international and supranational impact of these documents considering the intermediation of the legal constitutional culture and of the effects of the transborder spreading of this culture.[13]

We cannot stick only to the original intent of the authors and to the literal content of the legislative texts. We must consider that their historical relevance makes sense through their

[9] M Caravale, *Magna Carta Libertatum* (Bologna, Il mulino, 2020) 67–73.

[10] A Dicey, *Introduction to the Study of the Law of the Constitution* (London, Macmillan, 1908) passim.

[11] See Venice Commission, CDL-AD(2011)003 rev and CDL-AD(2016)007. For a critical analysis of the European Union approach, see A Magen, 'Cracks in the Foundations: Understanding the Great Rule of Law Debate in the EU' (2016) 54 *Journal of Common Market Studies* 5, 1050.

[12] A Reed Amar, *The Bill of Rights* (New Haven, Yale University Press, 1998) 299.

[13] For general presentations of the relevant problems, see K Tuori, *Critical Legal Positivism* (Farnham, Ashgate, 2009) 121; K Tuori, *Ratio and Voluntas* (Farnham, Ashgate 2011) 173.

cultural elaboration, which elucidates their meaning by identifying the ideological basis of the relative choices and their political orientations. Therefore, in some way, we can enlist the legal constitutional culture between the sources of the object of our research. At least, we may say that the products of the legal constitutional culture are part of the materials we must use in view of the identification of the European constitutional heritage in a historical perspective. From this point of view, the perception of the transborder reciprocal influences that are at the base of the yardsticks adopted by the Commission is becoming more evident. We cannot limit our research to the countries that participated in the active spread of the mentioned documents, but must also look at the experiences of the countries interested by the spreading of the influence of these documents.

Based on this conclusion, we cannot forget the contribution to the elaboration of the doctrine of the European constitutionalism by the experience of the USA and by the American legal and political literature accompanying the debate of the Philadelphia Convention. Within this literature, *The Federalist*[14] played a major role. The contribution of the first liberal and democratic constitutions of the nineteenth-century Western world cannot be missed, especially if we look at the developments of those documents and their legislative and judicial interpretations and transformations. In this frame, the reasoning of the Venice Commission benefits from the contributions of the liberal and democratic constitutionalism produced since the French Revolution to recent times. In fact, constitutional doctrines have been developed, step by step, through three different eras: (i) in the first part of the twentieth century, after World War I and after World War II; (ii) following the revolutionary changes of regime in the Mediterranean Sea in the second part of the twentieth century; and (iii) at the time of the fall of the Warsaw Pact, of the Soviet Union and of the Federal Republic of Yugoslavia at the end of the twentieth century. The passages from the initial historical declarations to the constitutions allows a deep understanding of the necessary steps and measures to be adopted in view of the implementation of the general statements that are the typical content of the formal documents and bills at the origin of constitutionalism.

For instance, Article 16 of the 1789 Déclaration does not say many things about the institutional arrangements that have to be adopted to establish a correct relation between the powers of the state in compliance with the principle of the separation of powers. In this matter, we can draw useful suggestions from the old constitutions of the nineteenth century. However, they concern constitutional designs that were compatible with monarchical regimes. Therefore, the above experiences need to be complemented and integrated with the analysis of more recent constitutional developments. In this way, the perspective adopted sheds light on the investigated problems from an operational point of view. Consequently, alternative constitutional designs may emerge and comply with the principle of the separation of powers in contemporary societies.

However, we also have to realise that, so far, the Venice Commission has not been concerned with one of the most characterising aspects of post-Weimar modern constitutionalism: the inclusion of social conflict within the constitution. This is surprising, as the supranational European Courts have had many opportunities to deal with relevant

[14] A Hamilton, J Madison and J Jay, *The Federalist Papers* (first published 1788, Dublin, OH, Coventry House Publishing, 2015).

aspects of the social and economic conflicts in contemporary Europe. Therefore, while the constitutional rights of the first generation are frequently dealt with by the Commission, the so-called social rights are not present in its 'case law'.[15] The developments of the contemporary constitutions are instead the focus of the Commission's attention when it reminds that 'since World War II, constitutional courts were typically established in Europe in the course of transformation to democracy; first in Germany and Italy, then in Spain and Portugal and finally in Central and Eastern Europe'.[16] These democratic transitions shared two essential purposes. On the one hand, the overcoming of the legacy of the previous regimes, and on the other hand, the protection of human rights violated in the past. To achieve these ends, it was necessary to substitute the system of the separation of powers for the principle of the unity of power centralised in the parliament and in the political bodies of the states. From the very beginning, a preference was expressed in favour of a constitutional jurisdiction exercised by a permanent special constitutional court.[17] Therefore, a preference emerged for the Kelsenian model of constitutional justice at the expense of the American model, which implied a diffuse system of judicial review involving ordinary judges. Thus, a new element of complexity was added to the doctrine of the separation of powers.

The findings resulting from constitutional experiences are not always univocal, so it is essential to find additional criteria to discern between them in view of their utilisation. A bright example of this ambiguity emerges from the indications that might be drawn from the principle of separation of powers with respect to the guarantee of independence of the judiciary. The Venice Commission distinguishes two systems of guarantee of independence of the judiciary. According to the first system, the functions of administration of the careers of judges are entrusted to independent judicial councils. Members of these councils are elected by the judges themselves and also by the parliament. According to the second system, the executive power has a strong influence over judicial appointments.[18] This system exists in some older democracies, and is considered dangerous for the independence of the judiciary from the point of view of an abstract constitutional doctrine. However, the Commission has conceded that the second system might work well as the executive is restrained not only by the law, but also by the legal culture and traditions that have developed over the years. The constitutional guarantee stays, in these ancient democracies, in old consolidated practices and in the adhesion to an established and shared body of values. In contrast, states where new democracies have been introduced only recently have historically missed a chance to develop those traditions that could prevent abuse. In other words, in the view of the Venice Commission, old democracies may maintain constitutional arrangements otherwise precluded to states lacking a long-established democratic and liberal tradition. In fact, the Commission takes into strong consideration value-oriented and historical criteria that might impact the concrete functioning of different constitutional arrangements.

[15] For the distinction, see J Waldron, *Liberal Rights. Collected Papers* (Cambridge, Cambridge University Press, 1993).

[16] Venice Commission, CDL-AD(2013)014.

[17] This trend starts from H Steinberger, *Models of Constitutional Jurisdiction* (Strasbourg, Council of Europe, 1994). The interesting precedent of the Czechoslovakian Constitutional Court is not mentioned. Established by a 1920 law, this example of judicial review of legislation misses the continuity that the embeddeness of a tradition requires. New judges were not appointed at the end of the mandate of the previous ones. The Court therefore no longer worked, and was swept away by the dissolution of the state in 1939.

[18] Venice Commission, CDL-AD(2007)028.

However, the Venice Commission is not always in a position to appreciate historical criteria by assessing institutional arrangements in the monitored countries. For instance, while it may be acceptable that the constitutional history and legal traditions of a given country may justify the allocation of non-criminal functions to the prosecution service, the Commission is of the opinion that this way of reasoning can only be applied with respect to legal traditions that are considered democratic and in line with Council of Europe values. Therefore, the preservation of the historical model of the prosecution service in Ukraine (the Soviet and czarist model of Prokuratura) is not justified. In fact, this model reflects a non-democratic past and is not compatible with European standards and Council of Europe values.[19] Moreover, the Commission criticised the Hungarian model of the so-called 'uniformity procedure'. According to this model, the Curia (the highest judicial authority in Hungary) is entrusted with the function of adopting obligatory uniformity decisions. These decisions must be applied in all courts. In this case, the fact that the roots of this model date back the nineteenth century is not considered as a justification of that choice by the Commission. On the contrary, the Commission focuses on the fact that such a procedure provides for the active interference of a 'superior' body in the administration of justice, which conflicts with lower courts' and tribunals' independence.[20]

III. The Dubious Contribution of the Central and Eastern European Countries

When one focuses on the legal constitutional culture, the question arises about the relevance of some documents that are not frequently mentioned in the main texts of the doctrine of constitutionalism. We might identify many documents that take centre stage in the history of some states but are probably less well known in the international debate. This is true, for example, with regard to the documents emerging from the exploration of historical developments of the ancient statehood of the Crown of Bohemia, the Georgian statehood and the Croatian Kingdom. This is also the case of the Polish Constitution of 3 May 1791, the Hungarian Bulla Aurea of the thirteenth century, the Lithuanian Statutes of the sixteenth century and other important texts. Did these documents contribute to the elaboration of European constitutionalism? It is convenient here to remember the arguments presented in previous pages of this book. These documents are certainly part of the history of some European countries; but is that enough to include them among the historical criteria steering the assessment, for instance, of a given constitutional reform by the Venice Commission? Or are we not allowed to treat those documents as constitutive factors of the European constitutional tradition? Certainly, the old Polish Constitution is part of Poland's national heritage; however, its inclusion in the European constitutional heritage is doubtful. Moreover, the compatibility of the historical and other local traditions of local self-government mentioned in Article 131.1 of the Russian Constitution is doubtful. The fact that these constitutional provisions are based on the roots of some ancient communal

[19] Venice Commission, CDL-AD(2009)048.
[20] Venice Commission, CDL-AD(2012)001.

institutions – preserved by the peasants and considered by Alexander Herzen as envisaging a specifically Russian socialism – is not enough to grant their compatibility with modern European constitutional yardsticks.

We cannot deny that the above-mentioned documents are part of the European constitutional history; however, if we want to answer the questions advanced in these pages, we must investigate the involvement of the concerned countries in the building of the modern state and its constitutional features. Looking at the history of the doctrines of constitutionalism from this point of view enables us to recognise that the statutes and constitutions of Central and Eastern Europe are rarely mentioned as constitutive elements of the European constitutional tradition. We can find an explanation for this by comparing, for instance, the different historical meanings and relevance of the Magna Carta and the Bulla Aurea. The Magna Carta was at the origin of the gradual extension of the protection of humans in England and, eventually, the UK. A crucial role in this process was played by the customs and freedoms of the UK. The connected enlargement of the powers of the parliament opened the way to a modern approach to the safeguarding of civil and political rights and freedoms. The Bulla Aurea was always interpreted according to a restricted idea of a corporative state, where the guarantees that it ensured were based on the exploitation of the land and concerned the protection and the prerogatives of the ruling class. Therefore, the Hungarian experience, as well as that of other Central and Eastern European documents, is correctly described in the European historical legal literature as having been peripheral with respect to other documents of the European constitutional civilisation.[21]

A similar reasoning can be developed regarding the constitutional statute of the judiciary. For example, Article VIII of the old Polish Constitution states that 'as judicial power is incompatible with the legislative, nor can be administered by the King, therefore tribunals and magistratures ought to be established and elected'. Unfortunately, Polish history did not allow a satisfying elaboration of the organisational models for its implementation. Therefore, the contribution of the Polish tradition to the constitutionalism regarding judicial matters is not very conspicuous. Furthermore, in Hungary, the substitution of the constitutional developments of the Austro-Hungarian Empire for the experience of the exercise of judicial power by the king and his *palatini comites* only partially complied with the doctrine of the separation of powers. It is true that the organisation of the judiciary and the careers of the judges also depended on the executive in some Western European countries until the end of World War II. However, in the second part of the twentieth century – while Central and Eastern Europe was held under communist regimes – France, Italy, Spain and Portugal adopted and implemented constitutional provisions that played a relevant role in forming the new models of judicial autonomy and independence. Therefore, the states that experienced communist regimes have had to accept an updating of their constitutional doctrines from external sources. In the presence of these new developments, reference to the old traditions is no longer credible or is completely inadmissible. Furthermore, the same can be said when the authoritarian regimes of the period following World War I are evoked.

[21] This conclusion is frequently mentioned in the legal literature as a result of the important contribution of Egidijus Jarasiunas concerning the European context of the 1992 Constitution of Lithuania and the history of constitutionalism in Central and Eastern Europe. See E Jarasiunas, 'The Prehistory of Constitutionalism: The Sources or the Archetype?' (2009) 118(4) *Jurisprudencija: Mokslo darbu Zurnalas* 21.

IV. Conclusions

Other legal sources must be considered among the yardsticks adopted by the Venice Commission. Some international documents are especially worthy of attention, principally the Charter of the United Nations of 26 June 1945; the United Nations Covenant on Human Rights; and the ECHR. These legal sources play an extremely important role, as they are the result of a common effort to summarise the main constitutional values and ideals that are largely shared in the contemporary world. It could be possible to read references to these documents as an openness to a globalisation centred point of view of the problems dealt with by the Venice Commission with the adoption of a universal perspective. However, it would be advisable to be careful in drawing such a conclusion. The geographical terms of reference of the Opinions of the Commission always refer to the constitutional experience of countries of Western Europe and the documents of the Council of Europe in particular. This is confirmed by the examples mentioned in the previous pages. This attitude can be easily explained if we consider the developments of the constitutional doctrines in the nineteenth century and have regard to Europe's political history. Taking these facts into consideration, the link connecting the take-off of the Council of Europe with the fall of the Nazi and fascist dictatorships after the World War II emerges. Similarly, a link emerges when the accession of new members to the Council of Europe is considered, particularly when the accession followed a democratic transition (as in the cases of Spain, Portugal and Greece). Conversely, the fall of the Soviet Union and of the Federal Republic of Yugoslavia had a significant impact within the picture of constitutional developments in Europe. These events took place within the international framework of the United Nations, but part of this story consisted in the accession of some of these new democracies to supranational institutions established by Western European liberal democracies. Within this picture, the accession of some of these states to the European Union was a landmark constitutional event in the story of their democratic transition. This is because the European Union may be considered as an institution that is developing and enriching the values and principles on which the Council of Europe was founded. We will return to the issue of the universal dimension of the Venice Commission perspective in the last chapter.

There are a great number of sources and materials that are considered by the Venice Commission in the elaboration of the yardsticks for the evaluation of documents submitted thereto. On this basis, it makes sense to sort the results of its activity (what we could call its 'case law') into different categories. First of all, there are principles of law that have a transnational relevance. These display their effects in the legal orders of all the concerned states insofar as they are transplanted from one system of law to another through the channels of the constitutional culture, the international relations and the activity of the international and supranational institutions in the frame of the strategy of conditionality. For instance, the establishment of the independence of the judiciary is affected by transnational principles in that important provisions of the international treaties concerning the safeguarding of the human rights are at stake, as they connect the guarantee of the human person to specific institutional arrangements of the judiciary. These principles are strictly binding on the legislators of states even if they are not expressed – according to Ronald Dworkin[22] – in

[22] R Dworkin, *Taking Rights Seriously* (London, Duckworth, 1977) 22.

an 'all or nothing fashion'. Therefore, they can be implemented in the frame of different organisational solutions, which can all be covered by the normative spectrum of the same principle.[23] Separation of powers is a principle that must be complied with inescapably. However, many models of implementation are concretely admissible. Among these are not only the so-called judiciary self-government model, but also the model requiring the establishment of the judiciary, subject to strict supervision by the executive, where the independence of judges is guaranteed through specific institutional and personal guarantees and the traditional legal culture.

The Venice Commission has an evident preference for the adoption of the judicial council model in the constitutions of the new democracies. However, it is prudent in suggesting the modalities of its application, even if it must recognise that the binding effects of the principles affect different practical implementations. In some cases, there are standards or guidelines of legislation that do not have the normative relevance of the principles, even if they are perceived as mandatory soft law by the addressees of the Opinions of the Commission through the machinery of conditionality. Therefore, the difference between standards and principles can be very vague. In other fields, the Commission recognises the existence of different legislative solutions to the constitutional problems that the states must deal with, but does not make an express choice and restrains its intervention to the identification of the limits that cannot be bypassed by the legislators. Parliaments and governments are free to choose the most convenient solution even if they must respect the general principles of law that are typical of a constitutional state. The principle of the rule of law is frequently mentioned in the Opinions of the Commission, which recognises that 'a challenge for the future is how the achievements of the rule of law can be preserved and further developed under circumstances where individuals are increasingly influenced by and linked to new modes of governance'.[24]

It could be said that in all the cases dealt with by the Venice Commission, the constitutional identity of the states must be preserved. This could imply a guarantee of their sovereignty; however, the experience of the Commission over the years has demonstrated that this exigency must be balanced with respect to the fundamental principles of European constitutionalism.[25]

This attitude explains the position of the Commission with regard to institutions that have a more recent history and have attracted the attention of legislators only in recent years. This is the case with the ombudsman, which has its origins in the experiences of the Nordic democracies and has been adopted in some modern European constitutions. There are only a few texts on the elaboration of materials concerning this institution, even if the Venice Commission suggested it as an alternative to the Soviet and czarist Prokuratura for the exercise of functions aimed at safeguarding public interests that do not fall within the scope of criminal law.[26] Another organisational model that is prudently dealt with by the

[23] This point is correctly highlighted by P Craig, 'Transnational Constitution-Making: The Contribution of the Venice Commission on Law and Democracy' (2017) 2 *UC Irvine Journal Transnational Law* 57, who remarks that 'the line between constitutional principles and their operationalization is not always easy to draw'.

[24] Venice Commission, CDL-AD(2011)003.

[25] Therefore, the correct position is that the European constitutional heritage 'implies respect for state sovereignty': S Bartole, 'Final Remarks: The Role of the Venice Commission' (2000) 26 *Review of Central and East European Law* 351.

[26] Venice Commission, CDL-AD(2009)048.

Commission is that of the budgetary and financial judicial autonomy practised by some Nordic countries. The 'case law' of the Commission in this field is not completely settled yet; however, some Opinions of the Commission support this Nordic model. Although Nordic countries are certainly not to be considered peripheral (as the Eastern and Central European countries are), the contribution of their constitutional experience in the identification of a European constitutional heritage has been limited. This is surprising, if one considers that, for example, the Constitution of Norway is one of the oldest constitutions of Europe.

The Commission's choices are sometimes pragmatic and flexible. An example of this pragmatism emerges from the remarks raised by the Commission on the Hungarian constitutional revision that was criticised for including provisions that did not develop the main principles of the organisation of the judiciary. The contested constitutional amendments left the adoption of the details of the regulation to cardinal laws (to be approved by a super-majority), whereas, according to the idea[27] of the Commission, it should have been left to ordinary laws. The criticised solution increases the risk of long-lasting political conflicts and causes undesirable pressure and costs for a society in case of possible future legislative change. This conclusion was argued on the basis of Article 3 of the First Protocol to the ECHR, which was read as requiring the participation of all the political forces – that is, the majority and the opposition – in the preparation and approval of the acts aimed at implementing the constitution. This claim can easily be connected to the idea frequently expressed by the Commission that constituent assemblies have to be elected according to a proportional electoral system to guarantee the presence of representatives of all the political parties and movements. Special attention has been paid to emerging democracies, where the initial identification of the nature and degree of segmentation of the political spectrum is considered as 'a necessary first step'. Therefore, a first general election under proportional representation should be required 'for a constituent assembly for example'.[28]

The establishment of the new democracies also required fundamental choices about the system of government to be adopted with the approval of the constitution.[29] One could consider it helpful to enlarge the scope of the research devoted by the Commission to this item. However, it has correctly abstained from expressing an explicit choice in favour of a parliamentary, presidential or semi-presidential government. Statements of general principles about this problem are lacking, the choice to be made is one of opportunity in view of the peculiarities of the concerned societies, and the states must have the freedom to select one solution over another. Notwithstanding these premises, the Commission has always evaluated the proposals submitted for its consideration, paying regard to the traditional models of government of Western European democracies and in the light of the connected experiences. Therefore, the Commission has frequently underlined the exigency that a system of checks and balances between powers and inter-institutional cooperation shall be ensured. Its approach certainly implies the reference to the models of the mentioned forms of government, which the legal doctrine and the political science have elaborated.

Furthermore, attention must be paid to these models insofar as they offer suggestions about the possible equilibrium between powers and the fair distribution of powers between

[27] Venice Commission, CDL-AD(2012)001.
[28] Venice Commission, CDL-AD(2004)003.
[29] See V Volpe, 'Drafting Counter-majoritarian Democracy. The Venice Commission Constitutional Assistance' (2016) 76 *Heidelberg Journal for International Law* 811.

the state's institutions.[30] The Commission favours institutional arrangements that avoid the uncontrolled growth of powers of the state authorities, especially where monocratic constitutional bodies are concerned, such as the President of the Republic (see the experience of Ukraine, and of other countries of the Commonwealth of Independent States).[31] From this perspective, the Commission has positively welcomed constitutional reforms aimed at substituting parliamentary or semi-presidential governments for previous presidential governments, as recently occurred in Armenia and Tunisia.[32]

From the above, it is apparent that, on the one hand, the sources of the Opinions of the Venice Commission have to be found in the mainstream developments of the European states that have adopted and implemented the doctrines of constitutionalism. On the other hand, we must identify the peculiarity of the use of these sources by the Commission, which is frequently mixing legal data, practical experiences and the doctrinal elaboration of these materials. It follows that the legal effects of the Opinions adopted is – as was underlined – necessarily diverse according to the different bases of the conclusions reached. Moreover, it is evident that the contribution of the Venice Commission to the internationalisation of constitutional law is Eurocentric, in that the main sources of its activity pertain to the developments of European constitutionalism even if there are still difficulties for their reception by all the European states.

[30] See the important remarks concerning Romania in Venice Commission, CDL-AD(2012)026.

[31] Bartole (n 25) 358.

[32] See the references to 'constitutional reforms' on the home page of the Commission, www.venice.coe.int/WebForms/pages/?p=02_Reforms&lang=EN.

6

The Venice Commission's Contribution to the Internationalisation of Constitutional Law Regarding States' Judicial Organisation

I. Introduction: The Separation of Powers and Its Implementation

The principles and standards regarding the judiciary's organisation are part of national constitutional law. The history of constitutionalism has taught us that these principles concern a fundamental power of the state. Judicial organisation has undergone developments that have kept the judiciary separate and distinct from the other branches of the state's organisation. This solution aims to ensure the independence and autonomy of the judiciary.

From a general and abstract point of view, the internationalisation of this chapter of constitutional law could be studied both with regard to the organisation of the judicial bodies of the international or supranational institutions and/or looking at the organisation of national judges within the framework of the national legal system. Both these points of view confirm the growing international relevance of the developments dealt with in this chapter, as they are strictly connected with the evolution of the safeguarding of human rights, the rule of law and democracy. The chapter explores the activity of the Venice Commission in the field of organisation of the judiciary. The focus is on the Commission's experience in the elaboration of international principles and standards regarding judicial organisation. Special attention is paid to the promotion of the adherence of the national legal systems to the so-called European constitutional heritage. The Commission's experience follows the path of the implementation of judicial independence in the frame of the Council of Europe and of the European Union insofar as it regards not only the national organisation of the judiciary, but also the relations between the states' judges and European judges.[1]

The intervention of the Venice Commission was frequently required in the transition to the adoption of new liberal-democratic constitutions by Central and Eastern European states. It had to settle many questions in its Opinions. The choice of model of judicial organisation had special relevance due to the multiplicity of its consequences. Since its inception, the Venice Commission has been confronted with the dilemma of two alternatives.

[1] A Seibert-Fohr, 'Judicial Independence in European Union Accessions: The Emergence of a European Basic Principle' (2009) 52 *German Yearbook of International Law* 405.

The first option was to reform the organisation of the judiciary, while keeping the old judicial personnel in office. The second option was to substitute new judges for the old ones, while reforming the judiciary. The first solution implied a constitutional reform aimed at ensuring as quickly as possible the prerogatives of independence and autonomy of the incumbent judges of the past regime. According to this solution, the old judicial personnel would have been kept in office without promoting the necessary processes of vetting and renewal of the judges. This option risked strengthening seniority and corporatist tendencies. However, if the second solution was preferred, there was a risk of the initial concentration of relevant administrative powers in the hands of the political bodies of the new democracies. The appointment of new judges could also be affected by political preferences. According to the Commission, 'choosing the appropriate system for judicial appointments is one of the primary challenges faced by the newly established democracies, where often concerns to the independence and political impartiality of the judiciary persist'.[2]

Therefore, the choice of entrusting the parliament with the power to appoint the ordinary (non-constitutional) judges could be justified if it was restricted to the start of the transition to constitutional democracy. In principle, 'political involvement in the appointment procedure may endanger the neutrality of the judiciary'.[3] The ideal solution should be rapid compliance with the principle of the separation of powers.[4]

The solutions finally adopted were not always satisfactory. Even when autonomy and independence of the judiciary were formally introduced in the constitutional transition, future experience cast serious doubts on the efficiency and integrity of judiciaries after the reforms. Some of the concerned states, such as Hungary, Ukraine, Poland and Albania, have started revising the legislation regulating the judiciary. Moreover, some of them have attempted to subject incumbent judges to a vetting procedure aimed at assessing their integrity and professional ability. However, this process has at times been conditioned by political concerns. As when designing the new judiciaries, these recent interventions have raised problems and questions in determining the guidelines of constitutionalism in the field of the organisation of the judiciary. What are the models that ensure the implementation of those principles? What are the justifications for and the limits of the possible processes of judicial reform? What is the basis for the legitimate 'lustration' of the judges currently in office?

As we have seen, the construction of the European constitutional heritage implies a historical approach. We have to look at the legal experiences of European countries to ascertain their common attitudes.[5] If our inquiry focuses on the safeguarding of rights and the rule of law, the starting point should be the Magna Carta. This is considered to be the cradle of the rule of law that implied an independent role of the judges in the formation of the common law. On this basis, it is necessary to focus initially on the principle of separation of powers and its effect on the organisation of the judiciary. Within this picture, a crucial role is played by Article 16 of the Déclaration des Droits de l'Homme et du Citoyen of 1789 and by the liberal constitutions of the nineteenth century. Article 16 proclaims the

[2] Venice Commission, CDL-AD(2007)028.

[3] ibid.

[4] ibid.

[5] For a general approach to these items, see M Cartabia, 'Separation of Powers and Judicial Independence: Current Challenges', paper presented at the European Court of Human Rights Seminar, 26 January 2018.

extremely general principle that a society in which the observance of the law is not assured, nor the separation of powers defined, has no constitution at all. This principle does not say much about the institutional machinery that has to be established for the implementation of the principle. The interconnection of the different branches of the state has to be taken into consideration in analysing the model, and in designing the separation of powers. Therefore, the link between the establishment of an independent and impartial judiciary and the arrangements concerning the other powers have also to be considered.[6]

It follows that we can certainly derive useful suggestions from the old constitutions of the nineteenth century. However, these constitutions were adopted in the frame of monarchical regimes. Therefore, any reference to these experiences has to be integrated – from an operational point of view – with the analysis of the constitutions adopted in twentieth century. Consideration also has to be paid to the new solutions adopted in order to comply with the principle of the separation of powers, for instance in the North European countries.[7] Moreover, an important role was played in the development of the European constitutional heritage by many international documents of the past century, especially in the field of the human rights, from the Charter of the United Nations of 26 June 1945 and the United Nations Covenant on Human Rights to the European Convention on Human Rights.[8] Their importance derives from the fact that they are the result of a common effort to summarise the main constitutional values and ideals that are shared by all the concerned countries. It is evident that when we mention the United Nations' documents, we widen our scope by including states that are not in Europe. From this perspective, we cannot forget the documents of the American Revolution and their historical evolution, the analysis of which is an essential part of the modern doctrines of constitutionalism. There are also important European documents, for instance the Council of Europe Recommendation CM/REC (2010) 12, adopted on 17 November 2010, the European Charter on the Statute for Judges of 8–10 July 1998 and the Consultative Council of European Judges (CCJE)'s Magna Carta of Judges of 17 November 2010.

Within this picture, important developments emerged in the process of accession of new Member States to the European Union. An interesting perspective emerges in the Presidency Conclusions of the Copenhagen European Council of 21–22 June 1993. In this document, there is a brief mention of the guidelines that have to be complied with by candidate states in order to achieve stability of the institutions in the fields of democracy, the rule of law and human rights.[9] The vagueness of this document was criticised from the beginning of the process of accession of the new Members to the European Union. The criticism was based on the realisation that 'Western European legal system provides *a plurality of models* of judicial independence'.[10] This pluralism made the a priori compromise difficult and was the

[6] A Pizzorusso, *Il patrimonio costituzionale europeo* (Bologna, Il mulino, 2002) 139.

[7] M Volpi, 'I Consigli di giustizia in Europa: un quadro comparativo' (2009) 2 *Diritto pubblico comparato ed europeo* 948.

[8] M Volpi, 'L'indipendenza della magistratura nei documenti del Consiglio d'Europa e della Rete europea dei Consigli di giustizia' (2010) 4 *Diritto pubblico comparato ed europeo* 1754.

[9] SN180/1/93REV1, www.consilium.europa.eu/ueDocs/cms_Data/docs/pressData/en/ec/72921.pdf.

[10] D Smilov, 'EU Enlargement and the Constitutional Principle of Judicial Independence' in W Sadurski, A Czarnota and M Krygier (eds), *Spreading Democracy and the Rule of Law* (Dordrecht, Springer, 2006) 313 (original emphasis).

starting point of a case-by-case approach. Gradually, the supranational monitoring bodies developed yardsticks that finally were treated as legal principles by the European Court of Justice. Furthermore, the dangers of arbitrariness and opportunism of the monitoring activity – indicated by Smilov – were bypassed in the concrete experience.

It is generally accepted that any reference to international political documents has to be carefully appreciated in the light of the intermediation of the legal constitutional culture.[11] In the judicial field, such international documents are usually extremely succinct. From the old historical acts and declarations to the resolutions of the European authorities, these documents are limited to the mere enunciation of the principles of separation of powers and of the independence of judges.[12] Historical acts and declarations only assume relevance through their cultural processing. Important results of this process were reached at the European level in the contributions elaborated in the frame of the Council of Europe by its governing bodies and by the CCJE. All these materials give evidence of the meaning of the documents identifying the ideological basis of a given institutional choice and its political background. Moreover, an important step in the constructive process is the determination of the practical and operational implementation of those principles. The constitutions adopted by the states concurring to the formation of the European constitutional heritage have to be considered. These materials have to be taken into consideration in the analysis of the interpreters of international constitutional law in relation to the judiciary.

Hungary and Poland have been at the centre of the discussion due to their recent judicial reforms. These interventions are considered to lack conformity with the European yardsticks. At the moment of accession of these states to the European Union many 'had believed that consolidated democracy was irreversible'[13] in those countries. On the contrary, their leaders forgot the initial engagements and adopted different political guidelines to safeguard their national sovereignty. Thus, the question arises whether these states will be allowed to claim their specific constitutional identity on the basis of some of their historical documents that are not frequently mentioned in the main texts of the doctrine of the constitutionalism. This question was addressed in chapter three.

Accordingly, both Hungary and Poland were at the periphery of the experience of European constitutionalism. In any case, in the judicial field, the Polish Constitution of 3 May 1791 offered an interesting suggestion. Article VIII of the Constitution states: 'as judicial power is incompatible with the legislative, nor can be administered by the King, therefore tribunals and magistratures ought to be established and elected'. However, additional rules for the implementation of these principles were not identified or were missing. It follows that the contribution of the Polish tradition appears to be not very conspicuous on the matter.

The same can be said with regard to the Hungarian Bulla Aurea of the thirteenth century, which reserved the exercise of the judicial power to the king and his *palatini comites* in cases

[11] K Tuori, *Critical Legal Positivism* (Farnharm, Ashgate, 2009) 121; K Tuori, *Ratio and Voluntas* (Farnham, Ashgate, 2011) 173.

[12] M Bobek and D Kosar, 'Global Solutions, Local Damages: A Critical Study in Judicial Councils in Central and Eastern Europe' (2014) 15 *German Law Journal* 1257; D Preshova, I Damjanovski and Z Nechev, 'The Effectiveness of the "European Model" of Judicial Independence in the Western Balkans: Judicial Councils as a Solution or a New Cause of Concern for Judicial Reforms' (2017) Centre for the Law of EU External Relations Cleer Papers 2017/1.

[13] K Kovacs and KL Scheppele, 'The Fragility of an Independent Judiciary: Lessons from Hungary and Poland – and the European Union' (2018) 51 *Communist and Post-Communist Studies* 189, 190.

concerning indifferently all people, with the exception of ecclesiastical matters. However, the members of the Hungarian nobility were not required to have a legal education, they had only to swear to accomplish the judicial tasks correctly before starting their mandate. Furthermore, the Hungarian historical tradition regarding the status of members of the judiciary was always very weak. Only in the nineteenth century did some interesting developments emerge. In fact, the organisation of the Hungarian judiciary (the *Gerichteverfassung in Ungarn*, in the words of Ludwig Gumplowicz[14]) was affected by the constitutional developments of the Austro-Hungarian Empire. These developments gradually pointed in the direction of parliamentary government. Article 1 of the Law of 27 October 1862 provided for the guarantee of the' lawful judge 'pre-established by the relevant legislation, which fell in the competence of the Council of the Empire as far as the fundamental traits of the organisation of the judicial authorities were concerned (§ 11, l of the Law of 21 December 1867). The Emperor retained a central position in the organisation of the judiciary. For instance, the Fundamental Law of the State of 21 December 1867 entrusted to him the appointment for life of the president and the vice-president of the Tribunal of the Empire and of its 12 effective and four substitute members nominated in equal number by the Chamber of the Deputies and the Chamber of the Nobles. Moreover, on the basis of Article 5 of the Fundamental Law of the State of 21 December 1867, No 144, the judges were appointed 'definitely and for life' by the Emperor or in his name. However, some guarantees were introduced. The dismissal of judges from office was only allowed in the cases provided for by the legislation and on the basis of a judicial decision. In addition, they could be transferred from one office to another only with their consent. Recently, Hungarian authorities have referred to these nineteenth-century historical roots in conflicts with the European authorities. Specifically, the Hungarian authorities used the historical argument to claim that legislative provisions allowing the so-called Curia (the national highest judicial authority) to issue decisions aimed at ensuring the uniformity of minor judges' judgments was based on traditional roots. The Venice Commission reacted by lamenting the violation of the individual independence of the affected magistrates in the exercise of their functions.[15]

The Venice Commission took into consideration the historical developments of the forms of government of the states concerned when it evaluated the appropriateness of organisational models for the judiciary. The Commission has recognised the existence of 'a variety of different systems for judicial appointments'.[16] In older democracies, the Commission conceded, 'systems may work well in practice and allow for an independent judiciary':[17] even if the executive sometimes has a decisive influence on judicial appointments, historically 'these powers are restrained by legal culture and traditions, which have grown over a long time'.[18] However, in other countries, a shift in the direction of establishment of an independent judiciary according to past solutions may not be sufficient if there is no demonstration of a satisfying compliance with the principles of European constitutional heritage. In these cases, any historical continuity is missing. Therefore, in the new democracies that 'did not

[14] L Gumplowicz, *Das Osterreichische Staatsrecht* (Vienna, Manz, 1907) 155.
[15] Venice Commission, CDL-AD(2012)001.
[16] Venice Commission, CDL-AD(2007)028.
[17] ibid.
[18] ibid.

have a chance to develop these traditions, which can prevent abuse … explicit constitutional and legal provisions are needed as a safeguard to prevent political abuse in the appointment of judges'.[19] The executive-centred solutions have to be excluded.

II. Judicial Councils and Other Solutions

This way of reasoning led the Commission to pay special attention to the historical European models of organisation of the judiciary. The identification of these models could offer an overview of the guidelines that steer the implementation of the principle of separation of powers and its consequences on the status of judges and relative offices. As we have seen, from its inception, the Venice Commission recognised the existence of at least two different organisational models in Europe. In principle, both could serve the aim of guaranteeing autonomous and independent judicial bodies.

The first example is the judicial self-management (or self-government) model, which was apparently patterned on the constitutions of some Western European states (Italy, France and Spain). In this model (the so-called Mediterranean model), most of the decisions on the careers of the judicial personnel are taken by a council. Members of the council are elected by the judges themselves. This was the preferred solution suggested by European authorities at the moment of accession of the ex-communist states to the Council of Europe and to the European Union. It seems that such a solution draws inspiration from the principle of self-government of the judiciary. According to this idea, members of the Council (elected by fellow judges) would take care of the interests of the judiciary in the same way that elective local authorities of the local government take care of the interests of the territorial communities. Recently, this approach was strongly criticised by scholars from Central and Eastern Europe. Consequently, the choice for this model was the will of the representatives of the judges themselves rather than the decisions of the responsible political authorities.[20] Therefore, the approach of the legislators and of the supranational monitoring bodies would have facilitated corporatist and seniority practices of the newly created judicial councils. This phenomenon could be explained by the ready submission of the states to the approach illustrated above. The decision to keep in office old judges of the communist regimes, with no lustrations or preventive vetting, led to dangerous consequences. This recent criticism of the authors referred to in the lines above is ill-founded. On the one hand, the choices of the legislators were the result of the political bodies of the concerned states that implied an evaluation of the orientations of the concerned judicial categories in conjunction with other purposes and interests. The judges did not take part in the political decisions. On the other

[19] ibid.

[20] Bobek and Kosar (n 12) passim; CE Parau, 'Explaining Governance of the Judiciary in Central and Eastern Europe: External Incentives, Transnational Elites and Parliamentary Inaction' (2015) 67 *Europe-Asia Studies* 409; Preshova et al (n 12) passim. The relevance of the contribution of internal stakeholders to the elaboration of the reforms is due to the vagueness of the EU yardsticks, according to D Bozhilova, 'Measuring Successes and Failure of EU-Europeanization in the Eastern Enlargement: Judicial Reform in Bulgaria' (2007) 9 *European Journal of Law Reform* 285. This paper underlines that in this way it has been easy 'to accuse the EU of subjectivity and *favouritism*' (original emphasis), at the same time promoting the criticism of the veto players.

hand, the guidelines of the supranational monitoring bodies were preceded or approved ex post by the competent authorities of the supranational institutions concerned.

The spreading of corporatist and seniority deviations in some countries can be explained by a poor understanding of the philosophy of the model. At the centre of the solution are not the interests of the judicial categories, but the state's interests aimed at avoiding interference from the political legislative and executive bodies in the functioning of the judiciary. Therefore, the interests dealt with by the members of the judicial councils should not be the corporatist interests of the judges. The comparison with the local self-government is ill-founded, as the councils were not established to take care of specific personal or corporativist interests of the category of judges. Moreover, the presence in the councils of a minority of members elected by the parliamentary assemblies is an obstacle to possible corporatist deviations. In fact, the mandate of these members is the checking and ensuring of the correct management of the interests entrusted to the care of the judicial councils themselves. Undoubtedly, the concrete implementation of this design might have encountered practical hurdles and difficulties in some countries. However, practical inconveniences do not justify the repudiation of the whole model. On the contrary, they require the reformation of the details of the implementing legislation that is incoherent with the model.

The guidelines that prevailed in the process of accession of new members to the European Union refused the alternative model of organisation of the judicial personnel. This model implied the assignment of the power of administration of the judiciary to the executive branch of the state. The intervention of the executive is counterbalanced by the recognition of special personal rights granted to individual judges, or by consultative interventions of the judicial ordinary bodies in the relevant decision-making procedures. Judges may uphold their specific rights or the observance of the relevant procedural rules by way of appeal before the appropriate judicial bodies. Thus, the independence of the judiciary is assured – according to the principle of the rule of law – by means of specific personal guarantees of the judges or by specific articulations of the procedural formation of the relevant decisions. In this way, the constitutional legislators avoid the concentration of a great deal of power in a body, separate from all other state organs, whose membership is made up, at least partially, by magistrates who are personally interested in the matter.

After the dissolution of the Warsaw Pact and of the Yugoslav and Soviet Federal Unions, former communist countries adopted a mixed or intermediate model of judicial organisation. Those countries provided for a coexistence of deliberative powers of the political state authorities and of the entrusting of specific technical functions to judicial councils or committees.[21] This solution was preferred, as it avoided a complete judicial self-government by the ex-communist judicial personnel. The political authorities were supposed to be in a better position than a body of elected magistrates to check the persisting old-fashioned corporatist attitudes of the judges of the past communist regimes who were still in office. Specific arrangements were introduced on the basis of two justifications: on the one hand, these arrangements were aimed at avoiding a general lustration of the incumbent judges and, on the other hand, the arrangements were accompanied by the political intention to modernise the organisation of the judiciary according to the Western principles of constitutionalism

[21] S Bartole, 'Organizing the Judiciary in Central and Eastern Europe' (1998) 7 *Eastern European Constitutional Review* 62.

in an ongoing slow process of reform. Even the Explanatory Memorandum to the European Charter on the Statute for Judges conceded that 'some countries would find it difficult to accept an independent body replacing the political body responsible for appointments' of judges.[22] The Venice Commission elaborated this point by underlining that the appointment of judges by the parliament is 'a method for constituting the judiciary which is highly democratic but … the balance might be tilted much too far towards the legislative power'. Therefore, as happens in the case of appointments made by the executive, some guarantees should be introduced to avoid the prevailment of political interference. 'It would be desirable,' the Commission said, 'that an expert body like an independent judicial council could give an opinion on the suitability or qualification of candidates for the office of judge.'[23]

The intervention of the elected parliamentary assemblies in the procedure for the appointment of judges could be justified by the peculiarities of the transition process from the old communist regimes to democratic and liberal systems of government.[24] The Venice Commission agreed that the question of the substitution of new judicial personnel for old was at stake. As reported in the previous pages, the Commission recognised that there are examples of interventions of political authorities in the judicial field: in some older democracies, systems exist in which the executive power has a strong influence on judicial appointments. The documents do not mention, for instance, the example of the UK, notwithstanding that it has provided interesting and peculiar evidence of this kind of organisational arrangement. A plausible reason for this is that older and established democracies such as the UK may adopt this kind of arrangement with success, 'because the executive is restrained by legal culture and traditions, which have grown over a long time'. In contrast, states where new democracies have been recently established missed 'a chance to develop these traditions, which can prevent abuse'.[25]

When distinguishing between older and new democracies in Europe, the Venice Commission adopts a more flexible approach than other international institutions. Thus, an important place is reserved for legal traditions and a constitutional culture, which are essentially identified as the traditions and culture of Western Europe. On the one hand, the contribution of the historical heritage of former communist states is considered irrelevant or insufficient to guarantee the independence and separateness of the judiciary. On the other hand, the choices of some older European democracies are appreciated, notwithstanding the decisive role played by the executive in the procedures for the appointment of judges. There is a positive evaluation of the organisation of the judiciary in these older democracies, even if they do not formally comply with the model in principle preferred by the Commission (ie the establishment of a self-governing body for the judiciary). Therefore, the position of the Venice Commission has to be distinguished from the conclusions drawn, for instance, by the Committee of Ministers of the Council of Europe in its Recommendation R (94) 12 and by the Consultative Council of European Judges in its Opinion Nos 1 and 10.

[22] DAJ/DOC898 23 of 8–10 July 1998.

[23] See Venice Commission, CDL-AD(2002)026 and CDL-AD(2005)005.

[24] The complexity of the transition is underlined by PC Magalhaes, 'The Politics of Judicial Reform in Eastern Europe' (1999) 32 *Comparative Politics* 43, who explains how the adoption of innovative models can be explained by the prevalence of the conservative interests of politicians and judges linked to the past communist regimes.

[25] Venice Commission, CDL-AD(2007)028.

This approach provides a significant answer to our initial question about the cradle of the European constitutional heritage, which is mainly indicated as residing in Western constitutionalism. Important historical signs of the presence of the rule of law doctrine in other European countries, especially in Central and Eastern Europe, are considered insufficient for the consolidation of a significant contribution to the European constitutional heritage. Central and Eastern European constitutional experiences lack continuity of compliance with principles of constitutionalism, principles that have not been accurately implemented in their legal systems. It is true that in the past, the judicial organisation and the recruitment of judges were left in the hands of the executive also in Mediterranean countries, such as France, Italy and Spain. Therefore, the independence of the judiciary was imperilled, as a clear implementation of the principles of constitutionalism was missing. However, the objection can be easily rejected by underlining the readiness in the adoption of democratic and liberal constitutions that characterised the transformation of these legal systems following World War II and the fall of the dictatorships.

Many international documents state that the fundamental principles of the professional status of the judges have to be set out in internal provisions at the highest level in the hierarchy of norms, and at least at the legislative level in the implementing rules. The Venice Commission agrees with this approach.[26] During the adoption of the new constitutions, most of the former communist countries opted for constitutional provisions establishing a judicial council, considering this institution as a basic guarantee of the independence of the judiciary. By doing so, these states refused their past tradition, where judges used to depend on the executive power. Prima facie, this model complied with the principle of separation of powers. It implied the creation of an independent authority that is separate from the other branches of the state. The membership of this body must comprise a large representative body, whose members are elected from the judges themselves. This body is entrusted by constitutional provisions with decisive functions in view of the adoption of acts concerning election, promotion, transfer and disciplinary decisions over fellow judges. This design is in line with the majority of the documents adopted by expert bodies of the international institutions in the field of organisation of the judiciary. The choice is not exclusively the fruit of the corporatist purposes of the judges; it also draws inspiration from the example of more recent and modern liberal and democratic constitutions. Evidence of this double origin of the Commission's orientation is given by the guidelines of the Reports adopted by the Commission on the subject.[27] These Reports present frequent quotations of international documents and of the basic principles of the Western constitutions. The use of these guidelines in the monitoring process of constitutional transitions in Central and Eastern Europe is justified by the general acceptance of the 'Mediterranean model' of judicial self-government. In contrast, it should be clear to the readers that the alternative model – entrusting the executive with functions otherwise attributed to judicial self-governing bodies – is consented to only in older democracies, its persistence possibly being explained by the fear of corporatist and seniority practices. In any case, while, in the older states, an appropriate legal culture and tradition have stabilised over a long time, this element is missing in new

[26] See Recommendation R (94) 12 of the Committee of Ministers of the Council of Europe; Opinions 1 (2001) and 10 (2007) of the Consultative Council of European Judges; Venice Commission, CDL-AD(2010)004.

[27] Venice Commission, CDL-PI(2019)008 on courts and judges; CDL-PI(2018)001 on prosecutors.

democracies. These developments have slowly induced a progressive evolution of what was seen as a sort of law derived from a complex of de facto binding norms.[28]

A relevant exception is the case of the Czech Republic, which has not been submitted to the Venice Commission. The Republic refused the adoption of the judicial council model, preferring instead the Central European model of the administration of the judiciary by the executive. This system has seen constant clashes between the legislature, the administration and the judiciary. In recent times, the Czech Republic has slowly became accustomed to the idea of the participation of judges in the exercise of relevant powers in the judicial field, especially with regard to the adoption of disciplinary measures.[29]

Notwithstanding the general preference accorded to the judicial council model, experts are conscious that it entails a clear danger of influence from corporatist prejudices and opinions. Two corrective elements are normally introduced in the configuration of the model, and the Venice Commission has underlined their importance in the elaboration of its position. First, to avoid the danger of corporatism, membership of the judicial governing institution 'should not necessarily be entirely in the hands of judges'.[30] The presence of members who are not part of the judiciary has to be provided for to ensure the presence of representatives of other state powers or of the academic or professional sectors of society.[31] These members have to be elected by the parliament. This arrangement does not aim to open the doors to the implementation of political guidelines of the parliamentary majority; on the contrary, its purpose is to check the coherence of the activity of the judicial Council with the general interests, so to avoid the prevalence of corporatist factors. Therefore, the basis is set up for a balanced functioning of the judicial self-governing body and for an appropriate exercise of its tasks. Direct participation of the members of the executive in the exercise of the relevant functions should be excluded, with the exception of the possible involvement of the Head of the State. An active role for the Minister of Justice is not advisable.[32]

The correct interpretation of the self-administration of the judiciary requires that 'all decisions concerning the appointment and professional careers of judges should be based on merit, applying objective criteria within the framework of the law'.[33] As political choices are excluded, the competent body must stick to the relevant objective legislative provisions. The appointed judges shall satisfy general legislative requirements.[34] In an Opinion of 2010, the Commission explicitly quotes Recommendation R (94) 12 of the Committee of Ministers of the Council of Europe, according to which 'there should be guarantees to ensure that the procedures to appoint judges are transparent and independent in practice and that the decisions will not be influenced by any reasons other than those related to the objective criteria mentioned'.[35]

[28] Bobek and Kosar (n 12) passim. The 'progressive development in the normativity of the concept of judicial independence in the European Union' is underlined by Seibert-Fohr (n 1) 407.

[29] M Bobek, 'The Administration of Courts in the Czech Republic – In Search of a Constitutional Balance' (2010) 16 *European Public Law* 251. Smilov (n 10) 322 correctly stated that bodies comprising judges are 'just consultative bodies with no formal powers'.

[30] Venice Commission, CDL-AD(2010)004.

[31] ibid.

[32] Venice Commission, CDL-AD(2007)028.

[33] Venice Commission, CDL-AD(2010)004.

[34] Venice Commission, CDL-AD(2014)008.

[35] Venice Commission, CDL-AD(2010)004.

III. The Functions of Judicial Councils

Many materials utilised by the Venice Commission in the field of the judiciary address the functions that have to be entrusted to a judicial council. The Commission 'is of the opinion that a judicial council should have a decisive influence on the appointment … of judges'. However, the decisions concerning the appointments have to be construed as a necessary part of the general competence that affects the professional careers of judges.[36]

Therefore, the implementation of the system of the separation of powers and of the independence of the judiciary requires the legislative identification of different functions involving the different stages of the careers of the judges. The relevant legislative provisions shall cover all the matters from the initial appointment to promotions and transfers to other offices, and from the disciplinary control of their behaviour and activity to the eventual termination of office or retirement. The exercise of these functions has its own peculiarities, which have to be singled out by the legislative provisions concerning the organisation of the judiciary. This is the main task of the parliament in the judicial field. In a constitutional system, compliance with the basic principles of independence and impartiality of the judiciary has to be integrated by the legislative regulation of the matter.

According to a guideline of the European Charter on the status of the judges,[37] the legislator has to provide 'for the conditions which guarantee, by requirements linked to educational qualifications or previous experience, the ability specifically to discharge judicial duties'. The Venice Commission fully agrees with this way of thinking, as demonstrated by frequent references to this guideline in the Commission's documents. The guideline requires the legislative identification of objective criteria which have to be applied in the adoption of the decisions concerning judges.[38] Objective criteria are considered an important element to avoid the risk of political or corporative interferences in the decision-making processes of the judicial councils. Entrusting the adoption of these criteria to the parliament clearly implies the separate role of self-administration of judicial councils. The criteria have to be adopted in the frame of the unity of the state's legal system. The opinions of the Commission contribute to the elaboration of transnational law of the judiciary as far as the core of the competence of the judicial councils is concerned. The values initially provided for in the European Treaties were rather abstract, but were further developed by the monitoring activity. It was the Venice Commission that gave concreteness of content to these principles.[39] This is true for substantive principles, but when procedural issues are at stake, the general relevance of the Opinions is minor, especially if they concern legislative drafting.

The task of the judicial councils is, first of all, the execution and application of the legislative provisions concerning the general requirements that judges need to satisfy at the moment of their appointment, during their career and possible transfers from one office to another.[40] In these cases, the council shall perform administrative functions, which means

[36] See Venice Commission, CDL-AD(2007)028 and CDL-AD(2010)004.
[37] DA-DOC(98)23.
[38] Venice Commission, CDL-AD(2010)004.
[39] Seibert-Fohr (n 1) 408; Preshova et al (n 12) passim.
[40] See, eg Venice Commission, CDL-AD(2014)008, CDL-AD(2014)031 and CDL(2012)001.

that the judicial self-administration has a substantial administrative content. The administrative nature of the council's decisions concerning the appointment, promotion and careers of the judges is at times especially emphasised in the national legislation by the participation of the Head of the State (President of the Republic) in the formal adoption of the relevant acts. The Venice Commission has not contested this solution, but has claimed that 'as long as the President is bound by a proposal made by an independent judicial council … the appointment by the President does not appear to be problematic'. In these cases, the President 'acts in a "ceremonial" way, only formalising the decision taken by the judicial council in substance'.[41]

The exclusion of any discretionary power of the President derives from the principle that the danger of the prevalence of political considerations over the objective merits of a candidate has to be avoided. This idea follows the guideline, according to which 'appointments of ordinary judges … are not an appropriate subject for a vote by parliament'.[42] Special attention needs to be paid to the disciplinary control of judges. The Venice Commission recognised that in this field 'internationally, there is no manifest approach'. Moreover, the Commission displayed a certain deal of creativity, drawing inspiration from the general principles of the rule of law. Important principles have been stated, especially with regard to the grounds for the disciplinary proceedings, to some basic elements of the procedural aspects of the disciplinary cases and to the relevant rights of the concerned judges.[43]

> There is no justification in principle for treating judges differently in matters of discipline and removal according to whether they are members of superior or inferior courts. All judges should enjoy equal guarantees of independence and equal immunities in the exercise of their functions.[44]

The principles of legality, respect for judicial neutrality and impartiality, procedural fairness, proportionality of the sanction with the committed offence and transparency shall be in line 'with international standards'. 'A good practice/approach in conformity with international standards' suggests compliance with the rule of law and avoidance of discretionary powers of the judicial councils. Moreover, 'an exhaustive list of specific disciplinary offences' should be drawn up 'rather than giving a general definition which may prove too vague'.[45] The purpose is always restraining the interpretative choices of the competent authorities. 'Disciplinary proceedings should deal with gross and inexcusable professional misconduct, but they should never extend to differences in legal interpretation of the law or judicial mistakes.' 'A judge may not be limited to applying the existing case law. The essence of his/her function is to independently interpret legal regulations.' 'It would be problematic to discipline judges for merely criticising judicial decisions … or assessments with regard to the activities of state authorities and of the heads of those authorities.'[46]

According to the Venice Commission, the procedure of adoption of the disciplinary measures is comparable to a jurisdictional procedure. It requires compliance with the

[41] See Venice Commission, CDL-AD(2007)028 and CDL-AD(2013)034. Venice Commission, CDL-AD(2015)027 concerns the contemporary approval of the removal of the Ukrainian parliament's power to appoint judges. For the role of Presidents in the field of the judiciary in the transition of some Eastern countries, see Magalhaes (n 24) 52.

[42] Venice Commission, CDL-AD(2007)028.

[43] Venice Commission, CDL-AD(2014)018.

[44] Venice Commission, CDL(1995)074.

[45] See Venice Commission, CDL-AD(2014)06.

[46] See Venice Commission, CDL-AD(2012)012, CDL-AD(2014)06 and CDL-AD(2013)035.

principle of the natural judge, which implies that disciplinary trials have to be conducted by a competent jurisdiction previously established in conformity with the law. This guideline excludes the ad hoc establishment of a disciplinary panel 'composed on a case-by-case basis'. The reporting member of the panel, 'whose position is similar to that of a prosecutor, should be excluded from the deliberations and the vote'.[47] The concerned judge shall have the right to be heard and represented in the procedure. Moreover, if the legislator dealing with disciplinary control does not regulate a procedural issue, 'one of the procedural codes can be applied by analogy … the fact that the criminal procedural codes provide generally better safeguards to ensure the fairness of the procedure should be taken into account'.[48]

IV. Budgetary and Financial Matters

Judicial councils do not have a decisive say about the remuneration of the judges. The main aspects on the matter should be addressed by ordinary legislation. The Venice Commission is of the opinion

> that for judges a level of remuneration should be guaranteed by law in conformity with the dignity of their office and the scope of their duties. Bonuses and non-financial benefits, the distribution of which involves a discretionary element, should be phased out.[49]

These guidelines have to be considered in connection with the general idea of the budgetary autonomy of the judiciary. The problem of the personal treatment of the judges is part of the problem of the financial independence of the judiciary. At times, the Commission has stressed the deliberative role of the parliament in the matter, and suggested that 'it would be more practical to entrust one institution as the judicial council with the competence to draft all the parts of the budget for the system of the judiciary as a whole'.[50] It could be advisable to restrain the power of the parliament from reducing the budget of the courts without the consent of the judicial council, except in the case of a general reduction of the state budget.[51]

This move is a sign of the enlargement of the scope of the functions of the judicial councils by extending them to cover not only the personal status of the judges, but also the organisation of the courts. This solution can imply the self-administration of the judicial budget by the courts.[52] Supervision of this activity of the courts by the judicial council may be envisaged. However, the line of the Venice Commission in this specific field is still hesitating between the idea of entrusting the judicial councils to represent the judiciary in the parliamentary budgetary procedures and the fear that the involvement of that body in the relative battles could endanger its position, engulfing it in the political debate. In any case, the problematic aspects of the judicial budgetary management deserve more attention. On one occasion, the Commission explicitly admitted that 'it would be advisable to ensure that the views of the judiciary are taken into consideration in budgetary procedures'. The judicial

[47] See Venice Commission, CDL-AD(2014)038 and CDL-AD(2010)026.
[48] See Venice Commission, CDL-AD(2009)011 and CDL_AD(2014)032.
[49] See Venice Commission, CDL(1995)074 rev. and CDL-AD(2010)04.
[50] Venice Commission, CDL-AD(2013)005.
[51] ibid.
[52] Venice Commission, CDL-AD(2013)15.

council 'could represent the judiciary in this regard and have some influence on budgetary decisions regarding the needs of the judiciary'.[53]

Eventually, a solution may be envisaged that looks similar to arrangements of the relationship between the judiciary and the parliaments in Northern European countries (such as Denmark, Norway and Sweden). However, the Commission has not yet elaborated the experience of the autonomous self-administration of the courts, or its extension to financial and budgetary matters that is practised in those countries.[54] Further developments in this direction cannot be excluded. According to the guidelines they adopted, the Northern European states are oriented to entrust the bodies in charge of the administration of the courts also with functions about the formation of and continuous professional formation of judges, the evaluation of their behaviour and the drafting of deontological codes. This tendency is counterbalanced by the growth of the alternative model of the Mediterranean judicial councils, which have a pluralistic membership and a peculiar constitutional status. Conversely, it is not clear if the preferences will go in the direction of the centralisation of self-administration of the judiciary in the hands of one body only or if a pluralistic approach will be adopted. For example, more than one body could be established in the field of judicial administration, as has happened in Northern European countries. The Venice Commission could be confronted by this alternative in the future.

V. The Prosecution Service

What the Venice Commission refers to as the prosecution service is not always a part of the judiciary. The different legal cultures and the different conceptions of the relations between the investigative activity and the judges have produced a variety of models throughout Europe. However, the Commission also recognises in the same Opinion[55] that over the centuries, the European criminal justice systems have borrowed extensively from each other. Today, there are probably no pure systems that have not imported important elements from outside. In principle, it is suggested that the prosecution service should not be overly powerful and should limit its competence to the criminal law field.[56] The Commission is of the opinion that the rebirth of a prosecution service designed according to the Soviet and czarist model of Prokuratura should be avoided as 'it reflects a non-democratic past and is not compatible with European standards and Council of Europe values'. In a case concerning Poland, it was said that, in light of the Commission's yardsticks, the Prokuratura model of general supervision powers was inadmissible.[57]

In any case – said the Commission – as far as the criminal prosecution is 'a core function of the state',[58] the prosecutors 'must act fairly and impartially',[59] even if they are not

[53] See Venice Commission, CDL-AD(2011)012 and CDL-AD(2002).
[54] Volpi, 'I Consigli di giustizia in Europa' (n 7) 954.
[55] Venice Commission, CDL-AD(2010)040.
[56] ibid.
[57] See Venice Commission, CDL-AD(2009)048 and CDL-AD(2017)028.
[58] See Venice Commission, CDL-AD(2010)040.
[59] ibid.

regarded as a part of the judiciary. Therefore, the constitutions and the consequent legislations have to guarantee the organisational and personal independence of the service and its personnel. When the independence of the prosecutorial branch from the executive is not guaranteed, safeguards shall be ensured at least 'at the level of individual case'[60] so that 'there will be transparency concerning any instructions [of the Executive power] which may be given'.[61] With regard to the internal and external independence of the prosecutor's office, the position of the Commission looks very complex. While the external independence shall reside 'in the impermissibility of the executive to give instructions in individual cases' to the service, the prevailing conception of the internal organisation allows a system of hierarchical subordination of the inferior offices to the superior ones.[62]

There are still systems where the Prosecutor General is elected by the parliament or appointed by the Head of the State in compliance with the legislative requirements of professional and ethical qualities. However, there is a growing tendency for the administration of the prosecutorial personnel to be undertaken by (or with the consultative intermediation of) a prosecutorial council, including prosecutors elected by their colleagues and lay members, including lawyers and legal scholars.[63] The establishment of such a separate body is suggested even with regard to countries where prosecutors are part of the judiciary. In these cases, the prosecutorial council could be designed as a special section or branch of the judicial council. However, the existence of a single body with general competence over judges and prosecutors is in any case admissible. The effects of the decisions of the prosecutorial councils can vary.

VI. Crises and Difficulties of the Mediterranean Model

A summary of the doctrines and practices explored in this chapter provides an idea of the Venice Commission's contribution to the elaboration of the international constitutional law of the judiciary. Slowly, those materials have achieved normative relevance, as demonstrated by a recent decision of the European Court of Justice. However, in the last years, the model of the independence, impartiality and efficiency of the judiciary based on the experience of the Mediterranean states has faced a number of difficulties, which may be signs of an oncoming crisis. On the one hand, the judicial councils established by the new democratic and liberal constitutions have been criticised for not always ensuring a real guarantee against the temptations of corporatism and seniority.[64] On the other hand, the economic difficulties of the concerned countries opened the way to a large increase in judicial corruption caused both by the exiguity of judicial salaries and by the great financial value of many questions submitted to the judges for decision.

The constitutional reform by Hungary in 2011 and the following cardinal acts aimed at its implementation offer an example of a transition from a model of judicial independence

[60] ibid.
[61] ibid.
[62] See Venice Commission, CDL-AD(2010)040.
[63] See Venice Commission, CDL-AD(2008)019 and CDL-AD(2010)040.
[64] See the contributions quoted in n 20 above.

based on the wide competences of a strong National Council of Judges to a different model of administration of the judiciary. The traditional functions of the executives of the pre-communist systems of government are no longer attributed to a judicial council, but to a new body. The President of the National Judicial Office is entrusted with the administration of the judiciary. The independence of this new authority from the executive and parliament should be ensured by the compliance with the principle of separation of powers. The reform was introduced to facilitate a great deal of turnover in the personnel of the judiciary by adopting new modalities for its enrolment and for the substitution of the old judges whose time for retirement was modified by the reduction of their upper age limit. This strategy could be considered as a kind of indirect lustration as far as the change in retirement age has affected many old judges who had started their career under the previous communist regime.[65]

The poor flexibility of the relevant acts that have to be adopted and revised with a two-thirds majority of the parliament (cardinal acts) was criticised by the Venice Commission. The difficulty in making possible but necessary amendments to the reform was emphasised. The novelty of this new constitutional arrangement of judicial independence was underlined by the Commission, and the body expressed 'serious doubts about the reform model chosen, which concentrates … very large competence in the hands of one individual person'[66] – the President of the newly established National Judicial Office. Therefore, amendments were necessary and urgent. In the same Opinion, the wideness of the range of functions of the National Judicial Office was also criticised. The exercise of many functions by a single person raised concern even if most of the relevant functions do not relate to adoption of judgments in individual actual cases. The accountability of the President of the National Judicial Office, which was presented as one of the main purposes of the new legislation, appeared 'clearly insufficient'.[67] The National Judicial Council, which was presented as the principal supervisory body, only had the power to adopt persuasive recommendations, was dependent on the initiative of the President of the National Judicial Office and was not apparently able to counterbalance the influence of the competence of the parliament to appoint the President. In fact, the functions of the Council appeared very limited and negligible. The reform claimed to offer 'guarantees that the appointment of judges' is based on objective criteria and especially on the merit of the concerned judges. However, the President of the National Judicial Office had significant powers of interference, as the regulation of said powers did 'not contain sufficient safeguards in order to exclude that improper considerations play a role'.[68] Analogous remarks were extended to the disciplinary proceedings.[69] Moreover, the Commission criticised the legislative provisions concerning the internal independence of judges in the light of the standardisation (uniformity) procedure falling in the competence of the central and superior judicial body. It was not admissible that the Curia could state binding guidelines of the case law. The procedure was defended by the Hungarian government by referring to precedents from the nineteenth century, but the Venice Commission did not accept the objection.[70]

[65] Venice Commission, CDL-AD(2012)001.
[66] ibid.
[67] ibid.
[68] ibid.
[69] ibid.
[70] ibid.

The Hungarian authorities took note of the Venice Commission's remarks. They adopted new provisions and attributed to the National Judicial Council the power of expressing a preliminary opinion on persons nominated as a candidate for the presidencies of the National Judicial Office and of the Curia. Important powers were transferred to the Council from the President of the Office, whose accountability was strengthened. Nonetheless, according to the Commission, the capacity of the National Judicial Council to control the activities of the President is very poor, notwithstanding the limitation of his interference in judicial appointments. Moreover, the Commission is still of the opinion that the internal independence of the judges is not sufficiently safeguarded in the frame of the controversial standardisation procedure. Therefore, the supervision of the judges by chairs and division heads of courts and tribunals should be abolished.[71]

The sudden reduction of the upper age limit for the retirement of the judges, whose unconstitutionality was declared by the Hungarian Constitutional Court,[72] had been producing unacceptable effects even after the adoption of the amendments of the reforms. The legislator had not yet adopted provisions reinstating the dismissed judges, whose right to regain their previous positions without going through a reappointment procedure was recognised. The question was submitted by the European Commission to the European Court of Justice, which stated that the compulsory retirement of judges at the age of 62 did not fulfil the obligation under the European normative for equal treatment in employment and occupation.[73] The decision was useful to the persons concerned, but did not address the question of the personal guarantees of the judges, which was dealt with by a successive judgment of the Court concerning Poland. On this occasion, the judgment focused on the guarantees of the judicial independence.

In January 2017, Poland started a comprehensive reform of the judiciary to increase its efficiency, enhance the accountability of the judges and combat corporatism in the name of strengthening their professionalism. Inter alia, the direct parliamentary election of the members of the National Council of the Judiciary and the reform of the Supreme Court were proposed, while new powers of the Minister of Justice concerning appointment and dismissal of judges were introduced. Moreover, the early retirement of judges was envisaged by the lowering of their retirement age. The purpose of this overall design was 'to make the courts politically dependent'.[74] Consequently, an Opinion of the Venice Commission was requested. According to its conclusions, there were severe risks of interference from the legislative and executive powers in the administration of justice.[75] Notwithstanding this admonishment, the Polish authorities adopted new legislation on the Supreme Court, which provided for the early retirement of judges at 65 years of age and allowed the President of the Republic to extend the mandate of the retired Supreme Court judges after having requested the advice of the newly created Disciplinary Chamber of the Supreme Court. The Polish authorities officially stated that this advice was provided to ensuring compliance with the rules ensuring the independence of the judges.

[71] Venice Commission, CDL-AD(2012)020.
[72] Hungarian Constitutional Court decision 16 July 2012.
[73] ECJ Case C-286/12 *Commission v Hungary* (2012) ECLI:EU:C:2012:687.
[74] Kovacs and Scheppele (n 13) 196.
[75] Venice Commission, CDL-AD(2017)031.

The European Court of Justice has dealt with three cases concerning Polish judges who lamented the violation of their retirement rights and contested the independence of the Chamber of the Polish Supreme Court, whose advice should have been a guarantee of the respect of their status. In a judgment of 19 November 2017, the judges of the Grand Chamber of the European Court recognised that the modalities of the formation of the Disciplinary Chamber of the Polish Supreme Court do not guarantee its independence. In fact, members of the Chamber are appointed by the President of the Republic on the basis of a proposal of the National Council of the Judiciary, whose members are mainly elected by political powers.[76] This arrangement imperils the implementation of the separation of powers. The decision is considered 'revolutionary' by the commentators.[77] It is especially important, as it recognises that the Member States are competent in the matter of the organisation of the judiciary[78] but are bound to respect the principles of the judicial protection when the compliance with European regulations of personal rights is at stake. The Court was evidently alluding to the powers of the national judges to apply European law directly, to submit preliminary questions and to decide on European mandates. Therefore, the European judges admitted that the matter was object of transnational European law as far as the principles they apply affect matters usually reserved for the national legislators. The legal relevance of all the materials elaborated by the supranational monitoring bodies in concurring with the integration and implementation of the relevant clauses of the Treaties is recognised.

VII. Corruption, Miscarriages and Vetting Procedures

In 1995, the Venice Commission observed that

> the low level of salaries of judges in Albania, relative to other professions and activities though not comparable positions in the civil service, was repeatedly identified as an objective factor contributing to corruption among judges and to the consequent reduction of public confidence in the courts.[79]

For a long time, this problem sparked the attention of the Albanian political authorities. A decision was eventually adopted with the purpose of a general vetting of all judges and prosecutors. The High Judicial Council and the High Prosecutorial Council were affected by this policy, which entailed the creation of a separate and distinct institutional organisation especially destined to the exercise of the relevant activities. In fact, the inescapable general vetting process concerning incumbent judges required the design of exceptional transitional bodies outside the frame of the ordinary self-government of the judiciary. Inter alia, the Albanian legislator introduced two levels of examination of the cases and established a two-instance Independent Qualification Commission at the centre of the system. After a first intervention in 2016, the Venice Commission recognised in 2018 the necessity of a

[76] ECJ Joined Cases C-585/18 *Sad Najwyzszy v Poland*, C-624/18 *AK v Krajova Rada Sadownictwa*, C-625/18 *v Sad Naywyzszy* (2018) ECLI:EU:C:2019:982.

[77] D Kochenov and P Bard, 'The Last Soldier Standing? Courts vs Politicians and the Rule of Law Crisis in the New Member States of the EU' (2018) 1 *European Yearbook of Constitutional Law* 243.

[78] Kovacs and Scheppele (n 13) 198.

[79] Venice Commission, CDL(1995)074 rev.

constitutional revision.[80] Therefore, a vetting process of the judges presently in office was started concurrently with the adoption of amendments of the constitution. The complexity of the choice was justified, and was destined to deal with the peculiar critical situation of the country's judiciary.[81]

In Ukraine, it was considered necessary to emphasise – in addition to the preservation of the frame of the traditional model of government of the judiciary (the High Judicial Council) – the role of a specific and peculiar institution, the High Qualification Commission of Judges. Corruption, professional incompetence and political miscarriages of justice among the judges justified the adoption of the extraordinary measures on the basis that 'a choice needed to be made between dismissing judges and inviting them to reapply for their position on the basis of a new evaluation, or assessing them'[82] and their qualification 'with respect to their professionalism, ethics and honesty'.[83] According to the Venice Commission, a form of assessment of the qualification of the judges or of the correctness of their decisions appeared as an exceptional measure. Therefore, the legislative intervention had to be adopted under the condition of extremely stringent safeguards to protect judges who were fit to occupy their position and the credibility of the judicial decisions made in accordance with the law.[84]

The phenomenon also concerns other new democracies. For instance, complaints have simultaneously been growing in Georgia. It was said that judicial decisions were adopted according to political choices and for political reasons, they constituted possible cases of miscarriages of justice and they raised questions about the way to restore law and justice. A temporary state commission was proposed by the Georgian authorities. Its examination of possible cases of miscarriages of justice was considered admissible by the Venice Commission. However, it had to be regulated in conformity with the principles of separation of powers and independence of the judiciary. The decisions on criminal charges against the interested persons had to be left to a court.[85]

A new case concerned the reactions of the Armenian authorities to the presence of the equally dangerous phenomenon of 'instructions or pressure on individual judges made by their fellow judges and vis-à-vis their judicial superiors'. In such a situation, the possible opening of disciplinary proceedings on the basis of the overall results of a specific evaluation was considered admissible, but only in case of the concerned judge's wrongful conduct and of the unlawful exercise of his/her functions.[86] Therefore, Armenia has not adopted extraordinary measures but has solved its problems through a reform of the system of administration of the judiciary and the ordinary institutions of that system.

The Venice Commission has been ready to accept the information provided by the authorities regarding the general problems of judicial corruption and inefficiency, which

[80] Venice Commission, CDL-AD(2016)009 and CDL-AD(2018)034.

[81] For general information on the Albanian developments, see S Hasanaj, 'L'Albania al bivio di un compromesso: la riforma della giustizia albanese e l'apertura dei negoziati con l'Unione europea' (2020) AIC Osservatorio costituzionale 3/2020.

[82] Venice Commission, CDL-AD(2015)027.

[83] ibid.

[84] ibid.

[85] Venice Commission, CDL-AD(2013)013.

[86] Venice Commission, CDL-AD(2014)007.

justified the adoption of exceptional constitutional measures. However, the Commission had always presented possible alternative interventions to settle the cases submitted to its attention. It was necessary to choose between constitutional reforms, the creation of a special ad hoc transitory institution or the activation of the existing machinery of judicial government. Moreover, there was often the risk of possible tensions between political authorities and judges. For instance, information of the Georgian authorities about the existence in that country of many cases of judicial miscarriages cast some doubts in the view of the Commission. The Commission refused to take a position on whether there really were miscarriages of justice in Georgia. If miscarriages were of a systemic nature, they required the creation of a temporary ad hoc state commission.[87] In these situations, the Commission admonished the concerned authorities to stick to the fundamental principles of constitutionalism, having regard both to the external aspects of its independence and impartiality, and to the internal organisation of the system of courts.

This attitude confirms the line adopted by the Venice Commission in the contemporary overview of the legislative drafts of judicial reform submitted to its attention by Montenegro and Macedonia. It took into consideration the preoccupation of the authorities of the two states about the efficiency and fairness of the exercise of the judicial functions. The Commission underlined that the criteria for the evaluation of the judges and their behaviour have to be primarily qualitative: in this sense, criteria should focus on the professional skills, personal competence and social knowledge of the judges.[88] Corruption, inefficiency, miscarriages of justice and lack of professional qualifications are signs of a poor ability to govern and administer the judiciary. The institutions established in the early days of new democracies have sometimes proved unsuccessful. Therefore, it was often necessary to reform the organisational system of the judiciary. In Montenegro and Macedonia, the scope of the reforms was restricted to the revision of the disciplinary rules for the judicial personnel and of the relevant disciplinary procedures. In other countries, it was considered necessary to emphasise the role of specific and peculiar institutions.

In analysing these developments, the Venice Commission was aware that these reforms should not become means of interference in the exercise of the judicial functions by the other state powers. Therefore, special qualification requirements had to be introduced, for instance, for the appointment of the members of the Albanian Independent Qualification Commission. Their election should depend on a qualified majority vote of the parliament, while specific rules have to guarantee their impartiality and independence. Moreover, specific substantive and procedural rules guarantee the rights of the judges and prosecutors subject to the vetting.

VIII. Conclusions

When asked for new Opinions in the future, the Venice Commission should learn from the crisis of its preferred model of self-administration by an independent judiciary. In light of the past experiences, the position of the Commission could be revised and rethought.

[87] Venice Commission, CDL-AD(2013)013.
[88] See Venice Commission, CDL-AD(2014)038 and CDL-AD(2015)042.

Certainly, dangers of corporatism and seniority connected with the continuous presence in the office of the old judicial personnel of the communist regimes disappear with time. However, these dangers can still be present even with new judges, as happens in some democracies in Western Europe.

Faced with a choice between the judicial council model and the executive centred model, a constitutional decision must be made. The elaboration of the traditional sources and materials of European constitutionalism in the process of supranational monitoring has concurred with the enrichment of international constitutional law in the matter. However, the adoption of one or another model has to be supplemented by choices that fall in the competence of the ordinary legislator. Objective criteria have to be identified and applied by the bodies entrusted with the administration of the judiciary. The fight against the corporatist and seniority tendencies of judicial personnel depends on the legislative decisions that are at the base of the measures affecting the careers of the judges.[89]

The elaboration of general guidelines for the above measures is relevant for the principal models that the Venice Commission has taken into consideration. The adoption of the necessary legislative provisions affects the careers of the judges whatever the model of judicial administration is adopted. The work of the Commission should draw inspiration from the experiences of diverse countries and from the mutual exchange of information and suggestions. Moreover, in these hypotheses, the Venice Commission can play an important role in the identification of criteria and standards that can ensure the status, independence and potential efficiency of the judiciaries of the states that seek its advice and support. The search for an organisational model should be complemented by the identification of the regulations that affect the individual status of judges and the content of the relevant administrative and disciplinary acts. This is the contribution that the Commission can offer to competent supranational authorities.

The purpose of the Commission's contribution should be the avoidance of situations that require a general lustration of judges as in Albania, or the modification of the terms of retirement of judges as in Hungary. These exceptional measures are not easily accepted by the Commission. The Commission shared the legal reasoning underpinning the declaration of the unconstitutionality of the early retirement of judges adopted by the Hungarian Constitutional Court and by the European Court of Justice. The Commission suggested that the Albanian authorities should introduce procedural and substantive guarantees in the general vetting of judges. Legislative interventions in these cases result in various measures, for instance, the request for a declaration of the patrimonial and financial situation of the judges whose adoption the Commission accepted.[90] The extensive spread of judicial corruption justified exceptional measures, even though the Commission maintained serious doubts about the measures, in light of the right to privacy. Conversely, such measures are frequently adopted in the case of holders of political and public offices.

Reducing the presence of judges on the judicial council is a frequently proposed arrangement. The Venice Commission prefers in any case arrangements that imply the presence of a majority of judges on the council. However, in some states, judicial members are in the

[89] Venice Commission, CDL-AD(2010)004.
[90] See Venice Commission, CDL-AD(2012)001, CDL-AD(2015)045 and CDL-AD(2015)057.

minority on the councils.[91] This situation can be dangerous and favours political interference in the life and functioning of the judiciary. If the purpose is the elimination of corporatist and seniority tendencies, a different legislative solution may be pursued. Moreover, at the level of institutional and organisational arrangements, the search for a strengthening of parliamentary control or the introduction of individual complaints by the persons affected by judicial miscarriages could be envisaged. Finally, the Georgian model of a Parliamentary Commission could be exceptionally accepted. However, it should generally be avoided, as it interferes with the treatment of individual cases. Perhaps it would be advisable to provide for a more flexible, fair and less intrusive machinery of parliamentary supervision of judicial activity. This supervision would have to deal with the systematic aspects of the phenomenon and not with individual judgments.

[91] Volpi, 'I Consigli di giustizia in Europa' (n 7) passim.

7

Constitutional Justice in the Frame of the Rule of Law

The Venice Commission has always paid a great deal of attention to constitutional justice across Europe. One of its initial meetings was devoted to the discussion of a working paper prepared by Helmut Steinberger on the models of constitutional jurisdiction. On that occasion, the presidents of the European constitutional courts and other equivalent bodies were invited to take part in a seminar organised in an old villa in Piazzola sul Brenta in October 1990.[1] In more recent times, the Secretariat of the Commission prepared a document entitled 'Compilation of the Venice Commission Opinions, Reports and Studies on Constitutional Justice',[2] which offers a clear idea of the Commission's interventions in the matter and the principles and standards followed in the adoption of the relevant documents. This compilation deserves special attention if we want to understand the fundamental choices at the base of the monitoring and consultative activity of the Commission with regard to the role of constitutional courts in the modern constitutional democracies. The documentation also helps us to gain an idea of the state of constitutional justice in European countries interested in the Venice Commission's guidelines. Before dealing with the principal conclusions adopted in the field by the Commission, some introductory remarks will be provided. Eventually, in the closing pages of this chapter, attention will be paid to recent developments that signal the tendency of some countries to deviate from the principles they adopted at the time of the commencement of their collaboration with the Venice Commission.

I. Setting the Scene

The Venice Commission has had a role in shaping the constitutional state in Europe, and especially in the ex-Member States of the Warsaw Pact after the fall of the Berlin Wall. Having regard to its focus on the overall aspects of the legal order of the state, its guidelines in the matter of constitutional jurisdiction must be read in the light of the teaching of the political philosopher John Rawls. According to Rawls, 'the constitution is not what the Court says it is. Rather it is what the people acting constitutionally through the other branches eventually allow the Court to say it is.'[3] This statement implies a reference to the

[1] The proceedings of the meeting as well as the working paper on the models of constitutional jurisdiction were published in the Science and Technique of Democracy collection: Venice Commission, CDL-STD(1990)001 and CDL-STD(1993)002.

[2] Venice Commission, CDL-PI(2017)008.

[3] J Rawls, *Political Liberalism* (New York, Columbia University Press, 1993) 237–38.

whole system of government of a state and clearly underlines the possibility of tensions and cooperation between the political bodies of the state and the system of judicial review. In fact, in shaping the judicial review of legislation, the constitutional legislator shall be bound to arrange a fair balance between the effectiveness of the political decisions of the representative bodies and the preservation of the constitutional frame chosen by the constitutional legislator.

The proceedings of the Piazzola seminar consequently emphasised the role of the courts as guarantor of the concrete compliance and implementation of the constitution in the judicial reviewing of the legislation and the settling of the conflicts between the other constitutional bodies of the state. The preferences of the participants were directed to the Kelsenian European model of constitutional jurisdiction. The American diffuse model of judicial review of legislation was not welcomed, notwithstanding the historical relevance of that model. In the opening pages of his paper, Steinberger suggested that, 'if a state wishes to introduce constitutional jurisdiction to its legal system … it appears preferable to entrust the decision of constitutional issues to a special institution, raised (to that extent) above the ordinary courts'.[4]

The legislator should recognise the courts'

> power to interpret the constitution, to affirm the question of the compatibility of a norm with the constitution, or to deny it; under this instrument it is only the power to declare an act of legislation violating the Constitution that is monopolised with the Constitutional Court.[5]

The Commission has always been faithful to this choice, even when it considered its position not to be mandatory for some countries, as was the case for Finland. In principle, however, it did not exclude the possibility of different alternative solutions of strong or weak systems of judicial review. Therefore, it has participated from its own peculiar position in the European debate on the matter. However, it has distanced its position from the discussion promoted on the other side of the Atlantic by some constitutional scholars who had taken a position against the present American system of judicial review[6] and proposed[7] alternative forms of judicial review with special attention to the possible adoption of a weak system of constitutional jurisdiction. There is substantial agreement that the distinction between strong and weak forms of judicial review opens up interesting avenues of research. However, the distinction is considered to be ambiguous in some ways, and can create misunderstandings. In fact, there are other elements that play a crucial role in this field, namely, the distinction between those legal orders that directly entrust to the parliament the power to react in an ordinary way to the decisions of the constitutional judge and those systems where the opening to a follow-up parliamentary ordinary intervention depends on a specific decision of the judge.

The European experience has rarely followed this way of thinking. This is despite presenting some interesting examples of arrangements that allow the ordinary legislative majorities to react to the judicial interpretation of the Constitution in a relatively short run,

[4] H Steinberger, *Models of Constitutional Jurisdiction* (Strasbourg, Council of Europe, 1994) 3–4.
[5] ibid.
[6] M Tushnet, 'Against Judicial Review' (2009) Harvard Law School Public Law & Legal Theory Working Papers Series No 09-20; J Waldron, 'The Core of the Case against Judicial Review' (2006) 115 *Yale Law Journal* 1345.
[7] M Tushnet, 'Alternative Forms of Judicial Review' (2003) 101 *Michigan Law Review* 2781.

for instance, where there is a transitory suspension of the effects of a court's decision. This is the case of Germany, which has a powerful judicial review. The German Constitutional Court can suspend the effects of its decisions in view of a corrective intervention by the legislator. This option will be further investigated in this chapter below, where I will take these alternative arrangements into account in exploring recent cases of interference of political bodies in the functioning of the constitutional jurisdiction in some Central and Eastern European countries. In these countries, a specific regulation is missing with regard to an ordered settlement of the tensions between those political bodies and the constitutional judge. However, it is convenient to start this chapter by taking into consideration the choices that inspired the proposed arrangements concerning the institutional position and composition of constitutional courts.

II. Institutional Position and Composition of Constitutional Courts

When analysing the principles and standards adopted by the Commission in the field, it must be kept in mind that they are the results of an elaboration of the Kelsenian model in light of the choices of the constitutions and the practices concerning constitutional jurisdiction adopted by the European democracies after the end of World War II. Moreover, these results deserve special attention insofar as they are accepted by the new liberal constitutional democracies in drafting their legislation on the matter as a follow-up to the choices made by the Commission in its consultative and monitoring activities. Therefore, Opinions and Reports of the Commission concur with the development of the internationalisation of national constitutional law with respect to constitutional justice.[8] They provide a clear picture of the status of constitutional jurisdiction in Europe, at least insofar as conflicts in recent times arose between some states and the European authorities with regard to the states' compliance with the guidelines of the Commission in the matter. This is why, in studying constitutional justice, we have to take into consideration the possibility of conflicts and tensions between the constitutional courts and the other branches of the state in the internal national legal systems.

The basic principle of the guidelines of the Commission is that constitutional courts should be 'specific, permanent and independent judicial bodies'. This is because their task is the prevention of the arbitrariness of the authorities, and their interpretations of the constitution have to be respected in that the other authorities shall recognise the supremacy of the document[9] and not amend it. It is important to note that the Opinions were adopted in respect of Ukraine. Ukraine is an example of a still very problematic transition from communism to constitutional democracy, with significant problems concerning, on the one side, the exigency of overcoming the legacy of the unity of power, which was typical of the previous regime, and on the other side, the establishment of a coherent system for the

[8] S Bartole, 'Comparative Constitutional Law – an Indispensable Tool for the Creation of Transnational Law' (2017) 13 *European Constitutional Law Review* 601. The text of the article is published as Appendix 2 at the end of this book.

[9] See Venice Commission, CDL-INF(1997)002 and CDL-AD(2013)014.

separation of powers. Moreover, when the constitutional jurisdiction is adopted, its continuity has to be preserved even in cases that would require the abstention of a large proportion of the members of the court who are personally affected by the legislation submitted to the judgment of that body: 'the possibility of excluding judges must not result in the inability of the Court to take a decision'.[10]

The objective of the independence of the courts requires that special attention be given to the regulations that have to be adopted for their establishment. The relevant constitutional provisions and the implementing legislation shall leave certain space to internal rules of organisation and procedure whose adoption by the courts implies the guarantee of a special autonomy of these bodies and could allow a modification of the minor regulation in force in the light of experience without the intervention of the legislator.[11] On the other side, a balanced composition of the body has to be achieved to establish its independence and neutrality with regard to today's pluralistic society. Special attention has also to be paid to a fair representation of ethnic minorities, the judges' qualifications and their age.[12] Experience on the ground shows that significant threats may come from rules concerning mandates, terms of office and choices related to the schedule of appointments of members of constitutional bodies, or of the election of new judges.[13] Moreover, we must pay regard to incompatibilities and disciplinary rules.[14] In principle, drastic reductions of the term of mandate of constitutional judges need to be avoided. This principle has been implicitly stated by the Commission, which appreciated the exclusion of constitutional judges from a Hungarian transitional regulation that brought forward the age of retirement of public officers.[15] The extension of this principle to ordinary judges has been stated by the European authorities, even in decisions of European judges concerning Poland and, again, Hungary.[16]

In the modern constitutional democracies, the selection of constitutional judges is especially affected by the presence of political groups in the parliaments. The parliamentary representatives of the political parties are mainly interested in solutions that guarantee the appointment of judges who share their political ideas and programmes. When judges of a court are elected by the representative legislative assemblies or appointed by one political authority of the concerned state only, there is a risk that the collegiality of the court does not

[10] Venice Commission, CDL-AD(2009)0444.

[11] Venice Commission, CDL-AD(2004)023.

[12] Venice Commission, CDL-STD(1997)020. The Commission argued that even 'an excessive legal specialization could undermine the diversity of the composition' of a court, especially if the recruitment is mainly restricted to professional judges: Venice Commission, CDL-STD(1997)020. See also Venice Commission, CDL-AD(2004)024. The possible exclusion of younger lawyers from a court should be avoided: Venice Commission, CDL-AD(2008)015.

[13] Venice Commission, CDL-AD(2009)042. The relative requirements are usually connected with the necessity of ensuring the efficiency of the constitutional jurisdiction when the election or appointment of judges is delayed; therefore, a judge should continue his or her functions until a successor is appointed or elected: Venice Commission, CDL-AD(2006)017. The problem of the choice of the time of renewal of judges was at the centre of the Polish case, which will be analysed in the following pages.

[14] Incompatibility affects not only the abstention from cases dealing with affairs previously dealt with by the judge in his professional activity, but also the shielding of the exercise of his functions from any political influence: Venice Commission, CDL-AD(2016)034. The Commission is oriented to reserving for the constitutional court itself the decision on disciplinary measures against its members, and a similar approach is adopted with regard to lifting the immunities guaranteed to the judges: Venice Commission, CDL-AD(2016)009 and CDL-AD(2016)014.

[15] Venice Commission, CDL-AD(2012)001.

[16] European Court of Justice Case C-286/12 *European Commission v Hungary* (2012) ECLI:EU:C:2012:687; Case C-619/18 *Commission v Poland* (2018) ECLI:EU:C:2018:910.

reflect the pluralism of the political, social and cultural orientations existing in the relevant society. At times, the inclusion of principles and guidelines concerning the professional and experiential requirements of the judges in a constitution with a view to ensuring a pluralistic membership of the court is not sufficient to produce a balanced composition of the judicial body. Judges are frequently elected by qualified majorities of the parliament. This requirement obliges the political parliamentary groups to agree on suitable solutions. In one Opinion, the Venice Commission remarked that the useful arrangement provided for in the German Law on the Constitutional Court by requiring a procedure for the election of judges by a two-thirds majority in parliament favours 'the agreement of the opposition party to any candidate for the position' at stake. The choice can certainly lead to a stalemate; however, it can be balanced by the adoption of a specific anti-deadlock mechanism.[17] In other cases, the Commission explicitly appreciated solutions that entrusted the task of recruiting the constitutional judges to different bodies of the state in accordance with the solution adopted by the Italian Constitution. It could be a way of balancing 'the possible influences of the different organs of the state participating as well as of the political forces behind them'.[18]

It is important to note that the compliance with these requirements, or at least with the most important ones, is an obligation not only of the ordinary, but also of the constitutional, legislator both in adopting a new constitution and when revising the constitution presently in force. There are supranational principles that bypass the wall of the sovereignty of the concerned states when the unity and coherence of the European community are at stake. In fact, the possibility of adopting constitutional amendments 'is an important counterweight to a constitutional court's power over legislation in a constitutional democracy'.[19] However, the revision of the Constitution is limited and circumscribed notwithstanding the fact that it is supposed to be an act of a sovereign power. A growing disagreement has emerged around these principles between some states and the bodies entrusted with the task of advising, checking and monitoring the behaviour of the Member States of the Council of Europe and of the EU.

These developments will be further investigated in this chapter, but from the very beginning it is sensible to underline the following point. Choices adopted by some states to ensure the coexistence of constitutional jurisdiction with the political choices of the state's other bodies have required the adoption of measures aimed at intruding indirectly, and in a covert way, in the formation of the decisions of the constitutional courts through interferences in the appointment of the judges or through arbitrary limitations to the functions of the courts. These solutions took into consideration the absence of alternative ways of settling possible conflicts, such as preventive conflict neutralisation or general regulations aimed at openly and explicitly intervening in the modalities and effects of sentences of the courts. It seems that the adoption of clear general rules providing for the coexistence of the correct exercise of constitutional jurisdiction, on the one side, and the democratic functioning of the new regimes, on the other side, would have been a preferable option. This option would have left room for more balanced solutions between the extreme alternatives of establishing strong or weak systems of judicial review. At this point, I will focus on the topic of jurisdiction and the functions of the courts.

[17] See Venice Commission, CDL-AD(2004)043 and CDL-AD(2017)001.
[18] Steinberger (n 4) 41–42. See also Venice Commission, CDL-AD(2009)024.
[19] Venice Commission, CDL-AD(2013)012.

III. Jurisdiction and Functions

Many Opinions devote great attention to judicial review of legislation. The introduction of direct constitutional complaint has been welcomed with regard to the comprehensive protection of individual rights, especially if it covers proceedings against individual acts. However, special preparation is required in the presence of a real risk of a strong growth in the number of cases the constitutional court should examine.[20]

The review is often conceived as an ex post control. According to the Commission, 'there is no common European standard'[21] regarding the initiators and the concrete modalities 'of an a priori control'.[22] The Commission further underlined that 'a clear disadvantage of a priori control by the Constitutional Court is that the Court has to decide without the benefit of knowing how the law is applied in practice'.[23] This way of reasoning shows a differentiation of the concept of judicial review suggested by the Commission from the old traditional idea of the abstract judicial review of legislation: it draws inspiration from the experience of the US model. On the other side, the possibility of giving a formal role to the constitutional court in the constitutional amendment procedures is seen as an alternative of a 'fairly rare procedural mechanism'. It cannot be considered as a requirement of the rule of law, and it appears – as happens with the ex ante review of the ordinary legislation – as a potentially dangerous involvement of the court in the political debate that has to be carefully dealt with. This way of thinking deserves attention if the legislator aims to avoid a politicisation of constitutional justice, and restricting 'the procedure before the Court only for serious cases in which supremacy of the constitution is actually at stake'. The Commission supports this line of prudence, even if it recognises that the Court 'can play an important role in the establishment of the rule of law and the reinforcement of law through the protection of a minoritarian group' in the parliamentary legislative process.[24]

States should avoid overburdening courts with work when designing their jurisdiction. This is a serious risk when their jurisdiction includes sub-legislative acts. In fact, ensuring respect for the entire hierarchy of norms is not a characteristic of the traditional model of constitutional justice adopted in the European continental legal systems.[25] Instead, the Commission has welcomed provisions that widen the competence to solve the disputes between constitutional bodies regarding their constitutional powers, and sometimes lamented the absence of similar provisions 'which could play an important role for the consolidation of constitutionalism'. The Commission suggested an neat solution to the Kyrgyzstan Court to bypass the difficulties caused by such an incompleteness.[26]

The modification of the constitutional provisions concerning the scope of the competence and the functions of a court is a sovereign decision by the constituent power of a state; however, this is a very delicate enterprise. 'A systematic approach of shielding ordinary law

[20] See Venice Commission, CDL-AD(2008)029 and CDL-AD(2014)026.
[21] Venice Commission, CDL-AD(2011)001.
[22] ibid.
[23] ibid.
[24] See Venice Commission, CDL-AD(2012)010, CDL-AD (2011)001, CDL-AD(2002)016 and CDL-INF(1996)010.
[25] Venice Commission, CDL-INF(1996)010.
[26] See Venice Commission, CDL-AD(2014)027, CDL-AD(1997)018 rev and CDL-AD(2008)029.

from constitutional review … results in a serious and worrisome undermining of the role of the Constitutional Court as the protector of the Constitution.'[27] This is the main substance of an Opinion expressed by the Commission about a fundamental law of Hungary that reformed a court that had a very broad range of functions. It clearly stated the principle that there are basic guidelines that cannot be disregarded by states in designing the jurisdiction of the constitutional court, otherwise an inacceptable infringement of democratic checks and balances and of the separation of powers would result.[28]

It could, however, be helpful to elaborate on the comparison between these remarks concerning Hungary and the conclusions of the Opinion on constitutional and legal review in Finland. In this case, the Venice Commission explicitly said that 'although … it has in the past emphasized the value of the adoption of a Kelsenian model of constitutional justice (ie a specialized constitutional court) this is clearly not mandatory'.[29] According to this line of reasoning, it follows that section 106 of the Finnish Constitution correctly complies with the objective of the protection of human rights as it states that 'if, in a matter being tried by a court of law, the application of an Act would be in evident conflict with the Constitution, the court of law shall give primacy to the provision in the Constitution'[30] and the relevant decisions of the major judges shall be respected by the minor ones. This peculiar arrangement is considered acceptable even if it does not ensure that the decision of the court applies *erga omnes*, as would be required by the principle of certainty of law.[31]

The recourse to constitutional traditions and culture supports this conclusion, as 'Finnish judicial culture displays a strong respect for the case law of the highest courts'.[32] This argument is not novel in the experience of the Venice Commission. In fact, it resembles the decision to justify the absence of a superior council of the judiciary in legal systems, where an established observance of the principles of rule of law and separation of powers guarantees the independence of judges.[33] In the view of the Commission, traditional legal culture and doctrine justify departure from the Mediterranean model of judicial autonomy and independence (frequently recommended by the Commission in the field). In fact, the recourse to tradition is considered valid and helpful also in the case of constitutional justice. However, it is evident that, if in a legal system, preference is given to the Kelsenian model, such as in Hungary, the adopted arrangements have to comply – according to the reasoning of the Venice Commission – with the main features of the model itself and shall entrust to the constitutional court all the functions that the fulfilment of its mandate requires. The legislator is bound by coherence and continuity when it has to find a fair balance between guaranteeing the efficiency of the judicial review and the exigencies of modern, democratic and representative government.

[27] Venice Commission, CDL-AD(2013)012.
[28] ibid.
[29] Venice Commission, CDL-AD(2008)010.
[30] ibid.
[31] ibid.
[32] ibid.
[33] S Bartole, 'The Contribution of the Venice Commission to the Internationalization of the National Constitutional Law on the Organization of the Judiciary' in I Motoc, P Pinto de Albuquerque and K Wojtjczek (eds), *New Developments in Constitutional Law. Essays in Honour of Andràs Sajò* (The Hague, Eleven International Publishing, 2018) 1.

IV. Effects of the Decisions of the Constitutional Courts

The Venice Commission did not explicitly take into consideration the possibility of leaving to the states the choice between strong and weak systems of judicial review. In some systems, courts have a general authority to interpret the constitution. Their decisions hold authoritative and binding effects on all other branches of the state. In other systems (eg in Canada), legislatures are allowed to respond to the judgments of the courts 'enforcing a constitutional constraint by reenacting' the legislation found invalid.[34]

In fact, the preference is to attribute generally binding effects to the decisions of courts that imply the nullification of unconstitutional legislative provisions. The entrustment to the courts of the mere competence of providing only an official interpretation of the constitution is criticised as in this case a law remains in force even if it is invalid in the light of the binding interpretation adopted by the court.[35] The attribution of both *ex tunc* and *ex nunc* effects to the decisions of nullification is 'sometimes found to need attenuation'.[36] However, as the *ex tunc* effects have to be limited to exceptional circumstances only, the solution requires great caution.[37] Vice versa, only exceptional circumstances could authorise transitory derogations of the rule of the *ex nunc* effects, which is normally accepted. This is because 'limiting the effects of the constitutional sentences to future cases and cases which have not yet been settled in final instance has an advantage from the viewpoint of legal certainty'.[38] These developments cannot be automatic; rather, they depend on a decision of the interested court providing for exceptional effects *ex tunc* or exceptionally derogating the rule of the *ex nunc* effects.

As was said in the introductory remarks, Germany is frequently quoted as an example of a constitution that authorises the constitutional court to introduce specific rules for transitory suspension of the *ex nunc* effects of its decisions in view of the modification of the invalid rules by the parliament. This example has been followed by Bosnia-Herzegovina and Ireland. In Austria, as in Poland, the court can adopt an 18-month delay of the effects of its decisions concerning legislative acts, while in Turkey the delay is restricted to one year, and in the Czech Republic, the court can decide the date for the commencement of the effects. In Greece, the court can give retroactive effects to its sentences. In Poland, the old constitution obliged the constitutional judge to ask the advice of the government with regard to fixing the date for the commencement of its decisions that had financial ramifications. In Slovakia, the parliament has a deadline of six months to modify the legislation in conformity with the decision of the court.

[34] M Tushnet, 'Forms of Judicial Review as Expressions of Constitutional Patriotism' (2003) 22 *Law and Philosophy* 353.

[35] Venice Commission, CDL-AD(2008)029.

[36] See Venice Commission, CDL-AD(2010)039 and CDL-AD(2011)018.

[37] ibid.

[38] Venice Commission, CDL-AD(2008)029.

V. Tensions between Constitutional Courts and Other Branches of the State

In the sections above, special attention was paid to some aspects of the regulation of the effects of the decisions of the constitutional courts with reference to the rules presently in force in different European countries. These countries are interesting examples of the possible normative ways of dealing with the tensions between constitutional courts and legislative assemblies without abandoning a strong form of judicial review in favour of a weak one. Recently, similar tensions have been frequent in the new democracies of Central and Eastern Europe since the newly adopted constitutional systems started functioning and conflicts often arose between the implementation of the principle of rule of law and the not always converging interests of the policies of the other state bodies.[39]

Constitutionalism spread in Europe after the fall of the Berlin Wall through the consultative and monitoring activities of the institutions of the Council of Europe and of the EU. Cases have frequently been submitted to the Venice Commission, especially since the beginning of the new century, when political movements and tendencies in some European countries started contesting the interpretation of constitutionalism. The concerned states disregarded the commonly accepted basic idea and construction of the European constitutional heritage by substituting it with different conceptions and principles and by looking for a different balancing of the exigencies at stake. These states claim to safeguard traditional features of their constitutional identity. On the one hand, they have justified contested measures by appealing to those provisions of the TEU that bind the EU to respect the constitutional identities of the Member States.[40] On the other hand, these states have claimed that the contested measures fell within a different interpretation of the main content of European constitutionalism. In any case, they claim to find new spaces for the exercise of the freedom and autonomy of their sovereign constitutional choice. Internal tensions between the constitutional judges and other bodies of the state are erroneously supposed to justify an unlimited exercise of the counterweight of the constitutional revision.[41] A fortiori, the Commission has criticised the decision of the Romanian Government to settle tensions with the Romanian Constitutional Court by reducing its jurisdiction through the adoption of an emergency ordinance.[42]

In the past, the above-described guidelines for the consultative and monitoring acts of the Venice Commission have offered a satisfying description of the commonly accepted guidelines for constitutional regulation in the field of constitutional justice in Europe. After the unprecedented developments reported above, compliance to these guidelines is not always certain, and that description does not perfectly mirror the current situation of the institutions in the Member States of the EU and of the Council of Europe.

[39] See P Blokker, 'Response to "Public Law and Populism"' (2019) 20 *German Law Journal* 284.

[40] L Besselink, 'National and Constitutional Identity before and after Lisbon' (2010) 6 *Utrecht Law Review* 3, 36.

[41] For remarks on the academic debate on the matter, see K Kovacs and GA Toth, 'The Age of Constitutional Barbarism' (*Verfassungsblog*, 7 September 2019).

[42] Venice Commission, CDL-AD(2012)026.

Some cases submitted to the Venice Commission have concerned the appointment of constitutional judges. With regard to Slovakia, the Commission stated that the newly elected President of the Republic did not have the power to refuse the oath to be taken by judges appointed by the outgoing President before the end of his mandate. Therefore, the new Chief of State should not be allowed to reject all the candidates nominated by the National Council in view of the presidential appointment and to require the submission of a new list. The main exigency is the preservation of the functionality of the constitutional justice system. Thus, the continuity of the membership of a court has to be ensured by providing that a judge remains in office until his or her successor takes over. It follows that 'a procedure of nomination of a new judge could start some time before the expiration of the mandate of the incumbent one'.[43] The Slovakian President was censured as he failed to take these exigencies into serious consideration.

A very serious conflict arose in Poland when the Sejm, in its last session of October 2015, before the calling of parliamentary elections, selected five judges to replace the outgoing ones within the next two months. This was made notwithstanding the fact that the electoral legislation provided for the election and commencement of the new Sejm in November 2016, in between the end of the mandate of three judges in November and of two judges in December. Regardless of the preventive measures adopted by the Constitutional Tribunal, the new Sejm elected five new judges as substitutes for the five judges that had been selected and recently installed by the outgoing Sejm. In this way, all the previous appointments were nullified. At the same time, various legislative interventions were approved to support the decisions of the parliament. The Venice Commission dealt with the problem of the successive appointments in connection with the evaluation of the legislative measures adopted by the Sejm to reform the rules concerning the functioning of the Constitutional Tribunal after the described events.[44]

It is evident that the conflicts arose both in Slovakia and in Poland as different constitutional political actors aimed to control the composition of the body entrusted with the functions of constitutional justice. The political actors involved pushed themselves to the point of anticipating the replacement of judges before the end of their office or of disregarding the choices made for the substitution by the incumbent authorities just in time before the end of their presidential or parliamentary mandate. In both cases, the tension between the constitutional bodies emerged from the attempt to interfere in the functioning of the courts, putting their independence and credibility at risk. Furthermore, in Hungary, tensions arose in relation to the reforms to the age of retirement of the ordinary judges that both the Hungarian Constitutional Court and the European Court of Justice declared not to be in compliance with the constitutional principles.[45]

According to the relevant Venice Commission Opinion, the cumulative election of five judges by the new Polish Sejm contradicted the pluralistic approach of constitutionalism. This doctrine rejects the simultaneous election of new judges, and requires measures that pay attention to the changeable political orientation of the representative assembly called

[43] See Venice Commission, CDL-AD(2014)015, CDL-AD(2006)016 and CDL-INF(2001)002.

[44] Venice Commission, CDL-AD(2016)001.

[45] Hungarian Constitutional Court, 16 July 2012, n 33(VII.17) AB h; *Commission v Hungary* (n 15) 687. A commentary in *Academia*, C-286/12 *Commission v Hungary* EUCJ.

to appoint judges. In particular, attention should be paid to the political orientation of the assembly at the time of the appointment of judges to be replaced. Generally speaking, a diversified composition of the body is desirable. Moreover, the Venice Commission rejected the argument made by the Polish authorities, claiming in support of their choice the existence of a customary constitutional rule in the field. The Venice Commission noted that a similar practice had been adopted only in one similar event and was not followed subsequently.[46] The appeal to tradition can be correct only where institutions have been consolidated.

Disregarding the pre-existing rules of the election of constitutional judges signals a strong interference in the functioning of a court through the appointment of persons whose positions are close to those of the transitory incumbent majority: it is a move a priori that does not imply any specific consideration of the caseload at stake, but puts in danger the neutrality of the court.

Moreover, the legislative reform of the rules concerning the functioning of the Constitutional Tribunal were evidently inspired by the purpose of restraining the freedom of decision of the Tribunal. These reforms violated the generally accepted constitutional principles insofar as they: (i) required an unusually high quorum of attendance of the judges in view of the valid adoption of a decision (13 out of 15); (ii) bounded the Tribunal to hold a hearing and to decide cases in a strict chronological order, disregarding the possible need of an urgent decision and compliance with the European standards; and (iii) fixed a qualified majority of two-thirds of the judges for the adoption of a decision, thus depriving a simple majority of the judges from being able to declare a law unconstitutional. Principles were also violated by the refusal of the Polish government to publish the decisions of the Tribunal, as their publication has to be a prerogative of the Tribunal itself. In these cases, the Venice Commission lamented that the new legislation put the efficiency of the Tribunal in danger and thus violated the principles of constitutionalism.

Similarly, a serious blow to these principles was identified by the Venice Commission in the Hungarian reforms of the constitutional justice system that affected the scope of its competence.[47] The Orbán government had already intervened and 'stacked the Constitutional Court with loyalist[s]', profiting from its parliamentary majority, which allowed it to avoid a consultation with the opposition in the appointment of the constitutional judges.[48] Moreover, the revision of constitutional rules favoured an additional 'package' of the body by increasing its membership from 11 to 15 judges. According to the Commission, the reform of the scope of the review of legislation submitted to it for monitoring aimed at restricting the competence of the constitutional court and countered the obvious purpose of the constitutional justice system. A sufficiently large scale of competences is essential to ensure the guarantees of the constitution, in that restraining the powers of the constitutional judge to 'review certain State Acts only with regard [to] a limited part of the Constitution' contradicts the logic of the choice of the judicial review of legislation. Therefore, the Commission identified a serious downgrading of the role of the court in measure that restricted the court's jurisdiction for certain acts. Among these were the state

[46] Venice Commission, CDL-AD(2016)001.
[47] See G Halmai, 'Dismantling Constitutional Review in Hungary' (2019) 1 *Rivista di Diritti Comparati* 31.
[48] According to the definition in *The New York Times*, 12 December 2018.

budget, state taxes, stamp duties and contributions, custom duties and state requirements related to local taxes whose review was admitted exclusively in connection with the rights to life and human dignity, the protection of personal data, the freedom of thought, conscience and religion, or with rights related to the Hungarian citizenship. Moreover, the massive 'constitutionalising' of provisions declared unconstitutional by the court deprived this body of its main function as the guardian of the constitutionality and as a control organ in the democratic system of checks and balances. Analogous remarks were advanced about the legislative choice of forbidding the possibility to base constitutional sentences on earlier case law, which 'interrupts the continuity of the court's case law on a body of principles' and therefore endangers the integrity of the constitutional system as such.[49]

Both the concerned states reacted to the critical position of the Venice Commission in a partially satisfying way, but adopted amendments complying with only some of the mentioned remarks. The introduction by the Hungarian parliament of the personal constitutional complaint was welcomed. Similarly, the cancellation of the *actio popularis* was considered a positive development. However, the shielding of potentially unconstitutional laws from constitutional review even when budgetary problems have subsided was kept. The Hungarian authorities nevertheless insisted that the abandonment of the special tax in case of unexpected expenditures resulting from the court's decisions be announced. The lowering of the quorum requirement from 13 to 11 judges in Poland was appreciated, but it still raised objections, as the requirement is still quite high. The modifications in the matter of the sequence rule do not allow enough flexibility for the work of the Tribunal, which is facilitated by the introduction of a simple majority of judges for the adoption of sentences.[50]

These developments and the mentioned reactions of the Venice Commission signal evident interventions of the political bodies to settle in advance and a priori (or better to neutralise) possible tensions between constitutional justice and the political branches of the state. This strategy falls short of considering the current agenda of the court and the merit of the currently pending questions of constitutionality. The Polish and Hungarian authorities enacted measures that disregarded those countries' previous commitment to the principles of constitutionalism. They did so with multiple measures, including the appointment of judges in violation of the applicable rules; the limitation of the efficiency of the constitutional jurisdiction by the introduction of heavy procedural constraints; and a reduction in the scope of the competences of the court. The contested legislative measures have not taken into consideration that the possibility of tensions is a natural feature of the contemporary pluralistic constitutional systems. They have moved from the idea that the original European model of constitutional justice conflicts with the constitutional identity and needs of the respective state.

Therefore, at their basis, there was an abstract and general evaluation of the inadequacy of the initial constitutional arrangements adopted at the moment of the transition after the fall of the Berlin Wall and confirmed at the time of the adhesion to the EU. Tensions between the court, on the one hand, and the parliament and the executive, on the other hand, required some compositions. Both states chose to not follow a piecemeal approach by

[49] See Venice Commission, CDL-AD(2011)016, CDL-AD(2011)001 and CDL-AD(2013)012.

[50] About Hungary, see Venice Commission, CDL-AD(2013)012 and CDL-AD(2013)020; about Poland, see Venice Commission, CDL-AD(2016)001 and CDL-AD(2016)026.

entrusting the court to correct and delay the effects of its individual decisions case by case, as in some European countries, or by allowing the parliament to intervene in the matter on a case-by-case basis, as in Canada. Instead, they opted for general preventive solutions. They violated the rules of appointment of judges with the purpose of appointing members of the court who were ideologically oriented in favour of the ruling parliamentary majority. They introduced constraints in the functioning of constitutional justice; and they reduced the scope of the competence of the court. Serious doubts about the alternative of choosing a weak or intermediate model of judicial review are certainly justified.[51] However, the ways Poland and Hungary have acted also differ – as reported above – from those adopted in some European countries to prevent serious constitutional conflicts without casting doubts about the adhesion to a strong model of judicial review.

The arrangements adopted in Poland and Hungary affect the functionality of constitutional justice; however, they do not allow case-by-case regulation of possible conflicts between the court and the parliament. These arrangements are based on a previous idea that some of the most important guarantees of constitutional courts – such as their continuous efficiency, a pluralistic appointment of their members and the jurisdiction of the court in some sensitive matters – are a priori dangerous and have to be avoided. Therefore, Poland and Hungary abandoned the ideal of a checks and balances system connoting parliamentary democracy and the principle of loyal cooperation between the branches of the state (which has a functional link to the implementation of the constitution[52]). As the court is excluded from the possibility of intervening case by case in the presence of constitutional tensions, the parliament is excluded from the possibility of intervening by adopting the eventual measures necessary in the developments at stake. These reforms signal a mistrust not only of the constitutional justice system, but also of the constitutional principles of a modern system of government.

VI. Constitutional Justice, Rule of Law and Dialogue between the Courts

Constitutional courts are judicial bodies. The Venice Commission has always been faithful to this approach, and the uniformity of the arrangements adopted by the new European democracies confirms the choice made at the commencement of the activity of the Commission. The growing importance of this approach is mirrored by the growing attention paid to the functional aspects of the constitutional justice system and by the interest devoted to the problems of the independence of these bodies and their members. This work avoided considering the details of these aspects to prevent the drawbacks of a lengthy discourse.

In the field of monitoring state measures in the matter of personal neutrality and the organisational independence of constitutional courts and of constitutional judges, the Venice Commission has clearly drawn inspiration from the elaboration of principles and standards concerning ordinary justice and judges. The Commission has developed the

[51] W Sinnot-Armstrong, 'Weak and Strong Judicial Review' (2003) 22 *Law and Philosophy* 381.
[52] Venice Commission, CDL-AD(2012)026.

teaching of this experience, after making the necessary adaptations. This way of reasoning and constructing the relevant materials is the result of the orientation aimed at the extension of the coverage of the rule of law to the constitutional justice system. The historical moment of change coincided with the advent of the modern constitutional state – that is, a state which has a rigid constitution providing the conditions necessary for the exercise of public power guarantees the rights of the humans and establishes an independent constitutional court.[53] Year after year, the change has interested the majority of European states and, after the fall of the Berlin Wall, also the new democracies of the Central and Eastern Europe.

In the past, the European legal doctrine circumscribed the scope of the rule of law to the administrative activity of the state. The rule of law required administrative acts of the state to be compliant with the ordinary legislation. According to this traditional view, ordinary judges were competent to guarantee this compliance. In the contemporary legal context, however, the extension of the judicial review to the conformity of the ordinary legislation with the constitution has appeared as a necessary move in the direction of guaranteeing the efficiency of the supremacy of the constitution as an aspect of the supremacy of the law. The relevance of this arrangement and its connection with the implementation of the rule of law is confirmed by the 'Rule of Law Checklist' adopted by the Venice Commission,[54] which is the basis for the European Parliament resolution of 25 October 2016 with recommendations to the Commission on the establishment of an EU mechanism on democracy, the rule of law and fundamental rights.[55] This document touches the field of the constitutional justice system insofar as it is aimed at ensuring that legislative and not only executive 'policy decisions by the institutions of the Union comply with the Union's core principles and values',[56] and requires 'an assessment of access to justice at Union level, including aspects such independence and impartiality of courts and judges'.[57] Insofar as the constitutional courts of the Member States are part of the European system of justice, they are affected by this document.[58]

The monitoring and consultative tasks of the Venice Commission cover all the geographical area of the Council of Europe, which is larger than the area of the EU. However, the importance that the Constitutional Courts of the Member States has had in promoting the developments of the legal system of the Union should be highlighted. Relevant interventions regarding both the pre-accession processes that guided the accession of the concerned states to the Union and the stage of the implementation of the accession through the establishment of a productive dialogue between the courts and the European Court of Justice. These developments required the conformity of the status of the courts with the consolidated principles and standards of the constitutionalism. In fact, only the full satisfaction of all those requirements has allowed the mutual confidence that is the basis of the dialogue and cooperation between the states and their judicial bodies. The European law gives a certain space to these cooperative moves of the courts regarding the dynamic character of

[53] J Weinrib, 'The Modern Constitutional State: A Defence' (2014) 40 *Queen's Law Journal* 165.

[54] Venice Commission, CDL-AD(2016)007.

[55] European Parliament decision, 25 October 2016, 2015/2254(INL).

[56] ibid § V.

[57] ibid § AL 15.

[58] D Piquani, 'Constitutional Courts in Central and Eastern Europe and their Attitude towards European Integration' (2007) 1(2) *European Journal of Legal Studies* 10.

the process of integration. Poiares Maduro correctly remarked that 'a political community may legitimately decide to exclude certain issues from the passions of the political process and "delegate" them to more insulated institutions'.[59] Thus, the participation of the constitutional courts in the processes of lawmaking should not be excluded. At the supranational level of international constitutional law, the difference between civil law judges and common law judges is gradually blurring.

The legal history of recent years has therefore signalled a new modality for exploiting the role of the constitutional justice system in modern democracies. The participation of the Venice Commission in these developments as a guarantor of the principles and values of constitutionalism offers clear evidence of the growing importance of that body in the European arena, as is demonstrated, inter alia, by the frequent requests for amicus curiae briefs submitted by the constitutional courts of the states to the Commission. Even if the Commission has correctly restricted its advice in these cases to European law related issues only, these interventions have underlined the continuity between the internal legal systems of the states as well as the principles and standards of European law.

[59] M Poiares Maduro, 'Interpreting European Law: Judicial Adjudication in a Context of Constititional Pluralism' (2007) IE Law School Working Papers 0802.

8

Conclusions and Perspectives

Notwithstanding the growing attention paid by the legal literature to legal pluralism and to supranational institutions, the contribution of the international monitoring bodies to the internationalisation of constitutional law is not very rich.[1] Studies devoted to the European Commission for Democracy through Law (the so-called Venice Commission)[2] are numerous, but they do not always devote attention to the legal effects of the Opinions and Reports of the Commission. Among the aspects that these studies frequently disregard is the appreciation of the contribution of the documents mentioned above to the evolution of international law. However, recent articles have criticised the activity of the Venice Commission for adopting political choices and giving up the original mandate of neutrality and scientific objectivity.[3] This book is entirely devoted to describing the contribution of the Venice Commission to the elaboration of international constitutional law. The contribution has been analysed as the result not of a political enterprise, but of an articulated process of legal reasoning. At this stage, summarising the conclusion of that narrative may be useful.

I. The Conclusions of the Research

The previous chapters took into account the involvement of the Commission in the transition of Central and Eastern European countries to a democratic and liberal system of government. This transition required basic constitutional choices that were made according to a conventional yardstick proposed by the fundamental documents of the Council of Europe and of the European Union. An important factor in these developments was the decision of the concerned states to become members of those institutions. Two elements were at the base of the interventions of the Commission, which is one of the bodies entrusted with the mandate of monitoring the accessions of the countries and the continuity of their memberships. On the one hand, the strategy of conditionality has inspired the exercise of

[1] An interesting exception is a contribution that explicitly speaks about transnational lawmaking: P Craig, 'Transnational Constitution-Making. The Contribution of the Venice Commission on Law and Democracy' (2017) 2 *UCI Irvine Journal of International, Transnational and Comparative Law* 57.

[2] A complete list of these contributions can be found on the home page of the Commission: https://www.venice.coe.int/.

[3] M Bobek and D Kosar, 'Global Solutions, Local Damages: A Critical Study in Judicial Councils in Central and Eastern Europe' (2014) 15 *German Law Journal* 1257; D Preshova, I Damjanovski and Z Nechev, 'The Effectiveness of the European Model of Judicial Independence in the Western Balkans: Judicial Councils as New Cause of Concern for Judicial Reforms' (2017) Centre for the Law of EU External Relations Cleer Papers 2017/1; B Iancu, 'Quod licet Jovi non licet Bovi? The Venice Commission as Norm Entrepreneur' (2019) 11 *The Hague Journal on the Rule of Law* 189.

the monitoring and advising functions by the Commission. On the other hand, this body was expected to base its choices on the concept of a European constitutional heritage and to draw inspiration, inter alia, from the case law of the European Courts.

The diversity of the constitutions of European states[4] was considered to be an obstacle for the construction of a common yardstick for the exercise of monitoring and advising functions. However, the cultural history of European constitutionalism helped the search for a common field of understanding.[5] The original ideas of the European constitutional principles and values offered the conceptual basis for the elaboration of the modalities of constitutional transition in the post-communist European states. The experience of Western Europe was the starting point for the construction of the parameters of the activity of the legal and political actors. The recognition of the continuity of the choices made by the states traditionally linked to the developments of constitutionalism favoured the identification of the yardstick to be adopted in the cases at hand. The exercise implied the choice between the preferred models of constitutional reforms. The bodies entrusted with the monitoring and advising functions were engaged in a true exercise of legal interpretation. The result has gone farther than the written text of the relevant law. However, it is not the result of a political choice, but of a functional approach to the legal construction.

The Commission has had to deal with what HLA Hart would have defined as the 'open texture'[6] of the written provisions and declarations of the concerned international treaties (see, for instance, the European Convention on Human Rights and the relevant case law of the European Court of Human Rights). In the case of the unwritten principles of European constitutionalism, even a written provision was missing. It is difficult to distinguish the formal legal materials and other materials that are taken into consideration in the process of the interpretation of the law. The materials that are at the base of the identification of the law to be applied in the legal practice also have legal relevance.[7] The vagueness of the written texts and of the unwritten principles had to be clarified by the legal and political actors. The relevant materials were offered by the constitutions of the European states and by supranational documents such as the Statute of the Council of Europe, the EU Treaties and the Copenhagen criteria.

The Commission's Opinions deal with individual cases. These Opinions are the results of the evaluation of the constitutional reforms of the candidate states and Member States that is made in the light of the described elaboration of the relevant yardsticks. Insofar as those documents concern specific and particular legislative acts, they have to envisage solutions covering detailed aspects of the institutions of the constitutional democracy. Therefore, they go beyond the basic principles that are their starting points. The legal theory of authors such as Hans Kelsen and Ota Weinberger agrees that detailed interpretative statements adopted with regard to the settlement of a single case are law, or better – notwithstanding that the expression may not look appropriate – the 'law of the case'.[8] The conclusions adopted by the

[4] A von Bogdandy, 'Basic Principles of States, Supranational and International Organizations' in J Isensee and P Kirchof (eds), *Handbuch des Staatsrecht* (Heidelberg, CF Müller, 2007) 275.

[5] D Rousseau, 'The Concept of European Constitutional Heritage' in *The Constitutional Heritage of Europe* (Strasbourg, Council of Europe, 1997) 16, 32.

[6] HLA Hart, *The Concept of Law* (Oxford, Clarendon Press, 1994) 124.

[7] K Tuori, *Ratio and Voluntas* (Farnham, Ashgate, 2011) 173.

[8] H Kelsen, *Reine Rechtslehre* (Leipzig, Deuticke, 1934) ch V, § 31c–e; O Weinberger, 'Die Norm als Gedanke und Realitat (The Norm as Thought and Reality)' (1970) 20 *Osterreichische Zeitschrift fÿr offentliches Recht* 203.

Commission for one case are frequently used to settle similar cases and obtain a general relevance. The reiteration gives way to a phenomenon of customary lawmaking supported by an intellectual and voluntary factor, that is, the initial acceptance of those precedents as law. An interesting example of these developments is given by the collections (Reports or Compilations) of its precedents published by the Commission. Accordingly, the law elaborated by the Commission and applied by the competent monitoring political authorities becomes a component part of international constitutional law. This law is not the result of an inescapable supremacy, but is the product of a mutual dialogue between all the participants, for instance, in the process of progressive Europeanisation of the ex-communist countries. The Venice Commission, the governing bodies of the concerned supranational institutions and – possibly – even the European Court of Justice (ECJ) and the European Court of Human Rights take part in this interpretative process. These actors cooperate in the implementation of the European constitutional principles and in the elaboration of the modalities of this implementation. The Venice Commission does not have the exclusive paternity of those results; however, it certainly shares a great deal of the responsibility for their elaboration.

The phenomenon has to be considered in the frame of the strategy of conditionality. It regards the position of all the Member States of the European supranational institutions, but especially concerns the course of the events that occurred after the fall of the Berlin Wall and the dissolution of the Soviet and Yugoslavian Federations. At that time, the ex-communist states looked for new international legitimacy and requested to be accepted as Member States of the Council of Europe and, successively, of the EU. Both requests implied the observance of constitutional principles and values whose compliance had to be monitored. The Venice Commission played an important role in the monitoring processes, but its interventions implied a political follow-up. The success of the strategy of conditionality depended on the results of the overall convergence of technical and political contributions. Recently, the results of the functioning of the conditionality were doubted.[9] The question deserves to be examined taking into account the critical remarks of the activity of the Venice Commission mentioned at the beginning of this chapter.

II. Tensions in the European Union and Symptoms of Backsliding

The ex-communist countries welcomed the interpretation of constitutionalism supported by the European institutions, and adopted the relevant concepts and models in approving their new constitutional legislation. As the previous chapters underlined, the constitutional policies of the Council of Europe and the EU substantially coincided with Western European constitutional traditions. In recent times, some of the ex-communist countries have started claiming an alternative constitutional policy. Therefore, they adopted many constitutional reforms, especially in the field of the judiciary and the constitutional justice

[9] D Kochenov, *EU Enlargement and the Failure of the Conditionality: Pre-accession Conditionality in the Fields of Democracy and the Rule of Law* (Alphen aan den Rijn, Kluwer, 2008).

system. These reforms put in danger the new European policy for the implementation of the rule of law.[10] For example, the reforms are at the centre of conflicts between Hungary and Poland, on the one side, and the European institutions, on the other. Both states have looked for a justification in the new text of the Treaty on the European Union. According to Article 2, the EU is founded on the values of human dignity, freedom, democracy, equality, rule of law and human rights, including the rights of persons belonging to minorities. This statement is qualified to some degree by Article 4(2), which binds the EU to respect the national identities of the Member States. According to an important doctrine,[11] these provisions testify 'a shift in emphasis from national identity as such to *constitutional* identity'.[12]

However, the claim for constitutional identity of the concerned states is not a good reason for the adoption of some recent reforms. A state may claim the safeguarding of its constitutional identity when a constitutional transformation is considered necessary to recover the previous state's identity that was cancelled or amended because of an external intervention. The aim of the transformation is the restoration of the original identity of the state. If we look at the past of Hungary and Poland, we have some difficulties in identifying a past identity compatible with membership to the EU. Both states underwent a constitutional transformation when they acceded to the Council of Europe and the EU. At the moment of accession, they abandoned their previous constitutional orders for the adoption of the values and principles of European constitutionalism. If they were to return to their previous constitutional traditions, they would go back to the communist system of government; or to the authoritarian regimes of the first part of the twentieth century;[13] or, eventually, to the imperial past of the Austro-Hungarian kingdom or the sad experiences of Polish in the nineteenth and twentieth centuries. If the claim of constitutional identity of both states were based on the re-establishment of one of these past constitutional orders, the consequent transformation would be unjustified. The adoption of those old values and principles would imply a retreat from the modern models and forms of constitutionalism.[14] Therefore, the abandonment of the patrimony of the European constitutional heritage would be the necessary consequence of transformative constitutional reforms.[15] Thus, the hypothetic call to safeguard the constitutional identity of those states would appear unfounded.

[10] See A Magen, 'Cracks in the Foundations: Understanding the Great Rule of Law Debate in the EU' (2016) 54 *Journal of Common Market Studies* 1050; D Kochenov and P Bard, 'Rule of Law Crisis in the New Member States of EU. The Pitfalls of Overemphasising Enforcement' (July 2018) Reconnect Working Paper No 1.

[11] L Besselink, 'National and Constitutional Identity before and after Lisbon' (2010) 6(3) *Utrecht Law Review* 36.

[12] ibid (original emphasis).

[13] Look the frequent references to the authoritarian regimes of Horty, Gombos and Pilsudski in B Mirkine-Guetzévitch, *Les nouvelles tendances du droit constitutionnel* (Paris, Giard, 1931); B Mirkine-Guetzévitch, 'L'echec du parlamentarisme "rationalize"' [1954] *Revue international d'histoire politique et constitutionnelle* 1.

[14] The decision of the Hungarian Constitutional Court 22/2016 AB stated that a European programme of distribution of the migrants violated the constitutional identity of Hungary. G Halmai, 'Abuse of Constitutional Identity. The Hungarian Constitutional Court on Interpretation of Article E) (2) of the Fundamental Law' (2018) 43 *Review of Central and East Europe* 23 criticised it and contested the opinion that constitutionalism was a living value of Hungary even at times of foreign occupation. According to Halmai, a prevailing authoritarian tradition is a characteristic of the Hungarian constitutional history with rare short exceptions (1848–1945 and after 1989).

[15] S Bartole, 'Identità e trasformazioni costituzionali' (2020) 1 *Diritto costituzionale* 11.

So long as a state does not leave the EU and the Council of Europe, its constitutional identity is the constitutional identity adopted at the moment of accession to the relevant supranational institution. Transformative developments are apparently taking place in Central and Eastern Europe. Some months ago, the President of Russia, Vladimir Putin, said that the Western European model of democracy is inadequate for dealing with the complexity of the economic and social problems of contemporary society.[16] This intervention revives the old category of the 'illiberal democracies' proposed more than 20 years ago by F Zakaria.[17] However, while Zakaria's term was used for the purpose of raising criticism, President Putin has meant it in a positive way. The conversion to illiberal democracy is not compatible with European membership. The claim for national constitutional identity according to Article 4(2) TEU could be justified only if a specific punctual minor element of the identity of a state's constitutional order is at stake, and only if this element does not affect the basic constitutional choices of European constitutionalism.[18]

The Central and Eastern European countries do not share these conclusions. It has been noted, for instance, that the European Commission's influence over Romanian authorities is limited following the constitutional crisis of 2012.[19] On 20 December 2017, the European Commission proposed to the Council of Europe the adoption of a decision on the existence of an evident risk of serious breach of the rule of law by the Republic of Poland. The document underlined the 'lack of an independent and legitimate constitutional review' and expressed 'serious concerns as regards judicial independence, the separation of powers and legal certainty'.[20] On 12 September 2018, the European Parliament invited the Council of Europe to determine the existence of a clear risk of serious breach by Hungary of the basic values of the EU. The Parliament's concerns were with regard to the safeguarding of human rights and fundamental freedoms, the functioning of the constitutional and electoral systems, and the independence of the judiciary. Both initiatives invited the Council

[16] In an interview published in *Financial Times*, 28 June 2019.

[17] F Zakaria, 'The Rise of Illiberal Democracy' (1997) 6 *Foreign Affairs* 22. Other authors prefer the expression 'autocratic legalism' or 'soft totalitarianism and populist convulsion': D Kochenov and P Bard, 'The Last Soldier Standing? Courts vs Politicians and the Rule of Law Crisis in the New Member States of the EU' (2019) 1 *European Yearbook of Constitutional Law* 243. On the question of the 'populist constitutionalism', some interesting interventions deserve to be mentioned: K Kovacs and A Toth, 'The Age of Constitutional Barbarism' (*Verfassungsblog*, 7 September 2019); P Blokker, 'Populist Constitutionalism and Meaningful Popular Engagement' (*FLJS*, 18 December 2018).

[18] As in the recent case of *Taricco* involving the European Court of Justice and the Italian Constitutional Court (CJEU, Case C-105/14 *Taricco et al*, 8 September 2015, ECLI:EU:C:2015:555; Corte costituzionale, ord 24/2017, CJEU, ECLI:EU:C:2017:936; 5 December 2017, *MAS MB*; Corte costituzionale, sent Corte costituzionale, sent. 115/2018, 31 May 2018): see P Faraguna, 'Constitutional Identity in the EU – a Shield or a Sword?' (2017) 18 *German Law Journal* 1617. An important contribution to an unexceptional interpretation of Art 7 is B Guastaferro, 'Beyond the Exceptionalism of Constitutional Conflicts: The Ordinary Function of the Identity Clause' (2012) Jean Monnet Working Paper 01/12. LD Spieker, 'Framing and Managing Constitutional Identity Conflicts: How to Stabilize the *modus vivendi* between the Court of Justice and National Constitutional Courts' (2020) 57 *CMLR* 361 concludes an overall analysis of the matter by stating that 'any recourse to Article (2) TEU is only permissible insofar as it respects the values enshrined in Article 2 TEU' (396).

[19] D Kochenov and L Pech, 'Monitoring and Enforcement of the Rule of Law in the EU: Rhetoric and Reality' (2015) 11 *European Constitutional Law Review* 518.

[20] The Chancellery of the Prime Minister of Poland reacted with the 'White Paper on the Reform of the Polish Judiciary' and defended the right of the country to make sovereign decisions in accordance with its constitutional identity. The White Paper stated that the reforms of the judiciary 'fully meet the European standards'.

to proceed in accordance with Article 7(1) TEU, which provides for a special procedure aimed at determining the existence of a risk of a serious breach of the EU's basic principles. The Council may open a procedure by a majority of four-fifths of its Member States. The concerned states are allowed to submit observations and can be required to reform their legislation. If the state does not comply with the requests of the European authorities, the Council has the power to determine by unanimous vote the serious breach by the state of basic EU principles and values. Moreover, the behaviour of the state may be sanctioned with a qualified majority of the Council.

Different political strategies adopted by the Member States, combined with the required qualified majorities when deciding upon these issues, have held up these initiatives. While 'the European Union simply did not have the tools to intervene', the Member States 'simply do not want to judge each other'.[21] The 'predominantly political nature of Article 7 TEU' has been correctly underlined in the legal literature.[22] The strategy to implement that Article needs an overall consideration of the constitutional order of the state in question. Within this framework, the concept of a living constitution can be useful again with regard to the exercise of monitoring functions and may help the interpreters again in their work. The treatment of the citizens' personal rights is also at stake. The above-mentioned Resolution of the European Parliament of September 2018 emphasises this aspect. Nevertheless, a general overview of the actual functioning of the institutions of a state requires something more than an evaluation according to a strictly legal yardstick. Thus, a political evaluation has to be adopted. In the meantime, the rule of law in Poland and Hungary has worsened. The EU's discussions with both countries have yet to result in a positive outcome. The European Parliament has suggested the introduction of 'an annual independent review aimed at assessing, on equal footing, the compliance of all Member States with the values stipulated in Article 2 TEU'.[23]

III. The Reaction of the European Judges

Rebus sic stantibus, the European bodies that do not have a political mandate and do not follow political guidelines have attracted new attention. This is true for monitoring neutral institutions, such as the Venice Commission, and it is especially true for the judges who are the guarantors of the division of competences between the European Union and the Member States. The task of the judges is also a piecemeal scrutiny of the detailed legislative acts and provisions according to a legal yardstick. Inter alia, the ECJ had the chance to deal with questions concerning the independence of the judiciary. Two judgments were given concerning the cutting of salaries of judges – one in Portugal and one in Spain. The legitimacy of those measures was contested in the name of the principle that judges shall have a fixed salary to protect them from an arbitrary decision of the political authorities of the

[21] K Kovacs and KL Scheppele, 'The Fragility of an Independent Judiciary: Lessons from Hungary and Poland – and the European Union' (2018) 51 *Communist and Post-Communist Studies* 189.

[22] ibid passim.

[23] European Parliament, Resolution of 16 January 2020.

state. In both cases, the Court recognised that judges have the right to have a salary adequate to the importance of their work. The ECJ considered that the measures adopted by Portugal and Spain were not discriminatory and were justified by a general policy of checking the state's expenses in a time of economic crisis.[24] Another important judgment had dealt with bringing forward the retirement of judges in Hungary in 2012.[25] However, notwithstanding the possible involvement of principles concerning the constitutional position of the judges, the Court restricted the focus of its decision to compliance with the EU's general principles in the matter of treatment of the employees. It was decided that the measure was an unqualified discrimination on the ground of age. Questions about the possible connection between the independence of the judges and the immutability of the age of their retirement during their mandate were avoided.

Recently, the problem of retirement age of judges was presented again to the ECJ in cases concerning Poland.[26] On the basis of a recourse of the European Commission, the Court decided that the bringing forward of the retirement age of the judges of the Supreme Court of Poland had infringed the European constitutional principles concerning judicial independence. The measure was considered to be an arbitrary interference in the functioning of the judiciary. The Polish legislator had made a choice lacking in any coherence or objectivity. The interested judges could avoid the curtailment of their mandate by asking the President of the Republic for an extension of their terms. The power of the President looked completely discretional in the absence of legislative criteria for its exercise. Moreover, no guarantee was offered by the provision that required the President to ask the advice of a special body of the Supreme Court. This body does not appear neutral and independent, as its members are appointed by the National Council of the Judiciary, whose members are elected by the parliament and are not independent of the legislative power.

Therefore, the ECJ concluded that Poland 'has failed to fulfil its obligations under the second subparagraph of Article 19(1) TEU'. The censure regarded both the bringing forward of the retirement age of judges of the Supreme Court and the discretion of the President of the Republic 'to extend the period of judicial activity of judges of that court beyond the newly fixed retirement age'. The ECJ reiterated this approach in three cases involving a preliminary ruling requested by the Supreme Court of Poland.[27] The European judge stated again that the independence of the courts forms part of the essence of the personal human right to effective judicial protection. In particular, the ECJ reiterated the negative evaluation that the modalities of the formation of the Polish National Council of the Judiciary do not guarantee the independence of this body or the judges governed by it.[28]

If we compare the conclusions of the ECJ with Article 19(1) and (2) TEU, it is evident that the yardstick of judgment adopted by the Court has a richer content than that provision.

[24] European Court of Justice 64/16 preliminary ruling adopted on the basis of a request of the Supreme Administrative Court of Portugal (2018) ECLI:EU:C:2018:117; C-49/18 preliminary ruling adopted on the basis of a request of the Superior Tribunal of Catalunya, Spain (2019) EU C 106.

[25] European Court of Justice C-286/12 *European Commission v Hungary* (2012) EU C 687.

[26] European Court of Justice C-619/18 Commission v Poland (2019) EU C 531.

[27] European Court of Justice Joined Cases C-585/18, C-624/18 and C-625/18 *AK v Sad Najwyzszy and others* (2019) EU C 982.

[28] Kochenov and Bard (n 17) 272 speak about 'the revolutionary case law of the Court of Justice on judicial independence and mutual trust'.

The Court considered certainty and stability of the retirement age of judges as an essential factor for the safeguarding of the independence of the judiciary. Moreover, the judgment stated that the bodies entrusted with the administration of the judicial personnel have to be independent from the other powers of the state. The independence of these bodies is guaranteed if a majority of their members are elected by the judges themselves. The relevant legislation has to restrain the discretion of the governing bodies of the judiciary. These statements enrich the content of Article 19(1) and (2), which obliges the Member State to 'provide[] remedies sufficient to ensure effective legal protection in the fields covered by Union law'. Even if we read this provision in connection with the guarantee of the rule of law stated in Article 2 TEU, we do not find an explicit statement of the principles identified by the ECJ. Therefore, the European Commission has correctly recognised that the ascertaining of 'the core meaning of the rule of law' depends on the case law of the European Courts and on the 'documents drawn up by the Council of Europe, building notably on the expertise of the European Commission for Democracy through Law ('*Venice Commission*').'[29] The Opinions of the Venice Commission are frequently quoted in the texts of the judgments of the ECJ and in the conclusions of the Advocates General concerning Poland. The European judges as well as the governing bodies of the EU recognise the contribution of the Venice Commission to the formation of international/transnational constitutional law. A similar attitude with regard to the Venice Commission was taken by the European Parliament when it asked the Council to determine the existence of a clear risk of a serious breach by Hungary of the values on which the EU is founded.[30] If we compare the initial meaning given by the interpreters to the yardstick of the European constitutional heritage with the results of the described interpretative process, we cannot help but recognise that today the yardstick looks enriched and articulate.

IV. International Constitutional Law: Principles, Norms or Standards?

The contribution of the Venice Commission is appreciated by political authorities not only with regard to its fact-findings missions concerning the cases at stake, but also in consideration of its identification of the principles whose observance is required. The prima facie evaluations made by the Commission are very important in helping the work of political authorities, and especially of the European judges. Both the Venice Commission and the European judges deal with specific individual cases that require identification of the detailed rules that are to be directly applied. The Commission provides for the applicable law by extracting it from European constitutional principles and adapting those principles to the given cases at hand. Therefore, we cannot contest that we are in the presence of a true expression of law. The Opinion of the Commission binds the concerned states insofar as it

[29] COM(2017)835 final, 2017/0360(NLE) Reasoned proposal in accordance with Article 7(1) of the Treaty on EU regarding the rule of law in Poland (original emphasis).

[30] Resolution of the European Parliament, 12 September 2018.

is adopted by the political monitoring bodies. Through the reiteration of its application, the interpretation of the Commission can acquire general relevance and may become part of transnational constitutional law. This final result is frequently shared by the ECJ as consolidated law. This is an obvious consequence of the fact that the Venice Commission deals with the identification of the rules that have to be applied in the individual cases, identification which also interests the judgments of the Court.

Some authors have tried to downgrade the legal status of the parameters referred to by the Venice Commission. These authors proposed to qualify these yardsticks as mere standards or guidelines concerning the modalities of the application of the European constitutional principles. Other authors have preferred the classification of those results as soft law.[31] Both of these viewpoints do not take into consideration the role of the Venice Commission's Opinions with regard to the states' admission to, and their continuous membership of, the Council of Europe and the EU. The strategy of conditionality – as far as it is implemented – has a concrete impact on those relations through the detailed concretisation of the European constitutional heritage in accordance with the interpretations of the Commission. In fact, the contribution of the reiterated observance of its precedents by the Commission avoids the day-to-day application of parameters that has been denounced.[32] This conclusion does not mean that the Commission's Opinions cannot sometimes be read with a degree of flexibility. The difficulty of distinguishing the constitutional principles and their practical operationalisation has been correctly underlined in the legal literature. Principles remain at a 'too high level of abstraction' if they are not considered in connection with the practical modalities of their implementation.[33] Nevertheless, it would be advisable to avoid a strict division between soft law and hard law. This distinction has a long history,[34] but even the legal positivists do not deny the integrating utility of soft law. Soft law is an instrument 'whose only rational[e] is to serve as a stepping stone to hard law',[35] because it is an important factor in view of the integration and, therefore, of the implementation of hard law.[36]

[31] W Hoffmann-Riem, 'The Venice Commission of the Council of Europe – Standards and Impact' (2014) 25 *European Journal of International Law* 579.

[32] D Kochenov, 'Overestimating Conditionality' (2014) University of Groningen Faculty of Law Research Paper Series 03/2014, 11–12.

[33] Craig (n 1) 57.

[34] KW Abbot and D Snidal, 'Hard and Soft Law in International Governance' (2000) 54 *International Law Organization* 421.

[35] G Shaffer and MA Pollack, 'Hard vs Soft Law: Alternatives, Complements and Antagonists in International Governance' (2010) 94 *Minnesota Law Review* 706.

[36] The experience of the Venice Commission offers good examples of the difficulty of distinguishing different kinds of rules and practices. This is the case of the documents concerning 'good practices' in electoral matters (CDL-AD(2002)023rev), on referendums (CDL-AD(2007)008rev-cor) and in the field of political parties (CDL-AD(2009)021). All these documents are presented as Codes and were adopted on the basis of requests of the governing bodies of the Council of Europe, which approved them after their adoption. Only the Code of good practices in the field of political parties explicitly refrains from providing legal norms. It does not have a mandatory character, but aims to promote the participation of the citizens to the political life through good practices and behaviours. The other two documents have a mixed content and gather practices and legal rules in the name of the European constitutional heritage without pretending to keep them completely distinct and separate. It is interesting that the Commission explicitly denies the presence of legal rules in the Code concerning political parties. The Commission evidently admits that legal rules are present in other Codes even if they are the result of its interpretative reasoning.

The recent developments in European monitoring activity emphasise the importance of the rule of law among all the European values and principles. Many of the conflicts that have been mentioned in this chapter regard the organisation of the judiciary and of the judicial review of legislation in European states. The content of the principle of rule of law was largely integrated by the contribution of the monitoring bodies and by the case law of the European judges. The rule of law is explicitly mentioned in fundamental documents of the Council of Europe and the EU. However, the meaning of the concept had to be determined through construction and interpretation. Many documents of European authorities identify the operational application of the rule of law, solemnly defined as 'the backbone of any modern democracy'.[37] The experience of the Venice Commission has been a pillar of the initiative of the Commission and of the European Parliament. The Commission's activities collaborated in designing a new and special policy aimed at strengthening the rule of law in the frame of the Union. A great contribution has been given by two of the Commission's documents in particular: the 'Report on the Rule of Law' and the 'Rule of Law Checklist'.[38] The Report drew inspiration from a resolution of the Parliamentary Assembly of the Council of Europe[39] and aimed 'to identify a consensual definition of the rule of law'. The Checklist intended 'to provide a tool for assessing the Rule of Law in a given country from the viewpoint of its constitutional and legal structures'. Both the documents have established a productive link between the activity of the Council of Europe and the policies of the EU. They offered the concerned supranational authorities elements to integrate and complete the yardstick of the public activities. The strict interconnection between hard law and soft law is especially present in this field, and in particular concerns the exercise of all the states' judicial functions.

The interest devoted by those institutions to the organisation of the judiciary and of the judicial review of legislation can also be explained by the important role played by the judges and constitutional courts in safeguarding human rights and fundamental freedoms. The regulation of states' judges and constitutional justice is not among the legal areas transferred to the competence of the EU. However, judges and judicial review provide the necessary 'remedies sufficient to ensure effective legal protection in the fields covered by Union law' (Article 19(1) TEU). Therefore, the involvement of the ECJ in the evaluation of the conformity of the behaviour of the Member States to the identified content of the rule of law is an essential part of the functioning of the overall European constitutional system.[40] The compliance with the rule of law implies, as a consequence, the independence of both ordinary and constitutional judges. Both principles concern aspects of the interpretation and application of the European Treaties. The judicial protection of the rights guaranteed by the EU, the functioning of the preliminary ruling and the correct developments of the judicial relations concerning the European criminal mandate deserve mention.

The practice of the EU signals that its constitutional doctrines assign a primary position to the rule of law. This principle is conceived as an essential component of the constitutional

[37] European Commission, 11.3.2014 Com(2014) 158 final.
[38] Venice Commission, CDL-AD(2011)003rev and CDL-AD(2016)007.
[39] Resolution 1594 (2007).
[40] Similar conclusions are reached by Kochenov and Pech (n 19) 520.

orders of the Member States. Thus, the concept of the rule of law is inclusive of the main principles of modern constitutionalism and incorporates them. The subjection of the state administration to the law, the requirement of the law to limit personal rights, the role of the law in regulating private relations and the independence of the judiciary are all important aspects of the rule of law. Quoting, inter alia, the documents of the Venice Commission, the European Parliament[41] has stated that EU institutions and bodies as well as the Member States

> should … move towards a shared culture of the rule of law as universal value … to be applied by all concerned even-handedly, while the full respect and promotion of those principles is the essential prerequisite for the legitimacy of the European project as a whole and the basic condition for building the citizens' trust in the Union.

If we take into consideration the described process of identification of the principles of the European constitutional heritage and of the rule of law, we could ask whether we are in the presence of a constitutional law without a constitution. This was the objection advanced by a number of authors who have regretted the compression of states' sovereignty emerging as a consequence of the monitoring strategy based on the mechanism of conditionality.[42] The objection could also be read as an admonishment of the possible accession to the EU of new Member States (western Balkans) and the progressively more frequent appeal for respect of the identity of the states concerned. However, it must be borne in mind that the expansion of the supranational constitutional law derives from the voluntary accession of the states to the EU and to the Council of Europe. These moves were based on the acceptance of the values identified in Article 2 TEU. Therefore, the machinery of the constitutional monitoring is not the result of any external imposition, but is required by the engagements that have bound the states from the moment of their accession and still bind them in view of the continuity of their membership. The epiphany of 'partial' or 'parallel' constitutions was already signalled more than 10 years ago by a seminal contribution which underlined that 'parallel constitutions exert a constitutionalising impact on the domestic constitutional order'.[43] The phenomenon is not exceptional, but is connected with the spreading of world constitutionalism and implies different strategies to legitimise the use of constitutional language and terminology. 'Constitution' may mean not only a formal document adopted by a constituent assembly, but also a basic complex of principles and values concerning the specific matters usually covered by formal national constitutions. As different developments are involved, so too may there be different actors of constitutionalism. Therefore, a limitation of the states' sovereignty is possible alongside the expansion of the powers of supranational institutions. We are faced with the consequences of international agreements and engagements. Taking care of the implementation of these agreements and engagements should be the task of the political authorities of those supranational institutions. However, experience shows that the supranational political authorities are not always able to comply

[41] Resolution of 25 October 2016 with recommendations to the Commission on the establishment of an EU mechanism on democracy, the rule of law and fundamental rights (2015/2254 (INL)).

[42] eg Bobek and Kosar (n 3); Iancu (n 3).

[43] O Diggelmann and T Alwicker, 'Is There Something Like a Constitution of International Law?' (2008) 68 *Zeitschrift für auslandisches offentliches Recht und Volkerrecht* 623.

with their mandate without the advice and support of the competent monitoring bodies (for instance, the Venice Commission). In that case, a corrective intervention of the competent European judges is necessary and justified. They are the guarantors of the compliance with the basic engagements subscribed by the Member States. Therefore, the critical evaluation of the 'modernist' imagery of the judges 'as the vehicles of an optimistic narrative of progress and equality'[44] cannot be shared. The role of the judges in the present situation of European transnational order is better described by those authors who have described the European judiciary as the 'last soldier standing'.[45]

Furthermore, we have seen that the identification of the European constitutional principles is not the result of an invention of the monitoring institutions but derives from the elaboration of the main principles of the European constitutions. We are not faced with a political process of constitutional lawmaking; rather, the decision-making is supported by processes of legal reasoning. The monitoring institutions have moved from the basic elements of European constitutionalism and are engaged in a progressive deduction of detailed rules derived from those basic elements.

V. European or Universal Perspectives?

Established in the frame of the Council of Europe, the Venice Commission is increasingly gaining the position of an institution whose mandate is giving support to European integration. The Commission is criticised because it is not coping with the geographical expansion of its membership and its prospects 'for its further evolution into a body with a genuinely universal dimension to its activities'.[46] These remarks do not take into consideration that, with the adoption of the revised Statute of the Commission, the link between this body and the Council of Europe was confirmed at the moment the door was opened to cooperation with states which are not Members of the Council of Europe.[47] Moreover, it is worth remembering that in the Opinion concerning the draft Constitution of the Republic of Tunisia, the Commission underlined the emphasis of the preamble of the draft on 'the three pillars of the Statute of the Council of Europe, namely human rights, democracy and the rule of law'.[48] Both these elements confirm the Eurocentric focus of the legal patrimony elaborated by the Commission. This does not mean that the Venice Commission is not in a position to take part in the universal spreading of the principles of constitutionalism. Nevertheless, the present European situation suggests focusing on the consolidation of the constitutional values in Europe while avoiding too ambitious a universal mission. The Commission's final contribution to these results is the underpinning of the case law of the European judges

[44] A Pin, 'The Transnational Drives of Populist Backlash in Europe: The Role of the Courts' (2019) 20 (special issue 2) *German Law Journal* 225.

[45] Kochenov and Bard (n 16) passim.

[46] M De Visser, 'A Critical Assessment of the Role of the Venice Commission in Processes of Domestic Constitutional Reform' (2015) 63 *American Journal of Comparative Law* 963, 1004–08.

[47] Resolution Res(2002)3 of the Committee of Ministers of the Council of Europe, 21 February 2002, 784th Meeting of the Ministers Deputies.

[48] Venice Commission, CDL-AD(2013)032.

insofar as its case-by-case monitoring approach allows a progressive enrichment of the actual European constitutional heritage. This is a perspective that cannot be devalued if we maintain the opinion that legal integration is a main factor of the European constitutional organisation.[49] It is not the first time in the history of Europe that the convergence of advice from professional and academic lawyers and the judgments of judges has enabled the difficulties encountered by the advent of a new legal order to be overcome.[50]

[49] M Kumm, 'Beyond Golf Clubs and the Judicialization of Politics: Why Europe has a Constitution Properly So Called (2006) 54 *American Journal of Comparative Law* 517.
[50] See the examples mentioned at the end of Appendix 2.

Appendix 1: Monitoring Committee and Venice Commission: 27 Years of Growing Interaction[1]

My speech is devoted to the European Commission for Democracy through Law, also known as the Venice Commission. The institution was established 20 years ago, as the result of a Partial Agreement between some Member States of the Council of Europe. The Agreement was then enlarged to all the states of the Council and other non-Member States. The Commission has a special position in the framework of the Council of Europe. Its budget is proportionally financed by the contributions of the Member States, ensuring autonomy and independence to the institution.

The Commission is entitled to participate in the monitoring procedures of the Parliamentary Assembly of the Council of Europe. This task has been developed and grown together with the extension and strengthening of the monitoring activity by the Assembly itself. In 1993, with Order No 488, the Assembly instructed its Committees to monitor the honouring of commitments entered into by the authorities of new Member States. Thus, the monitoring included the compliance with the conditions for accession to the Council of Europe. At that time, the Berlin Wall fell, and the Soviet Union and the Federal Republic of Yugoslavia broke up. The Venice Commission faced the constitutional reforms that the states resulting from the two Federations' dissolution undertook to deeply revise their constitutional legal order and adopt the *acquis communautaire* of the European constitutional heritage as it is expressed by the three ground principles of the Council of Europe: democracy, human rights and the rule of law. So, the role played by the Venice Commission was dual: on the one side, an advisory body and, on the other side, a monitoring body, checking the results of the reforms undertaken. Therefore, the Commission was involved in the machinery of the conditionality principle, which means that the membership to the Council of Europe has been conditional upon the respect of the values and principles enshrined in the founding documents of the Council of Europe that Member States committed to comply with. The Venice Commission is one of the players involved in the enforcement of the conditionality principle, but its role is only to advise the institutions of the Council of Europe responsible for deciding the appropriate measures appropriate for each state's behaviour, from accession to the Council to the adoption of the sanctions eventually relevant. 'Whether or not any additional sanctioning mechanism would be warranted is not an issue for the Venice Commission', President Buquicchio recently said. The Commission

[1] Report submitted by Sergio Bartole to the Council of Europe seminar 'The International Legal Order in a Changing World: Challenges for the Monitoring Procedure of the Parliamentary Assembly', Helsinki, 16 May 2017.

is essentially a technical body. Therefore, it is not part of its job to take measures that fall within the competence of the political bodies of the Council.

Special attention should be paid to the nature of the activities of the Commission. As a body responsible for constitutional assistance, the Commission is not able to intervene on its own initiative, except for carrying out studies and researches. Therefore, its work depends on the initiative of the Member States or the bodies of the Council of Europe – first of all the Parliamentary Assembly, the Committee of Ministers and the Congress of Local and Regional Authorities. It is fair to say that, for example, up to and including 2000, the Commission delivered 650 opinions and reports, 130 of which were on general issues, upon the requests submitted by the Parliamentary Assembly, and 56 in particular by the Monitoring Committee of the Assembly. These tasks directly relate the Commission to the requesting bodies and their activities, and mostly the monitoring one, which mainly concerns draft legislations and the assistance on Member States' domestic constitutional issues. And that is the activity that needs a parameter, a standard of evaluation.

This is a very sensitive point. We can easily say that the core activity of the Commission lies in the founding principles and values of the Council of Europe, ie the three fundamental pillars of democracy, human rights and the rule of law that I have just mentioned. Nevertheless, it is not easy to shape those principles in practical terms. Recently, following a resolution of the Parliamentary Assembly, the Commission adopted a report on the rule of law. The report highlighted that national legal provisions referring to the rule of law are of a very general character. To allow an application of the concept, the Commission than elaborated a Rule of Law Checklist in order to identify the core elements and the practical consequences of the application of the rule of law principle in different fields of constitutional interest. To draft the checklist, the Commission assessed the best practices of the Member States and shaped them through the doctrines of European constitutionalism. In this way, the Commission has provided the possibility to consider new criteria and standards for evaluation. If they were applied, those criteria and standards would, in one way or another, become part of the elements that the bodies responsible for the monitoring activity might use. As I wrote in another paper, through the machinery of the conditionality principle, the monitoring criteria become binding and commit the stakeholders concerned by the opinions of the Venice Commission and by the resolutions of the Council of Europe bodies, which are based on those opinions. Step by step, therefore, the criteria and standards constantly applied become part of the European constitutional heritage and serve as an example of the so-called 'transnational law'.

For the mentioned reasons, the participation of the Commission to the monitoring activities calls for a cautious and attentive approach, requiring a fair balance between the guidelines drawn from the fundamental principles and a prudent and monitored application of comparative constitutional law.

A clear example of this is the contribution of the Venice Commission to the internationalisation of domestic constitutional law concerning the organisation of the judiciary. The Commission collected information from the national constitutional traditions coming after the Second World War, as well as from the documents drawn up by the institutions of the Council of Europe or other similar bodies. As a result of the investigation, the Commission suggested the institution of a collective body, usually called 'Judiciary Council', as the better solution to ensure the independence of the judiciary. The body should be composed by judges elected by the judiciary itself and other members elected by parliament among qualified groups involved in judiciary activity (lawyers, law professors). The Council should take all administrative and judicial decisions on the career of judges and disciplinary measures against them. The office of President of the Council should not be held by the Ministry of Justice. The presidency should be headed by the head of state, except for presidential regimes in which the head of state is chief of the executive power. The aim is to safeguard the separation of the organisation of the judiciary from the government in systems where the independence of the judiciary is at least provided by law. It is easy to understand that the indications of the Venice Commission, as resumed in a report devoted to the organisation of the judiciary, go beyond the mere mention of the principle of independence and neutrality of the judiciary as provided by the most common theoretical definition of rule of law. These indications have been accepted several times and implemented at constitutional level by the Member States. In this way, they resulted in a *corpus* of transnational law that enforces one of the Council of Europe ground pillars.

A similar course was followed with the guidelines on the organisation and functions of constitutional courts, as part of the doctrine of the rule of law too. The Venice Commission gave many opinions about the judicial review of legislation. Among them, special attention should be paid to the recent ones concerning the reforms adopted by Poland, Slovakia and Hungary. On the matter of organisation and functions of constitutional courts, a short summary of the directives given to the legislations of Member States could be useful. A qualified majority is required for the election of constitutional judges by the parliament. In fact, these judges should not be considered as representatives of political parties, but, as a whole, they should be the expression of different interests and cultural backgrounds. In the mentioned cases of Poland, Slovakia and Hungary, the solution suggested was the Italian model. For instance, in Italy, one-third of the members are appointed by the President of the Republic, one-third are appointed by the judges of the higher ordinary and administrative courts, and the last third is elected by the parliament with a qualified majority. Constitutional courts should have organisational and budgetary autonomy. They should also be directly responsible for the election of their own President. At the expiry of the mandate, judges should be quickly replaced. An extension of their office should be provided in case of delay in the election or appointment of new judges. At the end of the term of office, re-election should be excluded. Constitutional courts should be given enough flexibility in the organisation of the agenda and they should not be bound by their own case law.

The effectiveness and continuity of the Venice Commission's contribution to the development of the European constitutional heritage rely on compliance of Member States. But sometimes this compliance is not voluntary, and it depends on the approach of the Council of Europe bodies. In some way, the relation between the Council of Europe bodies and a Member State is influenced by the relation between the same state and the Venice Commission. As I said before, the task of constitutional assistance and its advisory role exclude that the Commission might adopt any sanction. The Commission usually opens a dialogue with domestic authorities based on the submitted draft legislation or 'concept paper'. Prior to adopting an Opinion, it often happens that President Buquicchio (or one of the heads of the main bodies of the Council of Europe) makes a preliminary visit to the state in question and a channel of communication is opened with a Commission delegation going to the place. So, the final opinion of the Commission already considers the objections contrary to the given indications, expressed by local authorities, or their willingness to comply with and enforce the same indications. Generally, every opinion ends with a list of the main or key recommendations, to make easier its implementation.

It often happens that the Commission reanalyses the draft after the domestic authorities have suggested amendments and revisions. This is what happened, for example, in the case of the Albanian reform of the judiciary. Albanian authorities submitted a first draft and then requested the assessment of a second draft revised following the Commission's evaluation. In this way, the Commission had the chance to check the follow-up of its opinion. The task is somewhat sensitive, because the evaluation of the measure adopted by national authorities could imply concessions to the interplay of majorities and oppositions, while the Commission and its Secretariat, as an institutional choice, leave political questions outside. A good practice adopted by the Commission is now to put in the plenary session agenda a special point devoted to the follow-up to earlier opinions: the Commission is informed by the Secretariat about constitutional and legislative developments of Member States, related to previous opinions. That is the appropriate time for the plenum, at the formal request of a Member State, to hear explanations about the choice to implement or not to implement the Commission recommendations (as happened for Ukraine and Montenegro).

This plot of relations and interventions sometimes does not work well. The cases of Poland and Hungary, for example, are still open, despite, in the Hungarian case, the double check by the Commission of the draft legislation on the constitutional court, upon a first request from the President of the Monitoring Committee of the Parliamentary Assembly and a second one from the Secretary General of the Council of Europe. In the second Opinion, the Commission welcomed the fact that the Hungarian authorities had taken up the Commission's suggestions, but regretted that the Hungarian legislature repeatedly gave constitutional force to ordinary laws quashed by the constitutional court and criticised the prohibition of the use of case law prior to the constitutional reform, as well as the limitation of the constitutional court's powers of control in budgetary matters. At that stage, however, the following events were not a matter for the Commission, but fell within the competence of the political bodies of the Council of Europe.

My last point: the Poland and Hungary cases involve not only the Council of Europe, but also, as is well known, the European Union. The implementation of the Venice Commission's recommendations concerning Hungary was recommended, as well, in a recommendation of the European Parliament in 2013. Again, some recommendations of the European Commission adopted in July and December 2016 referred to the Venice Commission Opinions. So, the activity of the Venice Commission concerning the monitoring is important for the European Union too. The same happened for the Albanian reform of the judiciary. Further development should be expected concerning the Rule of Law Checklist. In fact, in the fundamental resolution of 25 October 2016 on democracy, the rule of law and fundamental rights, the European Parliament refers to the Venice Commission's Rule of Law Checklist, and the Commission is defined, among others, as a source and instrument for assessment, reporting and monitoring of Member States' activities. Even the resolution of 25 October 2016 pays special attention to the conditionality principle, in order to commit the Member States to the standards, values and democratic principles that they accepted at the time of accession. Furthermore, the same resolution suggests evaluating each Member State's behaviour in the framework of a continuous dialogue and to work towards a stronger consensus between the Union and its Member State. If the search for a stronger consensus is abandoned and the commitments are not honoured, the competent bodies of the Union should reflect and adopt all decisions concerning Article 7 TEU.

Appendix 2: Comparative Constitutional Law – An Indispensable Tool for the Creation of Transnational Law[1]

Growing attention is being paid to the study of comparative constitutional law due both to the expansion of transnational constitutional law and to the increasing relevance of the legal value of national constitutional identities. Other phenomena, such as the international monitoring of national constitutional systems, reflect, and simultaneously further contribute to, the evolution of cultural and political discussion on the matter. As recent academic contributions demonstrate, the field of comparative constitutional law remains open to debate. Some years ago, in an essay devoted to doctrinal constructivism in the field of constitutional law,[2] Armin von Bogdandy formulated a strategy for responding to the challenges facing European constitutional scholarship in which he emphasised the increasing importance of 'comparative constitutionalism in the European legal arena'. Recently, Mark Tushnet discussed the diminishing relevance of the traditional boundaries (subject matter, discipline and geography) of 'comparative law as a scholarly field'. The blurring of those boundaries has made it impossible to distinguish comparative law from the field of law in general.[3] An analytical comparison of these two authoritative positions offers an opportunity to reflect upon current discussions on the importance of the study of comparative constitutional law. I shall attempt here to expand upon the subject by framing it within the European context.

I. A European Perspective

One could justifiably wonder whether the differences between von Bogdandy and Tushnet derive from differences in the geographical and cultural areas in which the two authors frame their research and writings. It is evident that von Bogdandy's approach takes a European perspective and is especially concerned with the growing formation of a European legal order which can give – according to his research hypothesis – new currency to the project of the *ius publicum europaeum*: 'a solidified European context for discussion and reception', the doctrinal dimensions of which apparently go beyond the existence of the European Union

[1] Originally published as S Bartole, 'Comparative Constitutional Law – an Indispensable Tool for the Creation of Transnational Law' (2017) 13 *European Constitutional Law Review* 601.

[2] A von Bogdandy, 'The Past and Present of Doctrinal Constructivism: A Strategy for Responding to the Challenge Facing Constitutional Scholarship in Europe' (2009) 7 *International Journal of Constitutional Law* 364, 394 and 397.

[3] M Tushnet, 'The Boundaries of Comparative Law' (2017) 13 *European Constitutional Law Review* 13.

legal system. However, there is also an operational dimension to the discussion. Comparative law studies can make an important contribution to the identification of the basic features of European law held in common by the Member States of the Union and which bind them as well as the governing bodies of the Union. Legal literature has taken note of these developments with the introduction, as a term of reference within the European debate, of the concept of the so-called European constitutional heritage.

This concept, which 'refers to a collection of principles', is at the base of the collective constitutional cultures of Europe, even if its interpretation and application in the various national constitutional orders differ.[4] Within the European polity, the integration of the constitutional experiences of the concerned states is achieved by means of a constitutional discourse which 'must be conceived of as a conversation of many actors in a constitutional interpretative community'.[5] It involves in particular European and national judges. But the concept not only facilitates the consideration of the shared constitutional doctrines of the European states, it also has practical – and not merely cultural – relevance. It can be useful to remember that the origins of current thought on this concept are naturally linked to the ascent of the European Court of Justice's fundamental rights case law. For many years, the Court has undeniably been engaged in investigation into the common constitutional traditions of the various EU Member States.[6] The relevance of European constitutional traditions has even been recognised by the constitutional courts of the newer Member States. For instance, in its Lisbon decision, the Polish Constitutional Tribunal confirmed 'the solemn character of constitutional traditions, which are common to the member states'.[7] The implications of such judicial activity have not been lost on the constitutional and ordinary legislatures of the states concerned.

Alessandro Pizzorusso[8] rightly suggests that the European constitutional heritage can be identified with the use of comparative law techniques of research and construction, which in turn define the relevant features of the internal legal orders of the Member States. Not only judges and legislators are interested in the use of the concept. International bodies adopt a similar approach when they monitor member state compliance with their fundamental principles and values. The Venice Commission's advisory mandate entails setting up a dialogue with the states that are members of the Council of Europe and monitoring the implementation of the provisions of the Council's legal system aimed at ensuring compliance with the fundamental principles and values this institution was created to guarantee.[9]

[4] D Rousseau, 'European Constitutional Heritage: A Condition for European Constitutional Law' (1997) XXXIX *The federalist* 57.

[5] JHH Weiler, 'European Neo-constitutionalism: in Search of Foundations for the European Constitutional Order' (1996) XLIV *Political Studies* 517, 532.

[6] See, eg ECJ Case 11/70 *Internationale Handelsgesellschaft GmbH/Einfurh und Voratstelle fuer Gerteide und Futtermittel* (1970) EU C 114.

[7] M Wendel, 'Comparative Reasoning and the Making of a Common Constitutional Law' (2013) 11 *International Journal of Constitutional Law* 981, 1002. But, for example, in its decision of 5 December 2016 (No 22/2016 – XII. 5) concerning the rights of migrants and their treatment, the Constitutional Court of Hungary recognised that the protection of constitutional identity rests with the European Court of Justice and, at the same time, vindicated its power of guaranteeing the Hungarian sovereignty and traditional identity against measures adopted by the governing bodies of the European Union.

[8] A Pizzorusso, *Il patrimonio costituzionale europeo* (Bologna, Il mulino, 2002) 16.

[9] S Bartole, 'Conditionality and Living Constitution' in GG Harutyunyan (ed), *New Millennium Constitutionalism: Paradigms of Reality and Challenges* (Yerevan, NJAR Publishers, 2013) 157.

This is a well-known effect of the principle of conditionality.[10] Commentators recognised its importance in the years after the Berlin Wall fell, when former communist and Soviet states first started seeking admission to the Council of Europe, and later membership in the European Union. The Venice Commission played a crucial role in advising and supporting democratic transitions in Central and Eastern Europe. Other European bodies were involved in the process too. The institutions of the Council of Europe are allowed to deny accession requests or impose sanctions if its monitoring body finds that a Member State's actions breach accepted norms. In the context of OSCE (Organization for Security and Co-operation in Europe), the ODIHR (Office for Democratic Institutions and Human Rights of OSCE) supports and promotes democracy and the rule of law by observing elections, reviewing legislation and advising governments on the development of their democratic institutions. In both cases – the Council of Europe and OSCE – the functioning of the system implies the elaboration of guidelines of constitutional engineering and the establishment of yardsticks for the evaluation of the treatment of rights and freedoms based on the national traditions of European constitutionalism. The Commission of the European Union does the same when it supervises the implementation of the *acquis communautaire* by candidate states, or the reforms Member States must implement to comply with obligatory norms.[11]

II. The Continuing Importance of Comparative Constitutional Law

If we keep the European dimension of von Bogdandy's perspective in mind, we can better understand the conclusions Mark Tushnet reached in his contribution. When he considers the general expansion of the field of law in light of the 'inevitable globalization of constitutional law',[12] his research focuses on the end result in a process which is not limited to Europe and is characterised by a progressive blurring of the geographical boundaries which have traditionally defined the field of comparative law research. However, since this is an ongoing process, I do not believe that studying the varying national constitutional experiences has become irrelevant. In our view, the process towards the globalisation of constitutional law requires a comparative methodological approach. Even within the framework of the European Union, geographical boundaries still exist,[13] and we must take them into account if we want to understand the unavoidable and difficult balancing act involving the states' residual sovereignty and their basic constitutional features, on the one hand, and

[10] JT Checkel, 'Compliance and Conditionality' (2000) Arena Working Papers 00/18, 1.

[11] See, eg U Sedelmeier, 'Pre-accession Conditionality and Post-accession Compliance in the New Member States: A Research' in W Sadurski, J Ziller and K Zurek (eds), *Après Enlargement: Legal and Political Responses in Central and Eastern Europe* (Florence, European University Institute, RSCAS, 2006) 145.

[12] M Tushnet, 'The Inevitable Globalization of Constitutional Law' (2008) Harvard Law School Public Law & Legal Theory Working Papers Series 09-06.

[13] 'both normatively and institutionally, EU law remains intertwined with the legal systems of Member States': K Tuori, 'Transnational Law: on Legal Hybrids and Legal Perspectivism' in M Maduro, K Tuori and S Sankari (eds), *Trannational law Rethinking European Law and Legal Thinking* (Cambridge, Cambridge University Press, 2014) 21.

the exigency of the formation of the transnational (or international)[14] law of the Union, on the other. In this context, lawyers deal with provisions in the Treaty on the European Union that safeguard the constitutional identity of the Member States or demand compliance with the common principles and values whose observance is a *conditio sine qua non* of continued membership. Both require a comparative approach. The identification of the constitutional identity of a state implies a comparison with other states, and their common traditions are identified by surveying the multiplicity of traditions that exist in the states concerned. If we abandon a comparative constitutional perspective when considering European law, we run the risk of favouring a monistic approach at the risk of losing the advantages offered by the pluralist approach suggested by Miguel Maduro.[15]

The advent of a common, global legal space characterised by an absence of traditional boundaries will likely depend on the progressive expansion of the effects of globalisation. The expansion of the European Union may be considered – at the regional level – as the first, constituent, step in a long process. We may be observing a transition from the fragmentary experience of the various national legal orders to a global legal space constructed from the raw materials of national experiences – as we see happening today in Europe. Therefore, a comparative methodological approach is still important and productive, and not only for the sake of scientific research and knowledge. The comparative methodological approach might even prove more immediately practical and operationally useful than in the past, as demonstrated by the European experience. The European perspective provides a constructive point of view from this side of the Atlantic that is possibly more conducive to the study of the regional phase within a larger process. Superregional effects probably appear more frequently on the radar of researchers who approach the phenomenon from a different perspective.

III. Authoritarian Tendencies and the European Constitutional Traditions

Since 1989 and the fall of the Berlin Wall, the monitoring functions exercised by international institutions have gained in importance in the context of what has been defined – in a seminal article by Bruce Ackerman[16] – as 'the rise of world constitutionalism'. Monitoring bodies now also exercise advisory functions, which should facilitate the spread of constitutionalism into new areas. At the end of the twentieth century, the former members of the Warsaw Pact engaged in the process of accession to the Council of Europe, and later to the European Union. It was therefore necessary to ascertain whether they were in compliance with the fundamental principles and values of those European supranational institutions. Their sovereignty was never in danger as they had agreed to accept external advice and monitoring from the competent bodies as part of the accession package – it was not imposed.[17]

[14] On this terminological question, see Tuori (ibid) passim.

[15] M Maduro, 'Three Claims of Constitutional Pluralism' in M Avbelj and J Komarek (eds), *Constitutional Pluralism in the European Union and Beyond* (Oxford, Hart Publishing, 2012) 67.

[16] B Ackerman, 'The Rise of World Constitutionalism' (1997) 83 *Virginia Law Revue* 771.

[17] This aspect was not fully considered by M Tushnet, 'Some Skepticism about Normative Constitutional Advice' (2008) 49 *William & Mary Law Review* 1473.

In order to fulfil their monitoring task, the bodies developed a 'yardstick' to measure adherence to the European constitutional heritage, which assumed normative relevance as soon as it became binding through operation of the principle of conditionality. A dialogue has been maintained with the authorities concerned to avoid any hint of authoritarianism.

This led, little by little, to the burgeoning of transnational (or international) constitutional law, operating under the aforementioned principle of conditionality. However, its relevance to the Member States of both the Council of Europe and the European Union is threatened by the emergence of authoritarian tendencies, a backlash against liberal democracy supposedly justified by the primacy of state sovereignty and security, as demonstrated recently in Russia, Hungary and Poland.[18]

Conditionality is sometimes no guarantee of satisfying results. After admission to the Council of Europe or the European Union, certain states flouted recommendations: Poland has not yet fully acknowledged recommendations to reform its constitutional court made by the governing bodies of the Council of Europe and the European Union on the basis of opinions adopted by the Venice Commission, and Hungary has only partially accepted similar remarks on its judicial organisation.[19] The attitude of states that do not accept the prevailing norms or their sources put the credibility and usefulness of the comparative approach in defining the European constitutional heritage in peril. But even in these cases, comparative legal analysis and interpretation may yield positive results from a historical perspective. A complete evaluation of recent developments is only possible through exhaustive examination of the authoritarian aspects of the mentioned constitutional reforms in light of historical European traditions and the constitutional principles and values of the other European states that inspired the ongoing development of supranational institutions.

IV. The Importance of Interpretation and Application of Constitutional Provisions

Use of the comparative approach yields determinative suggestions for the identification of the basic elements of the relevant European legal doctrines in the frame of constructivism, as mentioned by von Bogdandy in his contribution. Comparison of the various legal orders also contributes to a better understanding of the national identities at stake – and of their differences. Although knowledge of the written constitutional and legislative provisions of the state concerned matters when compliance with the European constitutional heritage is

[18] A Cooley, 'Countering Democratic Norms' (2015) 26(3) *Journal of Democracy* 49.

[19] An important element to understand the overall situation is the interpretation of the behaviour of the institutions of the European Union. While the case of Hungary is still on hold after a resolution of the European Parliament adopted in July 2013, the European Commission both in July 2016 and in December 2016 invited Poland to reform the contested legislation concerning the Constitutional Tribunal. In both cases, the competent bodies have not yet considered the possible application of Art 7 TEU (at the time of the publication of the present text in 2017, but still in 2020). These developments bring into question the nature of the transnational law at stake. If the adoption of the follow-up sanctions depends on the political decisions of the European governing bodies, it could be reasonable to classify it as soft law. However, in other cases, we are in the presence of law which grants recourse to the judiciary. Recently on this point see W Sadurski, 'That *Other* Anniversary' (2017) 13 *European Constitutional Law Review* 417.

being monitored, its effective interpretation and application in light of the moral and philosophical traditions of constitutionalism are equally relevant, a point correctly appreciated by Tushnet. Giovanni Bognetti[20] emphasised the importance in comparative constitutional law studies of knowledge of the concrete application and interpretation of the constitutional provisions concerned. The same exigency is present in the field of constitutional monitoring. If we want to grasp the reality of constitutional experience, we must examine the socially effective result of the way the written texts are understood and the norms that emerge through their interpretation.[21] This is not necessarily an approach based on a realist theory of the law because even a formal take cannot avoid considering the concrete application of interpretations of legal provisions. The Kelsenian design of the *Stufenbau* of normative sources construes the practical judicial or administrative interpretation and application of constitutional and legislative texts as the last stage in the epiphany of the creation of law.[22] Comparative analysis only makes sense if we develop its doctrines while taking the concrete practical use of constitutional and legislative provisions into account.

The experience of the Venice Commission with organisational models of the judiciary clearly demonstrates that its approach is especially pertinent to the exercise of monitoring functions. The Commission frequently remarks that the judicial organisation needs to be kept separate from the other powers of state. The Mediterranean model of autonomous judicial councils has been proposed to the new democracies of Central and Eastern Europe as an institutional tool that could ensure the independence and neutrality of the judiciaries.[23] However, the Commission added that in countries where a judiciary dependent on the executive is a long-standing tradition, this arrangement will also suffice as long as the relevant practices respect judicial independence and neutrality.[24] It is evident that in this case the Venice Commission does not limit its analysis to the relevant written constitutional and legislative provisions, but also thinks ahead by taking their concrete interpretation into account. It explores whether their application is inspired by the constitutional principle of judicial independence.

Is the credibility of (hard) law being vanquished by soft law according to a contraposition postulated more than 30 years ago?[25] Soft law does not impinge upon the construction of legal theory insofar as it is similar to, or overlaps[26] with, well-known venerable concepts 'such as gentlemen's agreements, comity, non-binding agreements, or – in English constitutional

[20] G Bognetti, *Diritto costituzionale comparato. Approccio metodologico* (Modena, Mucchi, 2011).

[21] O Weinberger, 'Die Norm als Gedanke und Realitat' (1970) 20 *Osterreichische Zeitschfrot für offentliches Recht* 203.

[22] See H Kelsen, *Reine Rechtslehre* (Leipzig, F Deuticke, 1934) ch V, § 31c–e.

[23] On this choice, see critical remarks in M Bobek and D Kosar, 'Global Solutions, Local Damages: A Critical Study in Judicial Councils in Central and Eastern Europe' (2014) 15(7) *German Law Journal* 1257; B Iancu, 'Perils of Sloganised Constitutional Concepts Notably That of "Judicial Independence"' (2017) 13 *European Constitutional Law Review* 582.

[24] Venice Commission, CDL-PI(2015)001. However, it is convenient to remember that, for example, in the UK, normative provisions and administrative practices were recently reformed to avoid difficulties connected with their problematic application.

[25] See R Baxter, 'International Law in "Her Infinite Variety"' (1980) 29 *International and Comparative Law Quarterly* 549; P Weil, 'Towards Relative Normativity in International Law' (1983) 77 *American Journal of International Law* 413.

[26] A Peters and I Pagotto, 'Soft Law as a New Mode of Governance: A Legal Perspective' (2006) New Modes of Governance Project No CIT1-CT-2004-506392.

law – constitutional Conventions'. Moreover, after the contributions of Ronald Dworkin on the subject, the graduated effects due to the regulation of norms are a frequently studied phenomenon.[27]

In conclusion, recent experience suggests that it is not sufficient to develop a scientific theory; rather, one should also consider its practical application as a means of verifying the theory's development. Political and moral doctrines, as well as the historical experiences of constitutionalism, must be integrated in comparative constitutional law's studies and researches. For instance, the history of constitutional development in Europe allows us to distinguish between contributions of different states to the spread of constitutionalism by geographical area. Some states have, since the very beginning, been at the centre of the development and implementation of constitutional doctrines while other countries have remained – for varying political and social reasons – at the periphery of those developments or taken part in them in an ephemeral and occasional way. This is why Western European constitutional experience weighs so heavily upon the European constitutional heritage.[28] Political movements in certain European states have contested this orientation by appealing to ancient national traditions to interpret the doctrines of constitutionalism, but they run the risk of citing historical anachronisms.[29] Events in certain countries might be worthy of some attention, although, for various reasons, they cannot be construed as landmarks of European constitutional tradition. This is the case, for example, with the Polish Constitution of 1791, which was never applied.[30] Constitutionalism in that country only took root following the sad experiences of the twentieth century and the fall of the Soviet regime. Historical traditions cannot be invoked to explain the recent constitutional crisis, although the Polish authorities may think they do. The continuing relevance and development of the Magna Carta in the UK are entirely missing in the case of the Hungarian Bulla Aurea,[31] which was interpreted during the twentieth century as consistently awarding the nobility tremendous privileges. It disregarded the basic principle of equality of treatment and non-discrimination – it failed to recognise the dignity and rights of the individual. Therefore, the Bulla does not credibly create precedents for contemporary Hungarian constitutional choices. Recently, the Venice Commission declared that the traditional Russian and Ukrainian institution of the Prokuratura (office of the public prosecutor) is not in compliance with the guidelines that safeguard human rights and the rule of law.[32] Moreover, doubts arose about the compatibility with the principles of the European constitutional heritage of the references in

[27] R Dworkin, *Taking Rights Seriously* (London, Duckworth, 1977) 22–28, distinguishing principles from rules because they do not require an application in an 'all-or-nothing' fashion.

[28] S Bartole, 'Standards of Europe's Constitutional Heritage' (2015) 30(II) *Giornale di storia costituzionale/Journal of Constitutional History* 17.

[29] As is suggested by (as far as I can understand his position by reading the abstract of his contribution) E Jarasiunas, 'The Prehistory of Constitutionalism: the Sources or the Archetype?' (2009) 118(4) *Jurisprudence* 21. In an article published earlier, where Strauss lists the important constitutional changes introduced by decisions of the Supreme Court, he recognises that the distinction between Nations that have well established liberal traditions and those who have not, is more important than the distinction between written and unwritten constitutions: see D Strauss, 'Common Law Constitutional Interpretation' (1996) 63 *The University of Chicago Law Review*, 890.

[30] BM Palka, 'La Costituzione Polacca del 3 maggio 1791: tra tradizione e modernità' (2005) 6 *Historia Constitucional (revista electrònica)* 285.

[31] E Balogh, 'La formazione della Bolla d'oro e il suo contenuto istituzionale nella storia costituzionale e giuridica ungherese' in L Besenyei, G Erszgi and M Pedrazza Gorlero (eds), *De Bulla Aurea* (Verona, Valdonega, 1999) 129.

[32] Venice Commission, CDL-AD(2009)048. The Commission shares the opinion of the Consultative Council of European Prosecutors that the constitutional history and legal tradition of a given country may justify non-penal

the Russian Constitution (Article 131) to traditions of that local government, whose social orientation Alexander Herzen appreciated.[33]

V. A Common Endeavour

The examples given above all concern the organisation of the powers of state, which are closely monitored by the supranational institutions for compliance with relevant principles, such as those which are at the base of the rule of law policies adopted by the Parliament and Commission of the European Union.[34] Judges are especially concerned with safeguarding human rights and fundamental freedoms. Even in this field, and after the adoption of the EU Charter of Fundamental Rights, comparative constitutional law is still relevant. The European Court of Justice and other courts continue to rely on comparative studies in order to give content to the rights and principles by which the authorities and Member States of the European Union must abide. This arrangement is permanently in flux inasmuch as it is potentially affected by conflicting claims of supremacy of national versus European laws. Miguel Maduro, as quoted above, rightly emphasised that while 'the EU claim of supremacy forces national courts to reconstruct even their national constitutional law … national constitutional claims also shape how EU law is developed and sensitive to national constitutional traditions'.[35]

This implies that judges and lawyers taking part in these developments participate in the creation of law, in some way completing and integrating the written law of the relevant Treaties and national constitutions and legislation. Within this overall framework, we are witnessing a progressive convergence of the different national legal orders – even between civil law and common law, as Tushnet correctly remarks. For instance, the principle of stare decisis resonates through the decisions of civil law judges, particularly when they concern the development of normative innovations or when they are duty-bound to respect the decisions of supranational judges such as the European Court of Justice and the European Court of Human Rights.

Scholars and other legal professionals – even those not fulfilling formal legislative or judicial functions – have traditionally played a significant role in the creation of legal orders beyond the existing states, finding inspiration in the states' common legal heritage, and this is still the case. Contributions by constitutional and legislative authorities are sometimes lacking or insufficient – especially when there is a dearth of political initiative, or when intervention is limited to grandiose proclamations or the invocation of general principles, effectively leaving room for the other dramatis personae to develop the work in progress.

functions of the prosecutors, but considers the Ukrainian and Russian historical model of the Prokuratura not to conform with European standards and Council of Europe values: it reflects a non-democratic past, it is overly powerful and does not offer judicial guarantees comparable to those offered by similar institutions.

[33] See the two reviews of AM Kelly, *The Discovery of Chance: The Life and Thought of Alexander Herzen* (Cambrige MA, HUV, 2016) by M Ignatieff, *New York Times*, 20 May 2016 and GS Morson, 'Herzen: The Hero of Skeptical Idealism' (2016) 63 *New York Review of Books* 18.

[34] Communication from the Commission to the European Parliament and the Council (COM(2014) 158 final/2); European Parliament Resolution of 25 October 2016 (2015/2254(INL)).

[35] Maduro (n 15) 74.

European history may illustrate this. The contribution made by lawyers and scholars to the formation of international and transnational constitutional law in light of the spread and acceptance of commonly shared principles and values reminds us of the contribution to the development of the *jus commune* – in a different economic and social context – by jurists, judges, notaries and professional lawyers, and especially by scientists and legal academicians of the Middle Ages, who directly took part – as Paolo Grossi suggests[36] – in the reception of Roman law, which itself knew no geographical or political borders. And we must not forget the importance of Savigny's concept of the lawyer's *Beruf* for legislation and jurisprudence, which envisaged the formation of a common legal unity by taking a novel approach to the traditional legal experiences of the German states of the time.[37]

[36] P Grossi Paolo, *L'Europa del diritto* (Rome, Laterza, 2007) 48–54.

[37] FK von Savigny, *Von Beruf unserer Zeit fur Gesetzebung und Rechtwissenschaft* (Heidelberg, Mohr und Zimmer, 1814).

INDEX

www.ingramcontent.com/pod-product-compliance
Ingram Content Group UK Ltd.
Pitfield, Milton Keynes, MK11 3LW, UK
UKHW050944290926
15470UKWH00005B/1630

9 781509 941476